A TALK IN THE PARK

A TALK
IN THE PARK

*Nine Decades of Baseball Tales
from the Broadcast Booth*

Curt Smith

POTOMAC BOOKS
WASHINGTON, D.C.

Library of Congress Cataloging-in-Publication Data
Smith, Curt.
  A talk in the park: nine decades of baseball tales from the broadcast booth / Curt Smith.
      p. cm.
  Includes index.
  ISBN 978-1-59797-670-1 (hardcover)
  1. Baseball—United States—Anecdotes. 2. Radio broadcasting of sports—United States. 3. Sportscasters—United States—Biography. I. Title.
  GV873.S576 2011
  796.3570973—dc22

                                        2011014633

Printed in the United States of America on acid-free paper that meets the American National Standards Institute Z39-48 Standard.

Potomac Books, Inc.
22841 Quicksilver Drive
Dulles, Virginia 20166

First Edition

10 9 8 7 6 5 4 3 2

TO ERNIE HARWELL

(1918–2010)

Contents

Acknowledgments

Fifteen years ago, *The Storytellers* told tales from the previous six decades of baseball broadcasting: Bob Costas eating cheesecake, Charlie Jones inventing a twin brother, and Bob Uecker shagging fly balls with a tuba. Early Wynn lost a wheel off a speeding motor coach. Jerry Coleman cried, "They throw Winfield out at second, and he's safe!" However selective memory may be, the announcer links the public and its game.

Since then, a number of contributors have passed away, including Mel Allen, Jack Buck, Harry Caray, Ernie Harwell, and Harry Kalas, less indispensable than irreplaceable. Happily, many others have climbed baseball's radio/television stairway: huckster, reporter, statistician, cornball self, and/or personality of the home team in the flesh. *A Talk in the Park: Nine Decades of Baseball Tales from the Broadcast Booth* is theirs.

In 1921, radio play-by-play began on KDKA Pittsburgh. Six in ten U.S. households owned a set by 1933. In 1939, TV baseball debuted at Brooklyn's Ebbets Field. Here are yarns—by Voices active and retired—about the age since then: Bob Wolff, airing a longest-ever wild pitch; Howie Rose, using the '69 Mets to pass a Regents test; Charley Steiner, wearing a wrong-handed glove, explaining why George Steinbrenner "hired" Jason Giambi, and hearing Vin Scully's palm tree rhapsody.

Denny Matthews recalls George Scott's *faux* uniform No. 6-4-3. Ken Harrelson defends his one-handed catch: "With bad hands like mine, one hand was better than two." Eduardo Ortega announces for his mother, who is deaf. Pat Hughes etches Ron Santo's hairpiece on fire, a tea bag dangling from Caray's ear, and Uke meeting Richard Nixon—"Richie." Voices hail Lou Piniella: dressed, undressed, volatile, and lovable.

"There is nothing I wouldn't do for Hope," Bing Crosby vowed, "and there is nothing he wouldn't do for me. We spend our lives doing nothing for each other." By contrast, today Jon Miller spurs surpassing pleasure. Like Lindsey Nelson, Gary Cohen defines his Mets. Like Brooklyn's Red Barber, Milo Hamilton stirs yearning for time standing still. "On the field not a lot sometimes happens," mused the late Chuck Thompson. The best rarely let us notice.

In 1996, few Hispanic or other minority announcers existed. *A Talk in the Park* documents our fairer, if not flawless, time. Herein are other trends of the last fifteen years: ex-jocks' warp-speed rise; postmodern technology; 24/7 coverage including the MLB Network's; and separate radio, free video, and cable TV staff. Some have buoyed, others shrunk, baseball's audience beyond the lines.

To author Stephen Ambrose, "The act of writing is the act of learning." Several conclusions color *A Talk in the Park*. First, "Baseball fans know their sport better than any fans," as Jack Buck observed. By and large, announcers do too—almost every contributor to this book having loved it when they were young.

Second, persona's paddle navigates dead air. A three-hour game may put the ball in play ten minutes. "Other sports carry the announcer," said Hank Greenwald. "The announcer carries baseball." Kalas painted like a minimalist. Dick Enberg weds irony and melody. Felo Ramirez says grace around the Marlins' tank. Whatever the plot, each hauls a story from the shelf.

Third, *informing* demands *performing*. Lifting his hands, Franklin Roosevelt would drop them like a pianist. "Speaking, you strike a chord," he said. "Then you wait. Then you strike the chord again." In Depression-era Iowa, future *TIME* columnist Hugh Sidey walked his town's main street. It was hot, windows open. From a hundred radios the young boy heard other chords: Ronald "Dutch" Reagan making baseball less waif of a moon than bright noon sun.

Reagan said, "Tell fifteen facts, and it's the story you recall." Scully likens statistics to a drunk "using a lamppost for support, not illumination." Upon Harwell's death in 2010, Michael Rosenberg noted how Ernie, Vin, and Caray "created and perfected an American art form. It was as if the guys who invented paint also happened to be Monet, Rembrandt, and Picasso." Baseball should learn from another original, Dizzy Dean, who termed statistics *statics*. Be distinctive. Say something we didn't know. Make balls and strikes beguile.

Announcers forged this book by phone, Internet, MP3, in print, and in person. Five percent of these stories are public record; eight, past interview; the rest, told exclusively for *Talk*. Santo, Dave Niehaus, and Ron Menchine died several months after contributing stories which appear here, including Dave terming Cooperstown "Disneyland, except that you don't have to pay for rides." At least one past or present Voice represents each current big-league team and network. Others cover ball sporadically: CBS's Peter King, Westwood One's Jim Bohannon. Hockey's Dick Irvin tells a great tale about baseball's Jackie Robinson.

Andrew Blauner, John Church, Phil Hochberg, Jeff Scott, and my wife Sarah and our children Olivia and Travis were especially helpful. I cannot suitably thank Potomac Books' Laura Briggs, Elizabeth Demers, Sam Dorrance, Katie Neubauer, Claire Noble, Kathryn Owens, Melaina Phipps, and Jennifer Waldrop. David B. Breeding, Santos Garcia Hernandez, Eduardo Ortega, and Sal Rivera translated Spanish-speaking stories. Doug Gamble, a humor writer for Phyllis Diller, Bob Hope, and Reagan, among others, coined the title. Ken Samelson researched text with his customary skill.

I am indebted to the president of the Museum of Broadcast Communications and National Radio Hall of Fame, Bruce DuMont, for officially endorsing the book. I wrote where I am privileged to teach, at the University of Rochester in New York, and did research at the Library of Congress, *The Sporting News*, and the National Baseball Hall of Fame and Museum. Let me thank the latter's staff, including senior library associate Bill Francis; librarian Jim Gates; senior director, communication and education, Brad Horn; president Jeff Idelson; photo archivist Pat Kelly; and communications director Greg Mudder.

In *The Deerslayer*, James Fenimore Cooper wrote, "Here all was unchanged; the river still rushed through its bower of trees; the mountains stood in their native dress, dark, rich, and mysterious; while the sheet glistened in its solitude, a beautiful gem of the forest." Cooperstown remains a gem of photograph and memory. I am pleased that the Hall of Fame will receive half of all royalties accrued from the sales of this book.

The Voices

Parable built the Sermon on the Mount. Anecdote was always in Lincoln's season. "It's conversation," Bob Costas *similarly calls radio/TV baseball. "It's quirky. Tell us what you did today. Tell me about the guy sitting down at the end of the dugout. Is he a character? Does he come from some tiny little town in Arkansas somewhere? Did he always dream of being a big leaguer? It's a story-telling game."*

To teenage Ernie Harwell, 1930s Georgia meant community and oral density. "On the porch," he said, "you'd hear about the local banker and beauty parlor operator and who married whom," its rhythm baseball's, mythy and sweetly rural. Picture a drive to left-centerfield. "Mentally, you saw the runners, fielders chasing, shortstop relay, catcher bracing. Football's packaged for the screen" — baseball, the tongue.

Television's DNA can be still life, deadened by monotony. Radio's is a sonata, falling lightly on the ear. Many contributors to A Talk in the Park have aired both: beach bud, meet couch potato. All hope to make "baseball good company," as Jon Miller says. "It comforts you, and you enjoy it."

One day in 1929, President Hoover and Treasury Secretary Andrew Mellon began walking down the street. Suddenly, Hoover stopped.

"Andy, I came out this morning without a cent in my pocket" — a Depression truism. "Lend me a nickel, will you? I want to call up a friend."

Pausing, Mellon reached into his pocket. "Here's a dime," he said. "Call up both of them." By contrast, as a boy I heard Harwell cry, "That ball is nabbed by *a guy from Alma, Michigan!" Each day a different town fictively grabbed a foul. "Hey, Ernie," pled a bystander, "have someone from Hope [or Detroit or Sarnia] grab one!" Oblivious, I told Mom that Ernie must have a lot of friends. He did.*

Below: the largest number of radio/TV storytellers – 116 – gathered in any sports book. I hope that you find friends, too.

KENNY ALBERT has been a Fox TV figure since 1997: baseball postseason and *Saturday Game of the Week*, Fox Sports Net *Thursday Night*, FX *Saturday Night*, NFL regular- and postseason, and Sugar, Orange, and Pro Bowl. The son of announcer Marv Albert has called the Mets, Nationals, Orioles, and Yankees, and shiny sport of every sort: Rangers, Capitals, NHL Radio, and NBC men's and women's hockey at the 2002, 2006, and 2010 Winter Olympics.

NAT ALLBRIGHT broadcast to himself as a boy watching the Class-D Bi-State League: "The Dodgers were a natural. I'd re-created since seven!" In 1952–1957, the Texan announced the Brooklyn Dodgers Radio Network over up to 117 outlets, often licking big-league local ratings. It died in 1962 after the team's move west. Nat then voiced the 1978–1983 Class-A Alexandria, Virginia, Dukes, after which they, like Brooklyn's Bums, expired.

BRIAN ANDERSON is a Southern Man come north. In 1994, the former St. Mary's University catcher joined Double-A San Antonio radio/TV. In 1998, 2007, and 2008, he began ESPN TV Little League/minors, Milwaukee, and TBS Division Series coverage, respectively. In 2010, Anderson commenced TBS's *Sunday MLB*, a Sabbath rite sired by 1950s Dizzy Dean. The former NBA and Golf Channel Voice's brother, Mike, is a Texas Rangers scout.

JOE ANGEL played quarterback for a Bay Area high school, was O. J. Simpson's teammate, and found a happier fate than his troubled pal. The Colombian has broadcast ESPN, Giants, A's, Twins, Yankees, Marlins, and 1988–1990, 1992, and 2004– Orioles. "I can play it either way," the popular Birdman references English and Spanish. "Just tell me how to play it." Joe's "Hasta la vista pelota!" crosses Baltimore's bilingual divide.

JUAN ANGEL AVILA, post-1997 Padres radio/TV Hispanic Voice, also airs the weekly team magazine *Mas Cerca del Juego* and Fox Sports boxing. In 1992, Avila began play-by-play in his native Mazatlan, Sinaloa, Mexico, returning to telecast each 2000– winter league. The also-newspaper columnist has done the 1993–1995 and 2005 Caribbean Series and been inducted into the Mazatlan Baseball Hall of Fame in 2008.

ALAN ASHBY was the first player dealt to Toronto—November 5, 1976, by Cleveland—before the Blue Jays played a game. Later, after a decade at Houston, he was named all-time franchise catcher in 1999. Ashby covered TV's basketball Rockets, football Cougars, and *Inside Houston* show, then coached, managed, and did Astros radio. In 2007, he traded clubs, countries, and one retractable roof for another, joining Blue Jays wireless.

KRIS ATTEBERRY, a Bozeman, Montana, native, graduated Stanford '96. The English literature major brought classicism to Northern League Sioux Falls and the independent American Association St. Paul Saints. In 2007, the former Montana State football and basketball Voice joined a Twins radio network as anchored as 10,000 Lakes and widespread as Des Moines to Dickenson, North Datoka— in all, eighty outlets.

URI BERENGUER was diagnosed at age three with a rare form of blood cancer. A Panamanian doctor wanted to amputate his leg. Uri's mom Daisy took him to Dana-Farber Cancer Institute, where surgery saved his leg. Later Boston's Joe Castiglione made him radio statistician. Uri attended Boston Latin Academy and Northeastern University, became Sox Hispanic and New England Sports Network (NESN) Voice, and takes baseball like cancer: one day at a time.

STEVE BLASS heaps connotation on the term "class." The Connecticut right-hander signed with Pittsburgh in 1960, pitched in 1964 and 1966–1974, finished 103-76, and won twice in the 1971 World Series, including a 2–1 final: freeze-framed, in teammate Bob Robertson's arms. In 1983, Steve joined cable TV's Bob Prince, moving to radio in 1986. In 2009, the Pirates celebrated Blass's half-century with the team: the face and voice of Pittsburgh's blue-collar core.

JIM BOHANNON crashed radio in 1960, joined then-Mutual Radio in 1983, and a decade later succeeded Westwood One's prime time Larry King. The Missourian and Viet Nam veteran ferries talk, including baseball, to more than 500 Westwood affiliates on *The Jim Bohannon Show*, *America in the Morning*, and *America This Week*. Bohannon has made each of *Talkers Magazine*'s list of America's "100 Most Important Radio Talk Show Hosts."

DICK BREMER, a Lutheran pastor's son, spreads the Twins' Word throughout the Upper Midwest. Raised in population 135 Dumont, Minnesota, St. Cloud State '78 began as a disc jockey aka "Duke in the Dark," lighting 1983– Twins TV on Spectrum, TwinsVision, Midwest Sports Channel, and now Fox Sports Net. Bremer has braved the Metrodome, opened Target Field, and aired Minnesota college football, hoops, and hockey, and NHL North Stars.

MARTY BRENNAMAN, saying, "This one belongs to the Reds," has belonged to Cincinnati since 1974. In 2009, the American Sportscasters Association named him "among the top fifty all-time sportscasters": inducted into, among others, the Baseball, National Radio, and National Sportscasters and Sportswriters Halls of Fame. Brennaman is also an NCAA network postseason hoops staple. * Ford C. Frick Award 2000, given yearly for broadcast excellence.

BILL BROWN joined Astros TV a quarter-century after the 1962 expansion Colt .45s trained near Arizona's Superstition Mountain. In turn, 2011 marks Brown's quarter-century in Houston, having earlier aired or directed the Reds, Royals, and Cardinals. The ex-Financial News Network anchor and producer made the Texas Baseball Hall of Fame in 2004. A year later the 'Stros made their first World Series, losing to Chicago. At fifty, their superstition remains.

GREG BROWN followed such Pirates radio royalty as Rosey Rowswell, Bob Prince, Jim Woods, and Lanny Frattare. In 1979, interning as a Point Park College student, the Washington, DC, native started a decade in Bucs broadcasting, PR, and sales. Brown later voiced Buffalo's Triple-A Bisons, football Bills, University of Buffalo hoops, and Empire Sports TV Network, returning in 1994 to Pittsburgh: his once and future home.

ROBERT BUAN mocks Gertrude Stein's "There isn't any there there" critique of Oakland. He was the A's 1995–2010 broadcasting manager, hosting radio's pre-game *This Week in A's Baseball* and post-game *Extra Innings*. In 2008, the president and CEO of GT2 Entertainment won the Electronic Media's "best radio program" award for his syndicated two-hour *Country Fastball*, a mélange of country music and baseball interviews.

JOE BUCK grew up revering dad Jack. In 1991, fils joined the Cardinals, calling père's favorite sport "my stock market, my assembly line." Stock rose as Fox TV made Joe 1996 baseball duce: youngest World Series Voice since Vin Scully, twenty-five. In 2002, Buck replaced football's Pat Summerall. 2007: An each-*Saturday Game of the Week* returned for the first time since 1989. 2008: Joe's thirteenth TV Series passed Curt Gowdy's record twelve.

DAVE CAMPBELL, also known as "Soups," after the Campbell's brand, played at the University of Michigan, signed with Detroit in 1964, and made the 1967–1974 Tigers, Padres, Cardinals, and Astros. He called San Diego and Colorado, then ESPN TV's *Baseball Tonight*, *SportsCenter*, and Triple-A World Series, and radio's *Sunday Night Baseball*. Dave created the board game *Extra Bases*, also voiceovering the PlayStation portable game series *MLB: The Show*.

CHIP CARAY continues baseball's senior on-air clan. Granddad Harry bridged Bobby Soxers and the VCR. Dad Skip didn't force-feed a listener. The Chip off their block graduated Georgia '87, aired NBA Orlando, and did the Braves, Mariners, and *Game*. In 1998, he went to Wrigley Field to work with Harry. Instead, grandpère's death made Chip the Voice. Later joining Skip in Atlanta, he now daubs balls and strikes on Fox Sports South and SportSouth.

BOB CARPENTER, born in baseball's perceived capital, St. Louis, described its 1984–1985 and 1995–2005 Cardinals. In 2006, the ex-Twins, Mets, and Rangers mikeman left for the nation's capital. The Nationals TV ambassador has worked on CBS, ESPN, USA, and now Middle Atlantic Sports Network (MASN). Washington's last pennant was in Franklin Roosevelt's first year as President. For Carpenter, a bigs New Deal might help.

DUKE CASTIGLIONE is New York WWOR MY 9 Yankees post-game host and MY Fox 5 sports anchor and *Sports Extra* host; formerly, WHDH Boston anchor, ESPN's *SportsCenter* and *Around the Horn* guest host, and *Sunday Night Baseball*, World Baseball Classic, and WCBS New York reporter. In 2007, Joe Castiglione's son interviewed Kirk Radomski, ex-Mets employee, steroid dealer, and key source for the Mitchell Report, on the eve of publication.

JOE CASTIGLIONE, a young Yankees fan in Red Sox New England, visited Fenway Park in 1967 and converted: No Evil Empire could match The Impossible Dream. The Colgate and Syracuse graduate called the Indians and Brewers, joined the Olde Towne team in 1983, and wrote the 2004 book, *Broadcast Rites and Sites*. Joe's greatest sight was Boston sweeping that fall's Series. "Can you believe it?" he said of its first post-1918 title. Not even after '07.

GARY COHEN, visiting Shea Stadium as a boy, learned Metsomania from his dad. He made the Dean's List at Columbia, did the Durham Bulls and Triple-A Pawtucket, and joined Mets WFAN Radio and SNY TV in 1989 and 2006, respectively. Cohen has aired St. John's and Seton Hall basketball, CBS Radio baseball *Game of the Week,* and three Winter Olympics. Casey Stengel said, "Can't anybody *play* this here game?" Few ask if Gary can describe it.

JERRY COLEMAN once "worried about Colemanisms. Finally I figured they add to my sex appeal." Jesus Alou was "in the on-deck circus." Randy Jones "has a Karl Marx hairdo." "Put a star on that baby" for the World War II and Korea flyer, 1949–1957 infielder, then CBS, Yankees, Angels, and 1972–1979 and 1981– Padres play-by-play man. Hail evolution, going yard. "Sometimes big trees grow out of acorns. I think I heard that from a squirrel." * Frick 2005.

TOM COLLINS was as piquant as the drink. Born in Neenah, Wisconsin, the Three-I League player's son got his flying license at fourteen, spent much of World War II as a Marine at Midway Island, and announced the 1970–1972 Brewers on baseball's return to Milwaukee. The 1962–1970 Marquette University basketball Voice aired Al McGuire's 1970 National Invitation Tournament title, later heading Schlitz Brewery's broadcast division.

JACK CORRIGAN is Colorado's skilled utility infielder/Renaissance Man. Announcing: The NBA, soccer, college hoops and football, and Indians longest-running (1985–2001) TV Voice joined Rockies radio in 2002. Writing: Jack released a 2005 novel *Warning Track* about an aging player doing drugs and is working on two other books. Teaching: Cornell '74 and Kent State Masters Speech major coaches high school football, 24/7 before the term.

BOB COSTAS saw his first game at five at Ebbets Field. Later the Yankees fan carried a "religious artifact at all times": a dog-eared Mickey Mantle card. In 1983–1989, Bob sermonized NBC's Church of Baseball. When CBS got rights, he leapfrogged baseball for *Later With Bob Costas*, *Now*, Olympics, and NFL, virtually retiring the Emmy and Sportscaster of the Year award. In 2009, Costas joined the new MLB Network, again finding the big-league water fine.

TOM DAVIS, five-time Maryland Sportscaster of the Year, began on early-1970s WBAL Baltimore TV, buoyed 1984–2000 award-winning Home Team Sports, and now berths Orioles' pre- and post-game radio and video.

Davis has aired the NFL, USFL, Gator Bowl, and 1988 Summer Olympics: also, Cal Ripken Jr.'s 400th homer, Memorial Stadium's close, Oriole Park at Camden Yards' debut, and now MASN's *Take Me Out to the Ballgame*.

DAN DICKERSON deems Michigan summer solstice, not just winter wonderland. After Grand Rapids play-by-play, the native Wolverine called Detroit Lions and Michigan football, hosted Motown call-in radio, and was a WJR Detroit morning anchor. Tiger Stadium closed September 27, 1999, emcee Ernie Harwell saying, "Farewell, old friend." Next year Dickerson began radio at Comerica Park, passing from parent to child the joy of cheering Ernie's "Tiges."

BRETT DOLAN did 1994–2005 minors radio. In 2006, he took his Triple-A Tucson "Voice of the Sidewinders" pitch to the Astros, trading one nation-state (Canada, as 2003–2004 Montreal Expos fill-in) for another ("Don't Mess With Texas"). University of Iowa '92 and Arizona's 2002–2003 Sportscaster of the Year has done Arizona Fall League and Olympic qualifying baseball, University of Arizona and FSN Southwest hoops and football, and Texas Bowl PA.

GENE ELSTON economically ferried 1962–1986 Houston baseball from the Panhandle to Biloxi. The Iowan aired the 1980 League Championship Series (LCS), Nolan Ryan's record fifth no-hitter, and Astros (nee) Colt .45s first 1,600 games, having earlier done the 1950s Cubs and Mutual's *Game of the Day*. Later, Elston called 1985–1997's CBS Radio postseason and *Game of the Week*: still dry, like Lubbock, and pleasant, like a Gulf Coast breeze. * Frick 2006.

DICK ENBERG has covered the *Game of the Week*, World Series, NFL, Wimbledon, and college basketball, among other things. Born in Michigan, Dick got a doctorate, taught, and crashed broadcasting, adding the 1969 Angels to UCLA hoops and football Rams. In 1978, Enberg dealt the Halos for NBC and CBS, returning to "my favorite sport" on 2010 Padres TV. "I've always loved the game," Dick said of his first baseball since 1985. "I'm home." *Oh, my!*

DAVE FLEMMING was born in Alexandria, Virginia, graduated from Stanford and Syracuse Universities, and began teaching baseball in 2000 on Visalia Oaks radio and as assistant general manager. After three years at Pawtucket, the bi-coastal twenty-something joined Jon Miller and Duane Kuiper in 2005 on San Francisco's KNBR Radio. Dave also hosts, does selected Giants TV, and announces Stanford football and basketball.

SCOTT FRANZKE was Southern Methodist University '94, Prime Sports Radio talker, Kane County Class-A Voice, 2000 Summer Olympics reporter, and Rangers pre- and post-game host and play-by-player. In 2006, Scott joined Phillies radio, succeeding moving-to-TV Tom McCarthy. His dossier boasts a 2008–2009 pennant, 2008 world title, 2009 unassisted triple play, and Roy Halladay's 2010 perfect game and postseason no-hitter.

LANNY FRATTARE left Rochester, New York, in 1966 for Ithaca College, Triple-A Charleston, then confluence of the Allegheny, Monongahela, and Ohio. His task: replace Bob Prince, a ghost real as any relative's. Lanny became longest-running (1976–2008) Pirates Voice: his "statistical-heavy style," said Associated Press, calling Willie Stargell, Barry Bonds, and 1979's "We Are Family." He teaches at Waynesburg University, students his famille.

ANDY FREED makes even inside baseball—Tampa Bay's doughnut-shaped dome—seem like real baseball, after all. In 2005, he joined the then–Devil Rays from Pawtucket. Previously, Freed worked as Fox TV baseball statistician and researcher, at the Comcast Network, and on Orioles post-game WBAL Radio. Bred on the O's Chuck Thompson, the Towson State grad evokes his sun, breeze, and lore. It helps when your team wins: e.g., 2008 Rays.

JOE GARAGIOLA grew up "a pickoff away" from Yogi Berra, wrote *Baseball Is a Funny Game*, and became a funny man: ordinary on the field, extraordinary off. In 1955, the retired catcher turned to KMOX St. Louis, then NBC *Today* show, *Game of the Week*, Yankees, Angels, and a bat rack of other hits. Joe G. won a George Foster Peabody award, founded the Baseball Assistance Team, and at eighty-five, graces Arizona Diamondbacks TV. * Frick 1991.

GLENN GEFFNER knew that, as a proverb says, "East, west, home's best." The Miamian and Northwestern Medill School of Journalism '90 aired college, Class-A, Double-A, Triple-A Rochester, and San Diego radio. Next stop: Red Sox wireless and New England Sports Network (NESN) TV. Glenn looked homeward, angel, in 2008, joining Marlins radio. Gigs include pre-game *Marlins On Deck*, post-game *Tenth Inning*, and game-interrupted *Rain Delay Theater*.

HANK GREENWALD was born in Detroit, raised in Rochester, and attended Syracuse University, where he met Jim Brown, joined campus radio, and junked the law. Hank aired the 1979–2005 Giants, Yankees, A's, and CBS Radio. Humor bridged them: "In Montreal, when you ask for a non-smoking section, they send you to Buffalo." Greenwald turned fifty in 1985. "It's funny," he said of the toxic Giants. "When the season started I was only forty-three."

WAYNE HAGIN keyed ESPN's first baseball coverage: 1979's National Baseball Congress Tournament. Later, as Colorado's 1993–2002 Voice, he was named 1998 Players Choice Denver Media Man of the Year. Hagin also did the A's, Giants, White Sox, and Cardinals, two NL Division Series, and NBA Warriors and ESPN college basketball. Since 2008, you catch the former San Diego State University outfielder on Mets WFAN Radio.

MILO HAMILTON started at Armed Forces Radio, the University of Iowa, and the minor leagues, re-creating a thirty-seven-walk twin bill. At twenty-five, he joined the Browns, later Cardinals, Cubs, White Sox, Braves, Pirates, and 1985– Astros. Hamilton is a perfectionist: also, the Voice of Henry Aaron's crossing a most Ruthian line. "There's a new home run champion of all time," Milo sang famously in April 1974. To baseball's senior mikeman, Hank still is. * Frick 1992.

KEN HARRELSON follows his own drummer. Playing for four 1963–1971 teams, Ken popularized the batting glove, earned the name "Hawk," made each catch one-handed, and had 35 homers and a league-high 109 runs batted in for the 1968 Red Sox. Retiring, Harrelson tried golf, aired 1975–1981 Boston, and darned the 1982–1985 and post-1988 White Sox. "Put it on the board!" the five-time Emmy honoree says. On Pale Hose television, viewers put Hawk on theirs.

JERRY HOWARTH was born in Pennsylvania, grew up in San Francisco, graduated Santa Clara '68, and spent a decade calling baseball, football, and hoops. In 1981, the Blue Jays hired him. By turn, Jerry joined radio's Tom Cheek; Exhibition Stadium yielded to SkyDome; and the Jays won the 1992–1993 Series, lighting the Maritimes to Manitoba. Cheek's 2005 death ended the grand *Tom and Jerry Show*, making Howarth Canadian baseball's "on guard for thee."

PAT HUGHES stole as a teenager into Candlestick Park's visiting clubhouse, meeting Billy Williams, Ron Santo, and Ernie Banks. Their friendliness augured Pat's Cubs suzerainty. In 1996, he arrived at WGN Radio after twelve years as Bob Uecker's Brewers sidekick. Two years later Hughes etched the Sosa-McGwire homerthon, blooming like ivy at Wrigley Field: first-rate Second City Voice and eight-time Wisconsin and Illinois Sportscaster of the Year.

MARIO IMPEMBA joined Tigers video in 2003. In high school, Impemba placed third in Michigan's forensics final. At Michigan State, if a game were aired, Mario pined to air it, hiking through Peoria, Davenport, and Tucson to 1995–2001 Angels KLAA Radio and KCAL TV. In 2006, the website author of *The Sound of Baseball* got a Michigan Emmy award for his own sound on play-by-play.

DICK IRVIN is shorthand for Montreal hockey, but, as he writes, saw Jackie Robinson's baseball debut. The son of Canadiens coach Dick Irvin Sr. attended McGill, entered Montreal radio/TV, did *bleu, blanc, et rouge* color and play-by-play, and moored CBC's *Hockey Night In Canada*. Irvin is the author of six books, annual contributor to *Hockey Day in Canada*, and member of the Hockey Hall of Fame and the Canadian Association of Broadcasters Hall of Fame.

DARRIN JACKSON bridges each Chicago El baseball stop: drafted by and playing for the 1985–1989 Cubs; later, with six teams, including 1994 and 1999 White Sox, peaking at .312, 21 homers, and baseball-best eighteen outfield assists in a year. Jackson spent 1996–1997 with Japan's Seibu Lions. In 2000, he joined Ken Harrelson on Pale Hose WGN and cable TV, moving to its Illinois, Indiana, Iowa, and Missouri radio network in 2009.

DAVE JAGELER took Pawtucket's conveyer belt in 2006 to Washington, following Pawsoxer-turned-bigs Gary Cohen, Don Orsillo, Dave Flemming, and Andy Freed. Earlier, Dave did NBA, UNC–Charlotte, and Virginia Tech hoops, Texas and Florida football, *NHL Game of the Week*, and Triple-A Charlotte. In 1962, President Kennedy opened DC Stadium, saying, "I'm leaving you [Senators] in first place." Jageler's radio place is anywhere around the Beltway.

JAIME JARRIN migrated at nineteen in 1955 from Cayambe, Ecuador, to California to become a newscaster who later aired JFK's funeral and Winston Churchill's memorial service. In 1959, Jarrin began re-creating the Dodgers — *Esquivadores* — for Hispanic barrio, tract, and farm. In 1973, Jaime debuted their Spanish Network, relishing 1980s Fernandomania, LA's 1981 and 1988 World Series title, and Cooperstown. * Frick 1998.

ERNIE JOHNSON became cable television's first baseball star: son of Swedish immigrants, World War II Marine, 1950 and 1952–1959 Braves/ Orioles pitcher, and Milwaukee/Atlanta radio/TVer. In 1976, he replaced lead Braves Voice Milo Hamilton, invoking pops "that bring rain" and "give that one a blue star." WTBS Atlanta soon became a SuperStation, bulging baseball's and cable's clientele. In 1999, Ernie, seventy-five, retired, still missed a decade later.

ERNIE JOHNSON JR. aired the 1993–1996 Braves with his dad on Sport-South (now FSN South). By then, Georgia '78 had worked at WSB Atlanta, joined Turner Sports, and thrived as host and at play-by-play. On TBS, TNT, and NBC, "E. J." has done the Division Series and *Sunday MLB*, golf, NBA, pro and college football, Wimbledon, and the Olympics and Goodwill Games, winning two Emmies. In 2010, Johnson also doubled back to Peachtree TV's Braves.

LEN KASPER, born in Michigan, has aired the Bears, Packers, WTMJ Milwaukee talk, 1991–2001 Brewers, and 2002–2004 Marlins, Len's sole exception to the heartland's rule. Kasper's 2005– Cubs stage has been the Friendly Confines' bleachers, hand-operated scoreboard, and wind off Lake Michigan. Like Jack Brickhouse and Harry Caray, Marquette '93's window on the pastime is WGN TV.

MICHAEL KAY succeeded such Yanks TV grandees as Mel Allen, The Voice; Red Barber, Southern Gentleman; and Phil Rizzuto, shortstop-turned-character. Kay left the *New York Post* and *Daily News* for the MSG Network, WABC and ESPN New York radio, and WWOR MY 9 and YES Network play-by-play. Fordham '82 has won ten Emmys, "Best Sports Reporter" award, and Dick Young award for excellence, meriting Allen's self-description: "partisan, not prejudiced."

PAUL KEELS left Cincinnati's Moeller High School via Xavier University for hometown 50,000-watt WLW Radio, Marty Brennaman's, Waite Hoyt's, and Al Michaels' station. He has also done the Detroit Pistons, Michigan, Ohio State, and University of Cincinnati basketball and/or football. Keels was inducted into Ohio's Radio/TV Broadcasting Hall of Fame in 2007. Three years later he aired Reds play-by-play on Fox Sports Ohio.

RALPH KINER, said to have mused, "Home run hitters drive Cadillacs," each year led the 1946–1952 NL. In 1961, he moved to White Sox TV. Since 1962, Ralph has brought the Mets story, scene, and malapropism: "In Montreal, the Phillies again beat the Mets." WOR's post-game *Kiner's Korner* was an early black-and-white period piece: "interviews with big shots," wrote a critic, "few of them Mets." *Korner* ended in 1995. Kiner still does Amazin's video.

PETER KING is a CBS News Radio staff correspondent. Based in Orlando and at the Kennedy Space Center, he covers spring training, politics, hurricanes, "breaking news," and NASA, especially its space shuttle program. Ithaca College '78 worked in Upstate New York and Vermont before joining CBS in 1994. The five-time Florida Press Club Award recipient "would almost rather watch a meaningless exhibition game than the Final Four."

JEFF KINGERY, growing up a Dodgers fan in San Francisco, decided at fifteen to call ball. In 1981, Denver's Triple-A Bears made Kingery, thirty, lead announcer. In 1993, the NL expansion Colorado Rockies did the same. Two years later they opened Coors Field, of which Vin Scully said, "You don't need an official scorer. You need a certified public accountant." Baseball's first and longest-running big-league tie to the Rocky Mountain region retired in 2009.

KEN KORACH, a native Angeleno, began in the California League, called Phoenix baseball and San Jose football and basketball, and won the pot in Las Vegas, doing all three sports, including the Pacific Coast League Stars. *Las Vegas Life Magazine* named him among the city's "Best 100 People, Places, and Things." In 1992, Ken trekked to Comiskey Park, then Oakland in 1996. A decade later he was promoted to A's lead radio.

MIKE KRUKOW thrives on barb and brushback. Kruk was 124-117 with 1976–1989 NL Chicago, Philly, and San Francisco. In 1999, regional media named him the Giants' 1980s starting righty. The five-time Emmy awardee analyzes on KNTV, Comcast SportsNet Bay Area, and KNBR Radio. Hemingway coined "grace under pressure." The Giants 1991– good humor man is funny on command: as vital in a bad year (1996 68–94) as good (2010 world title).

TIM KURKJIAN is a cottage industry. The Marylander wrote for the *Washington Star, Dallas Morning News, Baltimore Sun, Sports Illustrated,* and *CNN/SI*, joining ESPN in 1998. He contributes to its *Baseball Tonight, SportsCenter, ESPN The Magazine, ESPN.com,* and *Mike & Mike in the Morning.* Tim's two books are *America's Game* and *Is This a Great Game, or What? From A-Rod's Heart to Zim's Head — My 25 Years in Baseball.* If he only got paid by the word.

RYAN LEFEBVRE grasps the philosopher Nietzsche's "What doesn't kill us makes us stronger." In 2006, he wrote a moving book, *The Shame of Me,* about depressive illness. Previously ex-bigs player and skipper Jim Lefebvre's son had played college baseball, signed with Cleveland, and entered media in 1995. Ryan aired the Twins through 1998, joined Royals radio, and a decade later added Fox Sports Net Kansas City: popular, deep, and brave.

JOSH LEWIN shows that youth isn't wasted on the young, at sixteen calling Triple-A Rochester radio. At twenty-five, Northwestern '90 became WBAL Baltimore sports director; twenty-seven, Fox *Saturday* and postseason Voice; twenty-eight, Cubs TV play-by-play man. Lewin has done 1998–2001 Tigers, 2002–2010 Rangers, Fox football and hockey, NFL local Chargers, and Big 12 and SMU hoops video. The wunderkind's two books are *Getting in the Game* and *You Never Forget Your First.*

TOM McCARTHY has lived to tell about I-95's Mets-Phils rivalry. The College of New Jersey '90 began in PR, turned minors assistant GM, and cracked radio/television in 2000: CBS College Sports Network, Westwood One, Atlantic 10, Princeton, Rutgers, St. Joseph's, and MLB's Caribbean Series. After Phillies 2001–2005 pre/post-game radio, Tom moved to Mets WFAN, then back to Philly, named TV Voice on Harry Kalas' 2009 death.

TIM McCARVER caught four 1959–1980 teams — one of seven to play four modern baseball decades — later airing the Phillies, Mets, Yankees, Giants, ABC, CBS, and 1996 Fox. McCarver has thrice won an Emmy, co-hosted the 1992 Olympics, and done twenty World Series. In 2003, his seventy-eighth

Classic telecast set a record. Some say Tim talks too much. Others think he has a lot to say, matched only by Jim Kaat and Tony Kubek as an analyst.

FRED MANFRA doubled in a 1964 American Legion game off Memorial Stadium's leftfield wall. By 1981, the Baltimorean reached ABC Radio Network via Tigers TV, Michigan/Iowa college hoops/football, and AP Radio, doing twenty-two shows each weekend: also, NBA, Olympics, Stanley Cup, Breeders' Cup, and Triple Crown. In 1993, Manfra, joining the O's, confirmed his high school yearbook: "Fred's . . . future plans are in . . . radio-TV work."

DENNY MATTHEWS quoted Jack Brickhouse on making Cooperstown: "Today, I feel like a man sixty feet, six inches tall." In 1976, he replaced Bud Blattner as Royals liegeman: Straightaway K.C. took three straight divisions. In 1980, it won the pennant; 1985, World Series; today, small towns and backcountry on an eight-state network. Denny's grandfather worked for the Chicago and Alton Railroad. Royals eighty-three-affiliate radio rarely goes off the track. * Frick 2007.

RON MENCHINE joined the 1969 Senators as Richard Nixon was inaugurated, Ted Williams became manager, and DC topped .500 for the first time since 1952. In 1971, a last-game forfeit preceded their move to Texas. Menchine moved to ABC, CBS, Mutual, and NBC, film's *All the President's Men* and *The Seduction of Joe Tynan*, and writing five books. In 2005, the Expos left *La Belle Province* for Washington, Ron no longer its last big-league Voice. He died in 2010, at seventy-six.

JON MILLER's sweetspot is priorities. At ten, Jon played *Strat-O-matic;* sixteen, broadcast sotto voce at Candlestick Park and Oakland Coliseum; twenty-two, joined the A's, then Rangers, Red Sox, Orioles, and 1997– Giants. Miller has gilded ESPN TV's and/or Radio's 1990–2011 *Sunday Night Baseball*, All-Star Game, LCS, Division Series, and World Series, winning two cable ACE Awards. If play dulls, he may mimic Vin Scully in English, Spanish, and Japanese. * Frick 2010.

MONTE MOORE welded an iron streak (3,001 games), three World Series (1972–1974), and 1962–1977, 1987, and 1989–1992 A's. NBC's and USA's TV *Game of the Week* capped the Oklahoman's *vitae*. Monte brooked Charles Finley's designated runner, mechanical rabbit, and orange baseball to call Jim Hunter's perfect game, Billy Martin's Billy Ball, and late-1980s and early-90s Bash Brothers. Their common chord was Monte's Gary Cooper twang.

JOE MORGAN left college to sign with Houston. "I told mom if she let me enter baseball, I'd get my degree." In 1990, Little Joe did—and entered Cooperstown: 1975–1976 MVP, seven-time division, league, and/or Series titlist, and first second baseman with 200 homers, 2,000 games, and 2,000 hits. Morgan announced the Reds, Giants, A's, and ESPN TV's 1990–2010 *Sunday Night Baseball* and Radio's Classic, LCS, and All-Star Game.

JEFF MUNN started Diamondbacks radio play-by-play in 2001: the franchise's then/now Everest. He also hosts KTAR's pre- and post-game show. The Phoenix native has aired Arizona State University basketball and baseball, Summer Olympics hoops, figure skating, NBA and WNBA, and MLB Radio's Arizona Fall League. Plus, of course, that not-to-be believed nor forgotten 2001 World Series.

ERIC NADEL joined Rangers radio/TV in 1979, outlasting Charlie Hough, Nolan Ryan's 5,000th K, and Arlington Stadium. Brown '72 is now the franchise's longest-running Voice. The four-time Texas Sportscaster of the Year graces the Texas Baseball Hall of Fame, is learning Spanish, and has written three books, including *Texas Rangers: The Authorized History*. Also recommended: Nadel's radio series *A Page From Baseball's Past*.

MARK NEELY grasps Arthur Hugh Clough's, "Westward, look, the land is bright." The St. Louis native and Kansas '87 worked Class-A Boise, Springfield, and Salem, Double-A Tulsa, Triple-A Louisville, and ESPN NCAA, big-league, and Little League baseball; also, Fox Big Ten Network hoops, football, volleyball, and soccer. In 2009, looking west, Mark became a Padres TV announcer on flagship Channel 4 San Diego.

DAVE NIEHAUS was Seattle's first and always Voice. Indiana '57 aired Armed Forces Radio/TV, joined Dick Enberg and Don Drysdale at Anaheim, and in 1977 fashioned the Mariners' Northwest Opening. The *Seattle Times* listed the Hoosier native among its Top 10 area "Most influential people of the century." "My, oh, my!" he said. "It will fly away!" Ex-M's outfielder Jay Buhner called Dave's November 2010 death at seventy-five of a heart attack "the saddest day of my life." * Frick 2008.

DAVE O'BRIEN is pitch-perfect for heavily Irish Boston. The Quincy native and Syracuse grad began Red Sox radio in 2007, having done the 1990–1991 Braves, 1993–2001 Marlins, 2003–2005 Mets, Georgia basketball, and Falcons football. Since 2002, O'Brien has covered ESPN's regular season, Division and World Series, college and pro hoops, and soccer, including World Cup. Top twin killing: Barry Bonds' numbers 755 and 756. On the seventh day Dave rests.

PAUL OLDEN succeeded the Yankees' two Voices of God. In 1994–1996, Olden telecast the pinstripes of 1940–1964 Hall of Famer Mel Allen. In 2009, he followed legendary Bombers public address announcer Bob Sheppard. A talented photographer, Olden has called baseball's 1998–2004 then–Devil Rays, Angels, and Indians, football Jets and Eagles, UCLA and Nets basketball, and Los Angeles sports talk. He also handled 1994–2005 Super Bowl PA.

DON ORSILLO grew up on a New England farm, attended Northeastern University with students from the Red Sox diaspora, and interned as Fenway Park booth statistician. In 1992, the Pittsfield Mets hired him. Ahead: Double-A Binghamton and Boston's Triple-A Pawtucket. In 2001, radio's child turned to TV's NESN, Hideo Nomo no-noing the O's in Orsillo's Sox debut. Don has broadcast TBS's post-season since 2007.

EDUARDO ORTEGA enters his twenty-sixth year of play-by-play, including Giants, post-1986 Padres, Tijuana, Torreon, Mexicali Eagles, CBS Hispanic Radio Network, Cadena Caracol, LBC Radio Network, and ESPN

Deportes. Ortega has aired ten Caribbean World Series, fourteen World Series, nine All-Star Games, Tony Gwynn hit 3,000, and Randy Johnson K 4,000, earning the Tijuana Sports Media Career Achievement award and Hispanic Heritage Baseball Museum and Hall of Fame.

RICO PETROCELLI still evokes "And there's pandemonium on the field!" — Ned Martin's sound track of the Boston shortstop's 1967 last-day flag-waving catch. The Brooklynite and 1963 and 1965–1976 Townie later played third base, was a two-time All-Star, made two World Series, hit forty homers in a season, and broadcast for the 1979 Red Sox. Rico now airs MLB Network Radio, '67 seldom wandering far away.

AMAURY PI-GONZALEZ left Cuba in 1961 at age seventeen: "I didn't want to. Castro's Communist Revolution left no choice." He joined the U.S. Army, cracked radio/TV, and is the sole Hispanic to air four big-league teams: Mariners, Giants, Angels, and 1977–1993 and 2009– A's. The actor, TV anchor, voiceover, and vice-president of the Hispanic Heritage Baseball Museum and Hall of Fame has done the Fall Classic, LCS, and Caribbean World Series.

ROSS PORTER as a child idolized Harry Caray, who treated statistics like beriberi. Strangely, the adult became The Stat Man. At twenty-seven, Ross left Oklahoma for LA, joining baseball's first-in-its-class in 1977. "I thought, with Vin [Scully] I'll be running water." Instead, he did that year's CBS Radio Fall Classic, soloed a 1989 1–0 twenty-two-inning match, and made the Southern California Broadcasters Hall of Fame. In 2004, Porter left play-by-play for philanthropy.

JIM POWELL bridges baseball's yin and yang. In 1996, the Peach State son joined the Milwaukee Brewers, born after the '60s Braves' move to Georgia. In 2009, history repeated itself, Atlanta luring Powell. Earlier, Jim broadcast the Twins, Charlotte, Columbia, college baseball and hoops, and CBS Radio football, including Sun Bowl. "Milwaukee understood my move," Powell said. Unlike the Braves, he was going, not leaving, home.

JIM PRICE, a reserve catcher, helped make 1968 The Year of The Tiger: Detroit's first world title since 1945. Signed by Pittsburgh, Price was bought by the Tigers, played through 1971, then entered broadcasting: White Sox and Detroit PASS cable, ESPN college baseball, WKBD Detroit analyst, and 1999– Bengals radio with Frank Beckmann and Dan Dickerson. Jim and wife Lisa founded Jack's Place, named for their son diagnosed with the Autism Spectrum Disorder.

MEL PROCTOR grasped Lucille Ball's advice: "The more you do, the more you find you can do." Mel acted: *Hawaii 5-O, Homicide,* and *The Young and the Restless.* Wrote: a well-received book on TV's series *The Fugitive.* Did radio/video: Rangers, Orioles, Padres, and Fox, enjoying Camden Yards' debut, Cal Ripken Jr.'s most homers by a shortstop, and Baltimore single-year attendance record. "If people sense *you're* having fun," Mel said, "*they'll* have fun naturally."

RAFAEL (FELO) RAMIREZ is larger than life, as his statue shows at Puerto Rico's National Sports Museum. The Cuba native *became* baseball in Puerto Rico, Nicaragua, and Venezuela, airing thirty-four Series and All-Star Games and all but nine post-1948 Caribbean World Series. Named expansion Florida's 1993– Spanish Voice, Ramirez announced its 1997 and 2003 title and entered Cooperstown, Felo's archived play-by-play already there. * Frick 2001.

JAY RANDOLPH, son of U.S. Senator Jennings Randolph, sat on Franklin Roosevelt's knee at an Easter egg hunt, ate at a White House state dinner, and inverted Ronald Reagan, trading politics for sportscasting: NBC's *Game of the Week,* college and pro football, golf, bowling, three Olympics, and 1967–1987 and 2007– Cardinals, 1988 Reds, and 1993–2000 Marlins. George Washington '58 has outlived twelve U.S. presidencies, including beloved FDR's.

KARL RAVECH graduated from Ithaca College and SUNY at Binghamton, worked in Upstate New York, Harrisburg, and Boston, and in 1993 matriculated as *SportsCenter* anchor at ESPN's Bristol, Connecticut, campus. In 1995, he became Emmy Award–winning *Baseball Tonight* host. Karl hosts World Series, playoff, College Hoops 2Night, college basketball studio, and major golf event coverage, overcoming a 1998 heart attack at thirty-three.

DAVE RAYMOND, Stanford senior class president, has served in the 1995–2005 minors, as a Giants and Orioles fill-in, and on 2006– Astros radio. Daily the former *Forbes* Magazine business reporter, nominated for a prestigious 2001 Loeb Award for coverage, reports Houston's bottom line. Dave also co-hosts a baseball variety show, *J.D. and Dave's Excellent Offseason Adventure*, with Houston TV's and former pitcher Jim Deshaies.

JOHN ROONEY debuted with boyhood idols. 1984: Jack Buck mentors the Triple-A Voice. 1985: John expects a neon coat on meeting Lindsey Nelson, who wears pale blue, terming it "a great coat for radio." 1986: Jerry Coleman says "It's so beautiful here in Kansas City you can see Missouri." John: "We're *in* Missouri." Such a man deserved, and got, network radio/TV's *Game of the Week*, NFL, college hoops, and Twins, White Sox, and 2006– Cardinals.

HOWIE ROSE, born in Brooklyn USA, has called its lineal descendant, the Mets, since 1995, including Mike Piazza's post–9/11 homer, 2006 Division Series, Tom Glavine's 300th victory, and Shea Stadium's close. The Queens College graduate swapped video for the wireless in 2004. Rose also voices radio/TV's hockey Islanders, having worked *Fox NHL Saturday* and Fox's *Saturday Game of the Week*, using his trademark "Put it in the books."

BILLY SAMPLE was a three-sport Salem, Virginia, high school star, attended James Madison University, and played for the 1978–1986 Rangers, Yankees, and Braves. Billy then decided upon another kind of resume, writing for *Sports Illustrated*, the *New York Times*, and *USA Today's Sports Weekly*, calling the Braves, Mariners, and Angels, and gracing NPR, ESPN, MLB.com, and SportsChannel as *The Art of Baseball* host.

RON SANTO bled Cubs red, white, and blue: 1960–1973 North Side third baseman; nine-time All-Star; 1964–1968 Gold Glover; Number 10 retired. From 1990–2010, the should-be-in Cooperstowner aided WGN's Harry Caray, Thom Brennaman, Steve Stone, and Pat Hughes: also raising more than $50 million for the Juvenile Diabetes Research Foundation. *Uber*popular, Ron died last year, at seventy, having become, like Ernie Banks, Mr. Cub.

GREG SCHULTE grew up in Cardinals Country, loved Caray and Jack Buck, and pined to paint America's once-westernmost and southernmost team. Instead, Arizona's 1998– first/still Voice rode the D'backs from Luis Gonzalez's single-year fifty-seven homers to Randy Johnson's Perfect Game. Coming full circle: The ex-NBA Suns, NFL Cardinals, and Arizona State mikeman now does only baseball.

VIN SCULLY graduated from Fordham, joined Red Barber at twenty-two, and aired Brooklyn's sole world title in 1955. Two years later, the Dodgers moved West, Vin hymning baseball as no one had, or has. His song ties Hank Aaron's number 715, Bill Buckner's Error, and Kirk Gibson going deep. In 2009, Scully became American Sportscasters Association "Top Sportscaster of All-Time": play-by-play's Roy Hobbs, the best there ever was. * Frick 1982.

DAN SHULMAN, Toronto-born and University of Western Ontario–educated, has covered America's pastime on Canada's The Sports Network (1995–2001 Blue Jays) and 2002-2011 ESPN Radio (*Sunday Night Baseball, Home Run Derby,* and All-Star Game) and TV (*Monday* and *Sunday Night*). Other hits: CTV 1994 Winter Olympics, The Fan 590 *Prime Time Sports,* and ESPN college and pro hoops. Shulman remains a citizen of his "home and native land."

LON SIMMONS pitched in the minors, hurt his back, became a carpenter, hated it, and turned to radio. In 1957, the Burbank native with a Kirk Douglas jaw became San Francisco KSFO sports director, next year inheriting the Giants. Lon aired them through 1979, did the 1981–1995 A's, and in

1996 returned to his cross-bay home, "a city's idealized self-image," wrote Leonard Koppett, "San Francisco to the core." * Frick 2004.

JOE SIMPSON, All-American at the University of Oklahoma, made the 1975–1983 bigs as Dodgers, Mariners, and Royals outfielder/first baseman. He has called 1987–1991 Seattle TV and 1992–2007 Braves TBS/radio, including Atlanta's first world title (1995), Turner Field's debut (1997), and All-Star Game (2000). Joe aired TBS's 2007 and 2009–2010 NL postseason, and the Braves now on Fox Sports South, SportSouth, and Peachtree TV.

DAVE SIMS was a Bethany College catcher, joined the *New York Daily News*, and segued to WCBS, MSG, WFAN, XM Satellite Radio, and ESPN TV Big East and Radio *Sunday Night Football*. In 1993–1994 and 2005–2006, the two-time Emmy Award recipient did ESPN baseball. Sims has telecast the Mariners since 2007, the view not seen in his native Philadelphia: Elliott Bay, Mount Rainier, and ferries, cargo ships, and sunsets from Albert Bierstadt.

KEN SINGLETON has worked elsewhere, but calls the Apple home: raised, Mt. Vernon; played Bronx youth baseball; entered Hofstra University. The Mets draftee became a 1972–1974 Expo and 1975–1984 Oriole: 246 homers, three-time All-Star and Bird MVP, and 1983 World Series ring. Ken then joined Expos radio and TSN, Fox, MLB International, and Yankees MSG and YES Network analysis and play-by-play.

CHARLIE SLOWES has called the Nationals since the Expos fled Montreal. Robert F. Kennedy Stadium housed the 1962–1971 Senators. After doing the transplanted 2005–2007 Nats there, Slowes moved to Nationals Park. "Bang zoom go the fireworks," he says. "A curly *W* is in the books." Fordham '83 knows DC (airing the 1986–1997 Bullets), and baseball (Cardinals, Orioles, Mets, NBC *Game of the Week*, and 1998–2004 expansion Tampa Bay).

DEWAYNE STAATS learned baseball in central Illinois' Bermuda Triangle: "Cubs, White Sox, Cardinals fans." At night, he heard the then-Colt

.45s over WWL New Orleans: to the ten-year-old, Houston might have been the moon. Staats has done the Astros, Cubs, Yankees, ESPN, and 1998– Rays, including Wade Boggs' hit 3,000, Rays' 2008 pennant, and that year's Series: his "easy-to-take pace perfect," said ex-partner Joe Magrane, "over 162 games."

CHARLEY STEINER. Bradley '71 peregrinated to the RKO Radio Network, USFL Generals and NFL Jets, and ESPN boxing, bigs postseason, *Sunday Night Baseball*, and 1988–2002 *SportsCenter*. In 2005, after three years at Yankee Stadium, the Brooklynite and Cable ACE recipient followed the Dodgers to California: the sole Voice save Dave Niehaus to air the Bombers *and* Angelenos. Charley's XM/Sirius Satellite 2005–2009 *Baseball Beat* is deeply missed.

DICK STOCKTON's career speaks for itself, but thankfully is still spoken for: Syracuse '64, then Pittsburgh, basketball Celtics, 1975–1978 Red Sox, and NBC TV, calling Carlton Fisk's homer. From 1978 to 1994, Dick telecast CBS baseball, Pan American Games, NFL, NBA, and Winter Olympics, later or still doing the A's, TBS baseball, Fox *Saturday Game*, football, hockey, and TNT hoops.

STEVE STONE pitched for four 1971–1981 teams, including Baltimore, winning the 1980 AL Cy Young Award. Stone and two Carays have supplied Cubs WGN viewing pleasure: Harry, 1983–1997, and grandfils Chip, 1998–2000 and 2003–2004. Since 2007, Steve has analyzed White Sox radio, now TV. Kent State '70s resume includes ESPN, TBS, and ABC's *Monday Night Baseball*, working with a likely record *circa* 100 play-by-play men.

RICK SUTCLIFFE clinched the Cubs' first post–1945 title September 24, 1984. "Now our lives are complete!" cried Harry Caray. At a minimum, Rick's life is full. The 1976 and 1978–1994 pitcher won the Cy Young, Roberto Clemente, Lou Gehrig, Rookie and each league's Comeback Player of the Year award. Retiring, he aired the Padres, became a pitching coach, beat colon cancer, did MLB Int. TV's postseason, and joined ESPN in 1998.

GARY THORNE became a Bangor, Maine, district attorney, made the bar of the U.S. Supreme Court, and turned from law to love: "Here I am," he said, "calling my two girls." One was baseball: Mets, White Sox, ABC, ESPN, MLB Int., and 2007– Orioles TV, ESPN Radio's *Sunday Night Baseball* and Division Series, and video game *Major League Baseball 2K9*. The other: hockey, including the NBC Olympics, ABC, ESPN, New Jersey Devils, and *Frozen Four*.

BOB UECKER was dubbed by *Sports Illustrated* "the funniest man in sports-casting" — Joe Garagiola with hair. Uke became a cult clown, film/TV actor, *Monday Night Baseball* and 1971– Brewers Voice, saying "Ah, those fans, I love 'em." In turn, they love the 1962–1967 .200 catcher, *Major League Baseball I, II,* and *III*er, and Lite Beer for Miller star: making Cooperstown Ueckerstown — as Howard Cosell said, still "bigger than the game." * Frick 2003.

DAVE VAN HORNE aired the bigs' first foreign game in 1969 at Jarry Park, the Montreal crowd singing "The Happy Wanderer" in French. Virginia's son soon became Canada's English-speaking Voice, outlasting Coco Laboy, Rusty Staub, and *L'Expos* bandbox to unveil a first: Internet play-by-play. In 2001, Dave joined the Marlins. The 2012 Fish will open a new park near the former Orange Bowl, hopefully redolent of *Parc Jarry*. * Frick 2011.

PETE VAN WIEREN wrote the work ethic large: "We're on the air so long. If you don't prep, you run out of things to say." The Cornell alumnus began with the *Washington Post*, Triple-A Tidewater, and 1976 Braves' rookie "double whammy": mikeman and traveling secretary. Often eliminated by Labor Day, '90s Atlanta remade itself into fourteen straight playoffs: the first to win a Series in three different cities. The Professor retired in late 2008.

MATT VASGERSIAN evokes *Pinocchio*'s "An Actor's Life for Me." At seven, he graced TV's *The Streets of San Francisco* and film's *The Candidate*. At USC, Matt appeared on *The New Dating Game*. Vasgersian began Brewers TV in 1997, shuffling to San Diego in 2002. He has hosted game and poker shows and MLB's 2009– *MLB Baseball Tonight* and aired Fox baseball and football and three NBC Olympics. Still sailing: "*Santa Maria!*" Matt's home run call.

RICH WALTZ played baseball at the University of California-Davis, etched it on ESPN TV/Radio, ABC, CBC, FX, MLB, and now Fox Sports Florida/Sun Sports, and added soccer, tennis college basketball, and Big 10, SEC, and pro football. In 2005, the ex-Mariners and Blue Jays fill-in and World Baseball Classic and Little League World Series Voice became the Marlins' TV angler, hoping to catch the club's third Fall Classic.

CHRIS WHEELER — "Wheels" — has driven baseball's highway since growing up in Philadelphia. Penn State '67 majored in journalism and broadcasting, got job one at hometown WCAU, and went to WBBM Chicago, CBS Network Radio, and Phillies publicity by 1971. In 1977, Chris began a still-running radio/TV niche, his team winning a division, league, and/or Series title in 1976–1978, 1980, 1983, 1993, and 2007–2010.

BILL WHITE braved much as an on/above-field pioneer. In the '50s Carolina League, he used "colored-only" restrooms, had his bus stoned, and stayed with black families on the road. White played for four 1956 and 1958–1969 bigs teams, most notably Cardinals. In 1971, the Yankees made the five-time All-Star baseball's first black play-by-play man. Hiram College '57 became the first minority to call a U.S. network Series (CBS Radio, 1977) and head a major league (NL, 1989–1994).

FRED WHITE has been heard on CBS, NBC, TBS, Raycom, and ESPN: above all, 1974–1998 Royals radio. Since 2001, the Eastern Illinois University product has headed the big league club's alumni group and broadcast services, also airing at one time or another the Big 10 and Big 12, Kansas City's twenty-four-hour channel Metro Sports, and occasional Royals wireless: Cardinals Nation's Radio Free American League, bridging George Brett and Zack Greinke.

DAVE WILLS was an Elmhurst College pitcher, called Midwest League radio, spent eleven years as White Sox pre- and post-game host and John Rooney's fill-in, and buoyed University of Illinois-Chicago basketball, Notre Dame football, and Chicago ESPN Radio 1000's *Kevin White Show*. In 2006, the 1988 Speech Communication and Urban Studies degree graduate joined Tampa Bay wireless, working with Andy Freed.

WARNER WOLF was ABC TV's 1976 first *Monday Night Baseball* host, joining Bob Prince and Bob Uecker, and televising that year's All-Star Game, LCS, and Olympics. Wolf's DC and New York stations include WABC, WCBS, WTOP, and now WPEN's ESPN Radio. *Primo* calling cards are *Gimme a Break!, A Boo of the Week!,* and hailing Yankees' reliever Mariano Rivera: "TRUST me . . . this guy can bring the heat!"

BOB WOLFF kept the 1947–1960 Senators from becoming the game's Atlantis. "I never had to say who was winning," he recalled. "I just gave the score." Wolff's consolation included Don Larsen's 1956 perfect game (Mutual Radio), NBC's 1960s *Major League Baseball* (partner, Joe Garagiola), and 1954– MSG, Sports Channel, and News-12 Long Island, luring awards like his Senators did defeat: at ninety, America's longest-running TV sportscaster. * Frick 1995.

Chapter One

A Little Child

Bob Prince, an army brat, followed baseball at six boyhood posts and fourteen or fifteen schools. Orphaned, Harry Caray saved money from selling papers to rent baseball books at a lending and leasing library. Joe Buck followed Pop to spring training and the road. Bob Costas played Little League near Hartford, Connecticut. "I was good field, no hit, and you know about guys who can't even hit their weight. That was true of me, and I weighed 118 pounds."

In Half Moon Bay, near San Francisco, Jon Miller, ten in 1961, absorbed base-ball, too. Playing the board game Strat-O-Matic, he mimicked the public address Voice, organist, crowd noise, and Giants' Russ Hodges. Hearing Jon through the door, a friend of his mother's asked who it was. Mom pled ignorance. "It sounds, though, like he has a little bronchial condition."

Next year Miller saw his first major league game, at Candlestick Park. Go figure: Los Angeles outhit San Francisco, 15–12, but lost, 19–8. Billy O'Dell threw a fifteen-hit complete game. The Giants' Willie Mays, Felipe Alou, and Jim Dav-enport homered. Attendance was 32,819. "Other than that I don't remember a thing," Jon said, sitting with Dad and a radio in Section 19, upper deck.

September 1962 became his "fan's coming of age." Frisco and LA played by day and night, respectively, vying for a pennant. After dark, Jon heard Russ re-create the Dodgers while Vin Scully did them live: "I'm on a hill, for reception, switching the car radio back and forth." Ultimately, the Jints lost the World Series to New York, Willie McCovey making Game 7's last out with Miller in a dentist's chair. "Pain everywhere. No wonder I almost bit his finger."

At fifteen, Jon fingered his first play-by-play. At twenty-one, he was hired by California Golden Seals hockey owner Charlie Finley to televise odd games. Thereafter the Falstaff joined the A's, Rangers, Red Sox, Orioles, Giants, and ESPN TV and Radio, in 1991 winning his first play-by-play cable ACE Award. Accepting it, Miller told the crowd, "What am I? I go to games and my best lines are, 'low, ball one,' or probably the line I'm most proud of — 'line drive, foul.'"

Scully likes the mot "In every childhood a door opens and the future appears briefly." With luck, it later reappears in the little child within the Voice.

In 1927, Babe Ruth hit sixty homers, Charles Lindbergh crossed the Atlantic, and I was born. Two out of three ain't bad. Growing up, baseball meant everything. Dad and his friends talked about it around an old pot-bellied stove. Bread cost six cents: Mom used to buy it a day late to save a penny, giving me the cent for candy. One year — 1938 — I saved fifteen cents to buy my first *Spalding Guide*: A year after Ducky Medwick won the Triple Crown, his picture was on the cover. I'm *still* a big Medwick fan, and he's been gone since 1975! After school I'd ride home on a bike, go to the news-stand, and see scores on the blackboard. In Iowa, every country school district had a team, families bringing food to the games. Our team played on a cleared-off cow pasture. There was no admission, but we'd pass the collection to buy balls and bats. That was our entertainment, baseball being with us all along. In Civil War photos, soldiers are playing a form of baseball. Southern prisoners learned it in the camps. At war's end, baseball spread from the Eastern Seaboard across the land. By the start of the twentieth century, you can almost trace hardship by the people who dominated the game — farm kids and players from Southern mill towns, then Irish, Italians, then blacks and Hispanics. Baseball was their ladder to a better life, which after all, is why people came. In World War I, Woodrow Wilson said: "Keep playing." World War II: Franklin Roosevelt said, "Keep playing." After 9/11, baseball brought us together. Think of it as U.S. history.
— *Milo Hamilton*

Come with me now to the front porch of 625 Northeast Street, Princeton, Indiana, on a hot sultry evening. About 8:30 at night, an eleven-year-old boy is chasing his lightning bugs, capturing them in a Mason jar, with holes punched into it with an ice pick. Every once in a while he would squish one between his thumb and forefinger just to see the glow. Dad is sitting on the porch with a cold slice of watermelon on one knee and a hot ear of buttered corn on the other, with a cold beverage sitting on the ground, and suddenly from the old, floor-model Zenith radio in the living room comes this voice [Harry Caray's] screaming, "It might be! It could be! It is!" And the young boy jumps about three or four inches off the ground with each halting phrase. Magic is happening in St. Louis, Missouri! Stan Musial has hit another home run about a zillion miles away! And a career had germinated that wound up in Cooperstown!

—*Dave Niehaus*

At 1:00 p.m. each Saturday, I opened a box of crackers, poured a glass of milk, and crawled under the radio—actually sat *underneath* it, putting a pillow on the crosspiece. I'd stay there all afternoon. The football teams were secondary. I mean, Alabama-Tennessee should have meant nothing to a kid in Washington Heights in New York. But I would listen and the crowd noise would come down like water out of a showerhead. I hadn't seen a crowd, but I had heard one. I loved its roar—I'd get goose bumps long before I saw them on my skinny arms. I used to think, "Oh, my gosh; that must be great." Even today, no sounds can possibly sum up a situation better.

—*Vin Scully*

In Little League, I woke every day in Falls Village, Connecticut, raced to the window, and made sure it wasn't raining—Game on!—then turned on the Yankees' Mel Allen, Les Keiter, and Jim Woods. I'd use a ruler to make a scorecard on a legal tablet, vainly hoping my Indians would beat the Yanks. Two or three times a year Dad and I went to Yankee Stadium, where players parked in an outside lot. You'd put a self-addressed stamped postcard in the crack some left in their car window. The player autographed, then returned it. 1950: a different world. I'd batboy in an old-guys Interstate League. Afterward they drove to a bar, left me in the car, got gassed, and brought me Coca-Cola. At nine, I wrote an essay, *The Smell of a Baseball Glove*: "Perfume is wonderful, a new car smells great, but ain't nothing like the smell of a Rawlings XTG 34 pitcher's glove." At sixty-nine, I still have one. Someone asked, "How do you hold a baseball?" I said: "I think you got it wrong. Baseball's had a lifelong hold on *me*."

    — *Steve Blass*

Princeton, population about seven thousand, was Gil Hodges' hometown, too, which is why he was my favorite player. I'd go into a little place called the Palace School Room, town square, in the Gibson County courthouse. And a man, D.A. Keimer, used to stick his chalk in a bucket of water, then put daily ball scores, including Gil's Dodgers, from Western Union on the blackboard. Some say watching paint dry is boring. Watching chalk dry was *thrilling*, because as it did, you saw the scores.

    — *Dave Niehaus*

"Be careful what you wish for" didn't apply to me. I was introduced to baseball in 1951 and after that dramatic season, capped by Bobby Thomson's Shot Heard 'Round the World, I wanted more. Thomson's poke against the Dodgers won the best-of-three pennant playoff. Yet the only World Series my Giants won before moving to San Francisco was 1954's sweep of the 111–43 regular-season Indians. No fan will forget the September 29 opener at the Polo Grounds, immortalized by Willie Mays's over-the-shoulder catch off Vic Wertz and Dusty Rhodes' game-winning, tenth-inning homer. I won't, since I was there, my father and I playing hooky from his job and school, respectively, our seats eight rows behind the Cleveland dugout. Like any Series game, celebrities and baseball notables were everywhere. Connie Mack wore his high-starched collar. After five straight Series titles, Yankees manager Casey Stengel finally had a Fall Classic to view instead of win. Giant fans Tallulah Bankhead and George Raft were nearby. So was Roy Cohn, Sen. Joseph McCarthy's aide, back from Washington's Army-McCarthy hearings. What a cast. My most memorable moment came in infield practice. Suddenly, photographers began to snap my picture. Turning, my father asked me to do the same. "Do you know who that gentleman is sitting right behind you?" he said. "General Douglas MacArthur. Those photographers think you're his *son*." Only later did I grasp MacArthur's impact — and meaning of that game. In baseball, anything can happen. Rhodes hit the ball 257 feet for a homer. Wertz went more than 460 for an out.

— *Dick Stockton*

As a Little League rookie, I was the only player ever traded, from the Yankees to the Giants, because the Yankees didn't have a uniform small enough. Quickly I found I was a horrible hitter. Once, in the on-deck circle, I knew I had to pee. I hadn't had a hit all year, so no problem: I'll make my usual out and head into the woods. Darn if I don't bloop the ball over the rightfielder's head, round first, and make second. My first hit! A double! I'm so happy until I realize I'd wet my pants. That's the bad news. The good: In 1950, we had on heavy gray wool uniforms, so nobody knew but me.

— *Steve Blass*

I knew what I wanted to be when I grew up the first time I heard Vin Scully's voice doing a Brooklyn Dodger game on radio. Had to be 1955 or '56. I was six or seven. I remember hearing the crowd, the crack of the bat, and that voice painting the picture. My eyes and ears must have grown to the size of the tubes in the back of the big brown Zenith radio. When I learned that was Scully's job — *job?* – my future life was clear. About this time my mother, who, to be charitable, was never much of a fan, bought me a new glove. Every kid remembers his (or her) first glove, almost as fondly as his (or her) first love. But my first glove and I were destined for a quickie divorce. I'm left-handed, which probably explains more than I care to admit. The moment mom gave me my mitt, I had to go out, play catch, and break it in. The glove felt fine. But my right arm didn't. For days the glove continued to feel fine, but I threw the ball like a ballerina. Then, missing one toss, I threw the *glove* hoping it would stop the rolling ball. (It didn't and never does.) I retrieved the ball, throwing it back to the kid with whom I was playing catch. Then an epiphany! I could easily throw the ball overhand, with mustard, better *without* the glove on my left hand. How could this be? Thinking, "My son is left-handed," Mom had assumed the glove should go there. It was a *right-handed* model, meaning that for the first couple of weeks of my ball-playing life I'd had to throw with that hand.

From the start, my baseball future was not on the field. Doubt vanished the first time I played a fungo softball game around the block from my house. I was five years old. The elm tree up the street on the right was first base. The elm tree across the street on the left was third base. A towel was second base. Home plate was a piece of cardboard. At this point an older neighborhood kid, Donnie Sorensen, eight or nine, hands me the bat and offers instruction. Toss the ball about shoulder high. When it drops, swing the bat, hit the ball, run to first base (the tree), then second, then third, and then home. I was nothing if not obedient. So I hit the ball. And ran to the tree. Then the towel. Then to the next tree. And then . . . home. I mean, *home!* All the way to my *house!* I couldn't figure out why everyone was chasing after me, laughing, screaming, and telling me I was running the wrong way. I tell you this, because it is with the innocence and pure joy without inhibition of that child, that I can still watch, broadcast, and enjoy this wonderful game. The first time I heard the game on the radio. The first glove I ever got. The first time I picked up a bat and hit the ball. And ran home.

— *Charley Steiner*

In my 1950s youth, New York had three teams. Who we liked defined what we were. Dad was a Dodger fan, our TV daily tuned to Channel 9, Jackie Robinson, Duke Snider, and Roy Campanella building a Hall of Fame resume: spring, summer, and, of course, fall. Turn the dial, see the Yankees. Tom Clancy wrote a book called *The Hunt for Red October.* Whitey Ford, Mickey Mantle, and Yogi Berra *owned* October. My favorite player was Willie Mays, who, like the others, made baseball seem so easy. It wasn't, as I later found, nor in my second career, influenced by those who broadcast: Russ Hodges, Vin Scully, Mel Allen, Red Barber, Ernie Harwell, Jim Woods, Phil Rizzuto, Connie Desmond, and Lindsey Nelson and Bob Murphy after the Giants and Dodgers left in '57 — possibly the greatest concentration of broadcast talent anywhere, anytime, their rhythm and pace fueling my baseball love. I try to make the game as informative and entertaining as they did after Dad introduced me to the game in 1951, when I was four. New York, New York's still a great place to grow up on ball.

— *Ken Singleton*

In New York, you inherit baseball passion. I inherited my dad's _Yankees_ passion, memorizing their batting order by age six. For instance, I knew that number 7 was Mickey Mantle, centerfield, and 8, Yogi Berra, catcher. This was crucial to the first baseball I remember—Game 7 of the 1960 World Series. Every Baby Boomer recalls Bill Mazeroski's home run over the leftfield wall at Forbes Field to make the Pirates champions. Berra was playing leftfield, with Johnny Blanchard catching, but all I knew of Yogi was his mask, chest protector, and shin guards. All winter, I tried to make sense of Berra's metamorphosis from behind the plate to the wall. How did he _get_ there so fast? Yogi must have taken his equipment off, raced to leftfield, and still might have caught the ball if only it had stayed in play! Eventually, I figured out that this day he played another position. It's a miracle I became a broadcaster, given how baseball confused my feeble, six-year-old brain.

—_Howie Rose_

I grew up loving Mantle, whose father had osteomyelitis, a degenerative bone disease. Chasing and carousing, Mickey expected to die by forty. At the time, we thought him a hero. Later Mick _became_ one, going dry, doing TV spots saying, "Kids, don't be like me." I interviewed him on [NBC's] _Dateline_, where as Mick was talking, I'm recalling how when he played, the Yankees let you on the field after every game, even to visit the monuments in deepest centerfield. I remember holding my father's hand there—the whole dimension of the place was so overwhelming for a child—and asking him, "Is this where Mickey Mantle plays? Can Mickey Mantle throw a ball from here all the way to home plate? Can Mickey Mantle hit a ball here?" Mick died at sixty-three, in 1995. I gave the eulogy at a Dallas memorial ("We wanted to crease our caps like him, kneel in an imaginary on-deck circle like him, run like him, heads down, elbows up.") but didn't know it would be televised. All I wanted was to be worthy of the family. Back in New York, I was approached by passersby. You don't feel boastful at a time like that, just gratified, that it was something that Mick hopefully would have liked. You pay back what you can.

—_Bob Costas_

In late '50s and early '60s Dumont, Minnesota, population 150, the Saints town team played twice a week, not in Yankee Stadium but Ralph Leslie Field. I never knew who Ralph Leslie was, nor what he got for naming rights, just that instead of bobblehead giveaways, a sandwich board sign was put in the middle of Main Street: "Baseball Today." Somehow it *worked*—the game drawing *twice* our population. Farmers parked their pickups behind the snow, or outfield, fence. Families sat on blankets, as likely to discuss Al Frisch's home run over a creek behind the fence as Harmon Killebrew's homer the night before. When the Saints scored, horns honked across town. Today, Lutherans no longer sit on the third-base side or Catholics on the first—remember, the early '60s. Yet as Dumont shrinks and Main Street erodes, the Saints remain its pulse, as they were at Ralph Leslie Field.

— *Dick Bremer*

As a kid, all I worried about was playing Kentucky basketball. Mama wanted me to play baseball: safer, more money. We compromised: I played baseball. I was a mama's boy, still miss her, she died in 1977. A single parent, she didn't make much a week. We lived in an itty bitty house in Savannah: no air-conditioning, holes in screens, open windows. Mama and I got through it together. We had a very special relationship, even when we argued. I was an All-American basketball player, but finally we took the money: a $30,000 bonus with the Kansas City Athletics. I join them in 1963, and that winter who do they acquire? Rocky Colavito, mama's favorite player.

— *Ken Harrelson*

If I hadn't made the majors, I wouldn't be broadcasting now. My high school coach was Ed Kirby of Housatonic Valley Regional School in northwest Connecticut, its six towns producing three big-league pitchers: me, Tom Parsons, and my brother-in-law, John Lamb, a fellow early-'70s Pirate. We had a mixed grill pitching staff: Moose [Bob], Veale [Bob], and Lamb. Signing in 1960, I left for the Bucs' Kingsport, Tennessee affiliate, where I had a lot to learn. One day, I took my six pair of underwear and six pair of socks on my first pilgrimage to a public Laundromat, which, unsurprisingly, sold soap. I thought: "Hum, twelve items, one box of soap for each, give me twelve." I fire the sucker up, add soap, and see suds flood the floor. Panicked, I ran away, ultimately sending laundry in a brown box to my mother, who washed and sent it back. It worked well until she decided to include cookies. Mom's package had melted chocolate chips all over it: God bless her, forgetting the August heat. I thought about returning to the Laundromat, except my picture was probably on the wall.

    — *Steve Blass*

    In 1961, the Washington Senators moved to Minnesota. In 1965, the renamed [Minnesota] Twins made the Series, but next year we moved to Missouri, maybe never to see my team again except for a relatively new invention that made baseball portable. My sister's rectangular transistor contraption had a folding wire stand, round dial, and volume control wheel on the side. It being hers, naturally what came out was Beatles music. Magically, one night I find that, at the southeasterly corner of our back porch, I can get the Twins' flagship station! True, the dial had to be rotated by thumb with surgical precision— but, once set, stuck. A satellite dish may take you everywhere, but can't compare to this little box, barely available a decade earlier, that deep in Cardinals country let me hear my Twins.

    — *Dick Bremer*

    About this time I'm a little kid in Salem, southwest Virginia. My grandparents could probably tell you how I used the rocks out of their yard. I'd be Willie Mays, right-handed, or Willie McCovey, left-handed. Spin the rocks, hitting sliders with them. The rest of the neighbors thought I was touched, which is probably true. Anything to play ball.

    — *Billy Sample*

    I, too, grew up far from a big-league city: in my case, St. Louis, along the Mississippi River. Silvis, Illinois, had little local TV baseball, so I turned my Philco to St. Louis' booming 50,000-watt KMOX, Jack Buck and Harry Caray winning me over, even when the Cardinals lost. In 1959, we drove to Busch Stadium, where Stan Musial happened by carrying a bat, glove, and ball. He flipped the baseball to the clubhouse guard, saying, "Give that young man there the ball." My mouth opened, but I couldn't speak. My father said, "Thank Stan," and I think I did, so shocked I can't remember. Two Cardinals were from our home, Gene Oliver and Dean Stone, whom my father asked if he could get some players to sign the ball. At Cincinnati, our next stop, Dean presented it, unbelievably signed by the *entire* Cardinals team. I still have it, in great condition, Dad coating with shellac names like Stan, Curt Flood, Bill White, Ken Boyer, and just called up Bob Gibson. One day I tell my parents I want to broadcast baseball. I'm eight, but they don't laugh, saying I can do anything I set my mind to. I set my mind to baseball. Like the Mississippi, nothing's changed.

    — *Greg Schulte*

In 2001, I broadcast Barry Bond's monumental seventy-three-home-run season. It reminded me of my incredible April 16, 1962 first game. I'd bugged my father to take me to Candlestick, and finally he relented. What a year to fall in love. The Yankees won another pennant. My Giants had great names— Mays, Orlando Cepeda, Willie McCovey, Felipe Alou— an exciting team, big crowds. The Dodgers lost Sandy Koufax in July and still had a 102–63 record. I often wonder if I'd love baseball as much if I'd grown up in a bad market with a boring team. Hitting traffic on the Bay Shore Freeway, we got to our seats late. From then it's one memory after another, the first how cold it was in the upper deck. Picking up binoculars, I had no feeling in my hands. I look out at Mays, then at Russ Hodges, to whom, like Lon Simmons, I'd been listening by radio. Russ says, "There's a curve ball, outside, ball two," then grabs some french fries. I *see* him do it— and *hear* him chew! Next pitch: "Fastball, outside, ball three." Russ grabs a cup, takes a swig, and at that moment I say, "This is the life for me!" Each inning I compared my scorebook to the scoreboard's scores and pitchers. In *our* game, Alou hit a sure double-play grounder, stopped running, then sped up on Junior Gilliam's wild throw. Dad said, "Look, he didn't run." I remember that when people now knock players, imagining guys always hustled when we were young. Dad taught me to keep score, and my scorebook was full: Giants, 19–3 in the ninth, when Billy O'Dell got wracked. Manager Alvin Dark later was asked if he minded having to ask Jim Duffalo to warm up. "No," Dark said. "I knew Billy wasn't tired because he'd _only_ thrown _150_ pitches." _Only_ 150! Writer Bob Stevens's account had the real number— 165— normal once upon a time. The Giants were four games out with seven left. The last day LA led by one. Our game ends first, Mays's homer beating Houston, 2–1. At Candlestick, people stayed for Russ's re-creation of the Dodgers game, St. Louis winning, 1–0. That day the 49ers played football at Kezar Stadium, where thousands were listening to the Giants by radio. The players'd break huddle, the crowd going nuts, the 49ers wondering what gives. In baseball, it's always something, like that incredible first game.

—_Jon Miller_

It _does_ matter where you grow up. Sports were nowhere on my family's radar until I stumbled, in 1979, on Chuck Thompson and Bill O'Donnell, who soon _became_ family, radio so personal, especially in a place like Baltimore, where pre–free agency Orioles and football Colts players owned local businesses, retired, and stayed. Chuck and Bill were a huge part of a big city with a small-town feel. At eight, I lay on my bed, eyes closed, as they let the sound wash over you, as great announcers do. Before long, I wanted to share a city's ups and downs, maybe affect a kid listening, like me. I know times differ from when I was young, my Baltimore gone for-ever. I'd also never presume to be as talented as Bill, dying in 1982, and Chuck, working another two decades. One night, interning with flagship WBAL, I saw Chuck awaiting the end of a post-game show, introduced myself, and found him true to form— warm and welcoming. I was struck by how Chuck meant so much to me, never _knowing_ me. How _did_ he create that feel? In 1993, entering Cooperstown, Chuck closed his speech by hop-ing that if someone was asked if they knew him, they'd say, "Yes, I did. He was a friend." In a twist of fate, my first big-league broadcast was the 2005 spring training day that Chuck died. Tampa Rays Vice President of Com-munications Rick Vaughn, former Orioles PR director, came up, tapped my shoulder, and said simply, "Chuck is gone." We had both lost a friend.

—_Andy Freed_

My parents met May 8, 1964, the first Friday night game at the Mets' new Shea Stadium. Marv Albert, twenty-two, hosted radio's pre-game show, interviewing Shea employees, including Benita Caress, nineteen, a stadium usherette. They were married fifteen months later. I was born in 1968, charting life by games on television and in person. At seven, I first saw the Yanks at Shea Stadium during Yankee Stadium's renovation. My third-grade teacher let a friend and me watch their TV opener while the rest of class did schoolwork, grasping my obsession. It peaked for Ron Guidry K-ing eighteen Angels, Reggie Jackson's three homers in a Series game, and Bucky Dent. By the '80s, I'd gravitated to radio, Shea closer to home, and took my recorder to practice play-by-play. As writer Leonard Koppett said, "I can imagine a world without baseball, but can't imagine wanting to live in one."

— *Kenny Albert*

Growing up, watching *Monday Night Baseball*, down goes the sound, out comes the soup ladle I used as a microphone. I had Captain Ahab single-mindedness. As a teen, I got creative enough to regularly get out of class, catching the number 7 bus from high school to Silver Stadium, where the [Triple-A Rochester] Red Wings played. I had notes, written in study hall instead of school work: the Wings against Syracuse, Tidewater, or whoever they were playing. Outside I set up a card table, spread out my notes, and talked into my recorder. Dan Logan, a 6-foot-7 first baseman, whom I had the temerity to interview on the field, encouraged, not mocked, me, though I was more terrified talking to him than later Cal Ripken or Barry Bonds. At fifteen one frigid night, I was invited by Rochester's GM into the press box to escape the cold. How big-time was this? The soup ladle was in the soup, where it belonged.

— *Josh Lewin*

In 1996, I graduated from Stanford just after Dave Raymond and ahead of David Flemming, now with the Astros and Giants, respectively, having written each minor league club and received a stack of rejection letters. I wound up doing high school sports and disc jockeying in Cody, Wyoming, starting the eight-year minor-league process that led finally to the Twins. Throughout, my wife supported me in every way. When Cody opened, we'd just started dating and she was perplexed about why I didn't get a job with the Giants so we could stay in San Francisco with her family and our friends. I explained how jobs just don't open, you have to pay dues, etc. In the next several years we had this conversation repeatedly. When Dave got the Giants job, I excitedly told my wife. Soon the other Dave joined the Orioles, and I proudly relayed that news. Her reaction to each bulletin was identical: "I thought you said it was hard to get to the big leagues. Are you sure you just aren't very good?"

— *Kris Atteberry*

I fell in love with baseball in West Virginia, where my dad [1933–1947 U.S. Congressman and 1958–1985 Sen. Jennings Randolph] was an athletic director and sportswriter before getting into politics. That continued in Washington, as with many presidents. [Abraham Lincoln often played hooky to watch amateur baseball teams play at the White Lott, or Ellipse. In 1909, ex-amateur pitcher William Howard Taft saw his first game as president. "The game was interrupted by cheering," read the *Washington Post*, "which spread from the grandstand to the bleachers as the crowd recognized him." Herbert Hoover loved baseball, even when a World Series crowd screamed "Beer! Beer!" at him during Prohibition. Harry Truman's wife Bess kept score by following the Senators on the radio. In 1960, John Kennedy, forty-two, met Stan Musial, forty. "They tell me I'm too young to be president and you're too old to play ball," said JFK. "Maybe we'll fool 'em." They did.] My Dad knew nine presidents, the most memorable his first. Once, Franklin Roosevelt greeted me at a White House Easter egg hunt. I sat on his knee, feeling FDR's steel leg braces. He was a great father figure. In 1942, Roosevelt wrote the wartime letter to Commissioner Kenesaw Mountain Landis: "I honestly feel it would the best for the country to keep baseball going." Due to dad, Griffith Stadium became a second home. I met Babe Ruth twice, the last when he had cancer, played with Williams and DiMaggio, and sat with Connie Mack — in ninety degrees, he wore a suit and tie. Even the lousy Senators had Mickey Vernon, Cecil Travis, and Eddie Yost. We all knew "First in War, First in Peace, and Last in the American League." What a time for baseball, if not always the Nationals, and every year FDR, pitching the opening day first ball.

— *Jay Randolph*

Chapter Two

Present at the Creation

Radio's 1920s and '30s resembled a two-headed Janus. On one hand, the wireless might lure people to the park. On the other, it might keep them home – why pay for something you could hear for free? Gradually, teams aired their entire home schedule. Away line charges were pricier. Solution: wireless telegraphy, like Western Union's Simplex machine, "[giving] play-by-play," wrote The Sporting News, "within three seconds of the time it occurs."

An operator at the park sent code to a station: B1L meant ball one, low; S2C, strike two, called. An announcer could "re-create" – soon a rite like gloves left on the field between innings. Arch McDonald worked three blocks from the White House. In Detroit, Ty Tyson called Hank Greenberg "Hankus Pancus." Cincinnati's Harry Hartman bayed whammo and bammo and socko and belto. Most used sound effects to hide being in studio.

A stick on hollow wood simulated bat v. ball. The sound track included background noise. Fielder: "Come on, bear down." Fan: "You couldn't hit my house!" None of it was real. Reality didn't matter. Only one Voice put the mike adjacent to the telegraph, amplifying its dot-dash. "No con," said Red Barber. "I wanted people to know I wasn't at the park."

By 1935, four Des Moines outlets aired the Chicago Cubs live. A fifth, WHO, re-created. Once, its wire on the fritz, "Dutch" Reagan considered returning to the station. "Then I thought, 'No, if we put music on people'll turn to another station doing it in person." What to do? Make a big to-do. "One thing doesn't make the box score, so for seven minutes I had the batter [Billy Jurges] set a record for foul balls."

Jurges fouled to the left and right. Pitcher Dizzy Dean tied a shoe, mopped his brow. Rain neared. A fight began. "None of this happened, but at home you couldn't tell." Finally the wire revived, Reagan laughing. Years later he bared its text: "Jurges popped out on the first ball pitched."

The 1939 Giants, Yankees, and Dodgers were the last teams to permit radio. In 1955, Pittsburgh became last to mint live road coverage. Looking back, the re-creation was among many of baseball's broadcast firsts.

The Pirates were first to use a tarpaulin, pad the outfield wall, host a night All-Star Game and World Series, and have a guy go 7-for-7: Rennie Stennett. They were also first to air baseball at Forbes Field on August 5, 1921. Talk about making up play-by-play on the fly. Few in western Pennsylvania had a radio. Listening, you heard the crowd often drown announcer Harold Arlin out. KDKA's announcer didn't even know if they'd *do* baseball again. In 1986 he said, "Hard to imagine how far the wireless has come." That year, Harold died at ninety, having helped.

— *Steve Blass*

Like the '20s, post-war radio invented itself. In 1949, the Liberty Broadcasting System started re-creating *Game of the Day*. Next year Mutual's [live] *Game* began. In '52, we launched the Brooklyn Dodgers Network from Cleveland to Miami, few knowing games weren't live! Mail went to, "Nat Allbright, Brooklyn Dodgers, Ebbets Field." *Brooklyn*?! We never left our studio in suburban DC! A direct line patched us into Dodgers flagship WMGM an hour before the game. Mutual did pitch-by-pitch. Re-creating gave me time for stories, but could leave me in the lurch. Once Brooklyn led, 3–1, when a guy in studio motions to cut my mike, saying somebody's on the phone. "I'm in a *game*!" I said. "Get the number, and I'll call later." A few minutes later the guy returns, still motioning: "This man wants to talk *now*." At inning's end, I pick up the phone. "Nat, this is so and so from Jacksonville," said a Dodgers affiliate head. "We have a Mutual station here, doing your game, and they're ahead of you by half-an-inning. I don't want to piss sponsors off, so catch up, okay?" I went back, and did. Art has its place, but not as big as profit's win and show.

— *Nat Allbright*

1950. I'm not forty-eight hours out of the University of Iowa, and I'm to broadcast my first boxing match—the first I ever saw! By 11 o'clock I've done all sixteen fights. I broke in in the Quad Cities, Iowa, area, where there was a joke that if you threw a ball in the air and blew a whistle, Milo'll be there. One day I did Tri-Cities Blackhawks—later Atlanta Hawks—basketball. Now the real work began: a B League doubleheader, played that afternoon. Getting to the station, I knew there'd been *thirty-seven* walks. I tell ya', re-creating I made first-pitch hits and outs. Sadly, every walk had four pitches. To keep the audience, you, well, embellished. In studio, the staff announcer played the anthem, then put his head into a waste basket to name starting lineups, trying to sound like the PA guy. You'd get "E-6" over the ticker, repeat on the air, "That looks like an error," move back from the mike, say "E-6" to simulate the PA, then lean back into it: "The official scorer says it's an error for the shortstop." *Whew!* Earlier we'd gone to the park to create sound effects: noise, staccato clapping, vendors crying, "Get your peanuts and your popcorn!" That was our baseball: re-create on command. It got me to the majors in three years.

—*Milo Hamilton*

Dodgers-Cincinnati, early '50s, 4-all, beautiful afternoon from Crosley Field. Gil Hodges singles, Jackie Robinson's at bat. I'm awaiting the next pitch when a guy tells me there *isn't* any. Recently, we'd enrolled with Western Union's new sports machine, which'd worked well—till today. Data's jumbled, so we call Western Union. Meanwhile, "get out the thundercloud"—sound effects. "See centerfield?" I ask my listener. "Look at that flag pole, stretching out. Man, I smell rain." Robinson's up, except we don't know what he's doing, so I have him break a bat, then another, talk to [manager] Walter Alston, who starts arguing with an ump: anything to buy time. Back then, smoking, I knew that if you took cellophane off a pack of cigarettes, crumpling it near the mike, it sounds like rain. "Hear those drops?" I said. "Move the scorebook back, can't get it wet." I'm dry in studio, but to the listener I'm drenched. "Man, it's dark out here! Oh-ho, here comes the tarp!" We go on a rain delay—of *one hour and forty-five minutes*—till the machine comes back. Dodgers win, 7–6. Next morning an amazing thing happened. The newspaper never mentioned our almost two-hour delay.

— *Nat Allbright*

Unable to play my way into the majors, I talked my way in. Jack Coombs was my coach at Duke. Breaking my leg freshman year, I was laid up, did radio, liked it, and asked Jack about my future. In effect, he said, "I've seen you play. Stick to radio." After World War II, I joined *Washington Post*–owned radio, leaving when the station turned all-music for television, still new. Studio lighting was so brutal, sweat poured from my forehead. Guests got ill on the set. In a wool suit, you lost ten pounds in a show. No wonder live sports thrived, making me the country's first TV sportscaster. I was also lucky to be twenty-seven. Older writers smoked cigars in the team bus rear. I sat in front, playing ukulele, like a college fraternity. The Senators let me pitch batting practice. In spring training I even hit, shocking camp by reaching the fence. That night, players staged a mock show of snubbing me. Finally one said, trying not to laugh, "That was a horrible thing you did to that pitcher, Bob. After you slammed that pitch they released him. They said that if Wolff can hit him, he must have nothing left."

— *Bob Wolff*

My career path differed from many [including Bob Wolff's story, previous]. By 1978, I'd aired hockey for six years in the minors, including Chicago's top affiliate, the Dallas Black Hawks. That July, Texas Rangers broadcast head Roy Parks asked if I'd done baseball. I lied, saying I had at Brown University, so he asked to hear a tape. Not having one, I auditioned for a TV opening. I'd played ball at Brown, attended Rangers games in Dallas, and had a decent command of the game's history and phraseology—enough to tape a four-game series—my tryout. I was exactly what they wanted: someone young and cheap. Roy figured that by 1979 I could do baseball without embarrassing him. If you like baseball on skates, hear my awful early tapes. With so much cash at risk, today my hiring could never happen. Think what I would have missed [notably, the fifty-year-old Rangers, nee Senators, franchise's first pennant in 2010].

— *Eric Nadel*

My first gig wasn't full-time—twenty-five home games at $25 per [game]—or in the bigs. In 1981, Angels minor leaguers trained in Casa Grande, fifty miles from Phoenix. That March I paid my way there to see my new team, the Class-A Redwood Pioneers. At the Single-A field, I introduce myself to a grizzled man with a two-day beard, "Hi, I'm Ken Korach, a Pioneers broadcaster." He says, "Nice to meet you, I'm Warren Spahn." I turn red, not recognizing the Hall of Famer. The then-Angels minor league pitching instructor forgave me, regularly touring our minors, patient with the usual questions about "Spahn and Sain and Pray for Rain" or complete-game 200 pitches he threw against the 1963 Giants and Juan Marichal, losing, 1-0, in sixteen innings. They say you never forget the first. Getting to know Spahn was my first encounter with a childhood icon: not names on a page or voices from a box, but real people, in *any* gig.
     — *Ken Korach*

My professional life began when I was twelve: August 4, 1966. At Shea, Juan Marichal was on the mound, whom the Metsies had never beaten, and behind, 5–0, looked like they never would. With two out in the sixth, Marichal had a perfect game. Scheduled to hit, Mets starter Dennis Ribant would surely be pinch-hit *for,* except that for some reason skipper Wes Westrum let him bat, Ribant bouncing a thirty-eight-hop single. In the ninth, Ron Swoboda pinch-homers off Bill Henry: Mets win, 8–6. Marichal wasn't the losing pitcher, but who cared after the best game a twelve-year-old could see? Most kids my age wanted to be Swoboda, mobbed by mates. Not me. I didn't ride the bus as much as float home, wondering about Bob Murphy on radio and Lindsey Nelson on TV. Did they go crazy? Think it gone right away? How would *I* have called it? I was envisioning my dream. When Shea closed in 2008, the Mets gave me Murph's chair, where I'd announced in the booth named after him, symbolizing my responsibility to be worthy of some Mets game-winning ninth-inning homer. Somewhere, for some young fan, that moment is *their* August fourth.
     — *Howie Rose*

The big leagues are easy. It's the minors where if you work around, through, or over obstacles, your education will be complete. In 1986, I broadcast the Carolina League Durham Bulls. One stop was playing at old Salem [Virginia] Municipal Field: a piece of work, in every way. The stands were built into a side of the Blue Ridge Mountains—for fans, beautiful; for broadcasters, grotesque. The grandstand had a visiting radio booth at its back. Topping everything was a roof from the booth to the end of the stands. All you could see was a sliver of light above the outfield fence, so any ball in the air was a mystery. Add poles blocking your view of first and third base and how this booth was shared by the home PA announcer and local sportswriter. Finally, consider that those two individuals carried on constant conversation over the broadcaster's— *my*—head for the entire game. My friends, if you can conduct nine innings of coherent baseball under those conditions, the majors are smooth sailing.

— *Gary Cohen*

Almost all players, coaches, managers, and umpires toil in the minors. So why do some unfairly stigmatize Voices who do the same? I spent twelve years doing everything there was to do: sell ads, write programs and game notes, paint grandstands, chip garbage and leaves from dugout ice, pull the tarp, and drive prisoners needed to pull it on rainy days in a van back to jail. Some games I got a nominal fee as official scorer and beat writer. I even gave plasma to make money, as the holes in my arms prove! I took two pay cuts in three years from my first radio job to work baseball. Plasma paid some bills, as did money saved by living in umpire dressing rooms some *Wisconsin* winters without heat. All this made me appreciate the majors, especially being befriended by our profession's heavyweights. I collect autographed baseballs of Ford C. Frick Award recipients, one of whom, Ernie Harwell, typically wouldn't take money for postage. By the way, he never looked down on minor-league announcers. Having worked with the '40s Atlanta Crackers, he'd been one himself!

— *Brett Dolan*

The minors teach humility, above all. In 1963, I'm at Pittsburgh's Carolina League Kinston. A teammate is a future big-league player and manager, five, six years older, good defense, can't hit, so he'd been sent down from Triple-A Columbus to learn how to pitch. Soon Gene Michael is Kinston's starting pitcher, shortstop, and $25 extra-a-month bus driver. At night I'd play blackjack to keep him awake, telling Gene between draws to watch the road. League trips were so long we seldom ate after a game, just slept on the floor or above on the suitcase rack, reaching town barely in time for next day's game. By then, we'd changed into our dirty, wet uniforms, waking up the bus. We'd go into a greasy spoon, all eighteen, nineteen, or twenty of us, sharing hamburgers. A little different than baseball's room service of today.

— *Jim Price*

My big-league debut almost didn't happen. In 1988, I aired Triple-A Pawtucket while Bob Murphy and Gary Thorne did the Mets. That offseason Gary aired hockey's New Jersey Devils, who, shockingly, made the playoffs. This led Mets broadcast director Mike Ryan to phone, saying that Gary had to air a playoff game and would I— *would I?* — fill in? I talked with my Pawtucket boss, who informed me the Pawsox played that night and I wouldn't be available. Happily, Mike called again, saying if the Devils made the next playoff round Gary'd miss a May 4 Mets game and would I call it? This time the Pawsox *weren't* scheduled — one of only three times all year! The night deciding the Devils' playoff destiny, I listened on radio from Massachusetts, reception fading in and out, vanishing with two minutes left, the Devils clinging to a one-goal lead. On May 4 I'm at Shea, as nervous as can be. Bob Murphy, who I'd never met before, introduced me as a fine young broadcaster. I was to give the lineups, which I did, then talk till Bob began the game. Instead, I was struck dumb. I didn't know what to do, or say. It was as if language had never come out of my mouth. Murph must have seen my panic, patting my hand with his to say that everything is okay. Bob's kindness let this lifelong Mets fan do a decent enough job that next year he made me his full-time partner, having saved my debut once it finally began.

— *Gary Cohen*

[As Bob Murphy showed] broadcasting is less important than treating people right. In 1992, I was a Trenton sportswriter heading to South Carolina for a story on a young South Jersey player. I'd done college, Babe

Ruth and high school radio, but wanted more, so I called the Charleston Rainbows Voice, say I'm a writer hoping to transition, and can I watch him air a game? Rich Jablonski said yes, even letting me do color and later play-by-play: barely knowing, yet helping, me. I used those tapes to land my first on-air job, often wondering if I would ever do the same thing if I were Rich. I hope so. I'm still not sure I've ever found how to express my gratitude for opening my door and never thinking twice, lighting the fire that yet burns today.

— Tom McCarthy

My door opened through a friend at Fordham, introducing me to the great hockey Voice Dan Kelly, who got my tape to KMOX, which hired me in '84. At ten, I'd found the transistor worked well under your pillow for late night games. At fourteen, I first thought that if you couldn't play, do-ing play-by-play in different cities would be cool. Many teams now have a separate radio, cable TV, and free TV crew. Then things differed, guys doing radio *and* TV, the Mets and Yanks each televising about 150 games. As I write, I'm watching Vin Scully call Dodgers-Diamondbacks on MLB Network. In '70s New York, you wouldn't see a non-Mets or Yankees game except for NBC. No problem. I turned back to radio, where irrespective of my team's luck, I awoke next day to a dead nine-volt battery.

— Charlie Slowes

Branch Rickey said, "Luck is the residue of design." At fifteen, finally allowed to practice in a booth in Rochester, I become an unpaid Red Wings intern: making popcorn, changing carbonated drink tanks, checking tele-type. When radio opens, I get it, crediting the tanks. In my twenties, I bad-ger then-parent Orioles' WBAL into a half-inning with Jon Miller. What a break, until the game's rained out, replaced by "Orioles Talk," which their Voices hate. "You do it!" they said, and I do: two-and-a-half call-in hours. Next week, WBAL requests a sports director and talk-show audition, ex-cept I don't have a tape, so I use a Rochester station, have friends call, and create one. At twenty-five, I'm off to Baltimore—as a talk host!—like the dog, chasing a car, then catching it. "What do I do now?" In 1996, Fox, start-ing baseball, wants a youngster, and luckily [coordinating producer] John

Filippelli had heard "Orioles Talk" nightly driving home. I'd never done TV, but John pitches me as a fresh face: my audition, an inning of '95's The Baseball Network Indians-Mariners playoff. Fortunately, when Fox calls I'm in Cleveland with the O's and I sweet-talk a PR friend into loaning me a VHS copy. At the hotel, I get a VCR machine, watch "my inning," and scribble stories to use about each batter. By the audition, I knew it cold: Jay Buhner would double—and it would hit high off the rightfield wall. Sure, I had the answer key to the test—but the chance was too big to miss. Without putting yourself in a position to be discovered, you don't make jack. You find luck. Luck doesn't find you.

—*Josh Lewin*

Between class, working, and playing Elmhurst College baseball, I didn't have time for early radio. Instead, my ticket to the bigs began in front of a PA mike in high school at Barnaby's and Nino's Pizza. I'm University of Chicago interim baseball coach when my college pitching coach, Mike Young, mentions a broadcast job. I make and send a demo tape to Class-A Kane County Cougars GM Bill Larsen, who hires me for sales, PR, and a little radio. Soon Bill gives me the full-time job. The clincher, says official scorer Marty Cusack, was when Larsen walked by a radio. "Who you listening to—Sox or Cubs?" he asked. Cusack said, "This is *our* game, that's *Dave*." Larsen said: "He's pretty good." Trust me—this doesn't happen without the PA "Number 34, your pizza's ready."

—*Dave Wills*

My first full big-league year was 1996, after seven full or part years of doing the PCL Las Vegas Stars. Since the Oakland Coliseum was being renovated, or compromised, for baseball, depending on your view, the A's season began in Vegas. People asked what my bigs debut was like, and I didn't know because I'm sitting where I'd sat since 1989! Things began as bizarrely for the A's leader, Mark McGwire: not yet a pariah, just trying to stay healthy. Each game I taped a clubhouse interview with a starter removed earlier, spending little time with Mac, who'd hurt his foot that spring. Relationships take time to cultivate, and the last thing I needed was a sign on my back: "I'm the new broadcaster!" Imagine when after a March

game, I hear a loud voice: "Hey, you, come over here, what the heck are you *talking* about?" Yep, McGwire, having heard us discuss on the piped-in clubhouse broadcast how long he might be out. Clearly I don't need the star player pissed off at me, especially one 6-foot-5 and 260 pounds. "Mac, I know I'm new," I begin, "and if there's a problem, let's talk," having repeated on air what team doctors said about his return: four to six weeks. McGwire shook his head, saying a timetable produced unfair pressure. If he didn't return on the expected date: 1) People'd say he wasn't working hard enough; 2) He was injury-prone and not tough enough; and/or 3) He was selfish and not thinking about the team. I said: "If you were me, what would *you* say?" Mac said, "That I'll be back when I'm back," making enough sense that ever since I've tried to avoid speculation. Timetables can be nebulous, four to six weeks becoming three or four months. A doctor wouldn't try to broadcast. A broadcaster shouldn't try to doctor.
    — *Ken Korach*

In 1997, I weekly fill in for the White Sox' John Rooney. That fall I had a scratchy throat, the broadcaster's bane, but didn't dare rest — one chance a week to shine. In Boston, we trailed, ninth inning, bases full, Albert Belle up. "Swing," I said, "and a drive to deep right-centerfield!" I tried to add, "It's a grand slam!" but nothing happens. I hit the cough button, trying to clear my voice. Same result. Back in Chicago, the doctor diagnosed acute bronchitis and slight walking pneumonia. Worse, our station made a promo of my botched call, comparing it to Harry Caray's throat-clearing in his final days. How ridiculous. Harry's legendary career was winding down. My un-legendary career already seemed washed up. Silence may be golden, but not on the air.
    — *Dave Wills*

Starting '96 on the disabled list, McGwire returned to the lineup in April, not talking to the press. The speculation sent him into shutdown, but once back his bat awoke. On May 25, Mac had a huge night in Baltimore. Before this, I hadn't asked him on the post-game show, but now a bell goes off: It's time. Before leaving for the field, I get advice from partner

Ray Fosse. "Don't ask Mac about himself. You won't get much. Ask about the A's." Game over, I congratulate Mac, asking for an interview. No response. I sit on the bench, McGwire comes over. I ask again. More silence, failure flashing before my eyes. I have to start, but what if I get dead air or one-word answers? "Thanks for joining us, nice game, must feel great to be back," I finally say, placing the mike in Mac's face. The face is blank: a nightmare, coming true. After an eternity, he turns to me, laughing: "It's about time you asked. I've been trying all year to get on your show." As Ray predicted, McGwire was effusive about his teammates, manager Art Howe, and the fun he was having. New A's owner Steve Schott even wanted to cut it up into sound bites to use as a commercial, which thankfully never happened. Next year Mac was traded to the Cardinals. As Paul Harvey said, we know the rest of the story. I liked what came before.

— *Ken Korach*

I wanted to be a pitching coach until televising a 2001 game. The Diamondbacks are getting bombed at home, 18 to 0. Looking at the pen, I say: "Arizona's bringing in a possible future Hall of Fame lefty to pitch the ninth." Who, the booth wonders? Randy Johnson, someone ambidextrous? Nope. Mark Grace, left-handed first baseman, my ex-Cubs teammate. Gracey hits the mound, looks up, and mouths, "What do I do *now*?" Deciding to help, I signal fastball: Gracey throws a strike. Another fastball: fly out. Next guy, I signal inside: Mark hits the target. Then, changeup: Mission accomplished, batter grounds to third. Two up, two down, and way too easy. David Ross comes up: a rookie, so I motion curve. Gracey mouths: "I don't have one." I try again: fastball. Ross hits it off the restaurant facing. In His infinite wisdom, God, having just closed one career — pitching coach — had opened another in the booth.

— *Rick Sutcliffe*

In 2010, I returned to baseball [as Padres TV Voice] after twenty-five years away. I made this decision, basically, because I love the game. And here's an opportunity at this stage of my career that I didn't think was possible in my favorite sport. I broadcast the Angels for about a decade

[1969–1978 and 1985]. In 2002, flying from Buffalo to Los Angeles, I learn about their first pennant after, of all things, doing a football game! It was so emotional I began to weep. Seeing this, the passenger in the next seat caressed a crucifix and held my hand. Laughing, I tried to calm her, explaining why it meant so much— the Angels!—after all this time.

—*Dick Enberg*

Chapter Three

The Play[er]'s the Thing

Before interleague play, centralized umpiring, and a one-stop hierarchy, baseball regularly referenced the Junior or Senior Circuit, an American League-type park, a National's kind of game. In 2009, MLB Network's Hot Stove *named the past decade's nine best players, judged by skill, not league. Albert Pujols led, trailed by Barry Bonds, Alex Rodriguez, Manny being Manny, Derek Jeter, Ichiro Suzuki, Mariano Rivera, Chipper Jones, and Jeff Kent. Unlike in Florida, recounts are not allowed.*

Next year MLB's Prime Nine *ranked "Top 9 Centerfielders," Willie Mays topping Ty Cobb, Mickey Mantle, and Tris Speaker. Joe DiMaggio was fifth — his number. Sixth: Ken Griffey, Jr., belting fifty-six homers (twice), hitting the Warehouse at Camden Yards (the first), and, like Mick, unanimous AL MVP. Edwin Snider was the Duke; Jim Edmonds, a highlight reel; Kirby Puckett, the hinge around whom two Series swung.*

Only centerfield tops shortstop's marquee. The latter's "Top 9" named Honus Wagner, Arky Vaughan, Cal Ripken, Jr., and A-Rod one through four. Next: sweet-tempered Ernie Banks — Mr. Cub — an amalgam of, among other things, 512 home runs, Wrigley Field's breeze off Lake Michigan, and "Let's Play Two." Jeter was sixth, followed by Luke Appling, Old Aches and Pains. Ozzie Smith and Barry Larkin finished eighth-ninth. Not to quibble, but where is Luis Aparicio?

Growing up in baseball's last full nine-man decade, I liked the "All-1960s Team." So far, so good: catcher, Bill Freehan; first base, Willie McCovey; second base, Pete Rose. Even better: Ron Santo, third base. Less good: Maury Wills, shortstop. (Not to beat a dead horse, but what about Little Looie?) Donning 1967's

Superman's cape, Carl Yastrzemski was in leftfield; Mays, center; Hank Aaron, right. I would regretfully drop Yaz, rename the category outfield, and add Roberto Clemente's best-ever rightfield arm.

It is fine that the starting pitcher is Juan Marichal, high-kicking like Gwen Verdon via Gower Champion. Bob Gibson would be even finer: 251–174, 3,117 Ks, and a 1968 of 1.12 ERA, 13 shutouts, and 28 complete games. Jim Britt, a 1940s and '50s big-league Roget's, *liked to say, "There are [X number of] persons here." Someone asked, "Is there a reason you don't say people or fans?" Jim stiffened: "Yes, people is correct. And fans are correct. But persons is more correct."*

Either way, Britt knew, like Shakespeare, that "the play[er]'s the thing."

People say hero this, hero that. Hey, what about DiMaggio? Take 1949. Our team splits camp in Florida, we go to Texas, hop a train north, and there's a guy missing. Joe D. had a heel spur, had it operated on, and missed the first sixty-five games. In June the Yanks go to Boston: you're talking Ted Williams, Bobby Doerr, Johnny Pesky, Dom DiMaggio. A terrific Red Sox team—but not as great as Joe. He hasn't swung a bat all year. First game of the series: home run, we win. Next day Joe belts two more. Ask Pesky: "One of them went over the [leftfield] Wall, the screen, and everything: It might have gone to the Hotel Kenmore." We win. Next day he hits the light tower: Yanks sweep. *LIFE* magazine puts him on the cover. You saw it, not believing it.

— *Jerry Coleman*

Billy Crystal, a New York native and a huge Yankee fan, was asked at Yankee Stadium before Game 1 of the 2003 LCS between the Red Sox and Yankees about his first recollection of their rivalry. "I was sitting right up there [first-base side, upper deck]," Crystal said. "Second game of a doubleheader, Ted Williams strikes out against Bobby Shantz. Thirty years later, I meet Mr. Williams. I said, 'I have home movies of you striking out against Bobby Shantz in the second game of a doubleheader at The Stadium.' He looked at me and I swear, Tim, he says, 'Curveball, low and away. Ellie [catcher Elston Howard] dropped it and tagged me, right?' I said, 'Yes, that's it!'"

— *Tim Kurkjian*

Williams hated us: "Christ, I wanted to beat the Yankees!" In 1949, our last two games are against Boston at The Stadium: one win, they take the pennant. On Saturday, Allie Reynolds gets bombed, Joe Page comes on in the third, Red Sox up, 4–0, and he shuts the door. We came back a run at a time. In the eighth, Johnny Lindell homers to win, 5–4, tying the race, and next day what noise: You could hear it in _Ashtabula_. In the first, Williams misplays Phil Rizzuto's triple, Tommy Henrich scores him, and we're up, 1–0. Inning by inning zeroes mount. In the eighth, [Boston skipper Joe] McCarthy pinch-hits for Ellis Kinder, but doesn't score. In our half, two guys get on and my triple knocks 'em in. "What a rinky dink," Williams told me, "that little Texas Leaguer." Number 9 was so pissed. I said, "Ted, you just saw the cover of the baseball. Its core is still in orbit." We win the pennant, 5–3. Ted never did stop fuming. What got him were all their superstars, and little Phil and I beat him. I said, "Scooter, we're carrying this club, it's just that nobody knows it."

— _Jerry Coleman_

[In 1968, dedicating a statue of Stan Musial outside Busch Stadium, former Commissioner Ford Frick said: "Here stands baseball's perfect warrior. Here stands baseball's perfect knight."] I grew up following Musial, then broadcast the '50s Cardinals, and saw how classily he behaved: Stan never really left Donora, Pennsylvania. You look at his average [.331, seven batting titles, and amazing 1,815 hits at home _and_ on the road], the pitchers he faced, his longevity [twenty-two years], starting as a gimpy-armed pitcher, becoming an all-time hitter: How could he _not_ be my favorite player?

— _Milo Hamilton_

A summer evening in 1963. I had a date with a beautiful girl. I was going to take her to see Musial make his final appearance in Los Angeles. I took her to dinner first, asked her to marry me, and never made it to the game. You know she had to be special to make me forsake The Man.

— _Dave Niehaus_

No sport matches baseball for fathers teaching sons. My dad, in the printing business, had selected season tickets at the Polo Grounds. In 1951, he brought home my first packets of Bowman baseball cards: five in a pack, flanked by a slab of bubble gum. I had a card, of course, of Stan, but my first card was my all-time favorite: Al "Red" Schoendienst, Cardinals' second baseman. Bubble gum pictures were vertical or horizontal. Red's was a horizontal close-up, bat over his shoulder, wearing the blue cap with red peak and intertwined *STL*. My dad took me to my first game, a beautiful Sunday, in May. I'll never forget seeing the light towers above the upper deck, each team's pennant floating in the breeze, and walking from the Speedway on Coogan's Bluff. What a feast for the senses: the sound of scorecard hawkers, echo of soda cups being stepped on, and smell of cigar smoke. Through the dark runway I saw centerfield's Chesterfield cigarettes sign, the bright green stands, and brilliant green grass: what's more, I heard the crack of the bat in batting practice. My eyes settled on two persons, each with one foot on the tire supporting the cage. They wore the Cardinals' road uniforms: gray with red numbers trimmed in blue, red stockings with blue and white stripes, and the familiar cap I knew so well from the cards. One wore Number 6: Musial. The other wore Number 2: Red Schoendienst, second base, St. Louis Cardinals, bats switch, throws right, born Germantown, Illinois. At the moment, my card came alive. Close my eyes, and it's yesterday.

— *Dick Stockton*

My 1947–1960 Senators never made the first division. Harmon Killebrew was an exception to the talent drought, but shared their horrific luck. In 1959, he led the American League with forty-two homers. That year *LIFE* magazine planned a feature. They put adhesive tape into every spot at Griffith Stadium where he'd homered — then, had a plane take a shot of where and how far the homers went. For days *LIFE* waited for Harmon to go long. President Eisenhower came to a game and on cue Number 3 went deep. Wouldn't you know it? That same week — May 26, 1959 — Harvey Haddix hurled a twelve-inning perfect game to KO Killebrew's cover. If we didn't have bad luck, we'd have had no luck at all.

— *Bob Wolff*

People debate if golfers are athletes — and if pitchers are players. Less than two weeks after his 1961 graduation, Lew Krausse, eighteen, the first

real "bonus baby," started for the Kansas City A's and blanked the Angels in his inaugural. Lew went 2-for-3 at the plate, expecting to be in the lineup *next* day as an outfielder! Krausse was just a few days out of high school, where that schedule is normal and where the pitcher *is* a player. Tigers pitcher Hank Aguirre once went 1-for-62 as a batter. I'm not sure that he'd agree.
— *Denny Matthews*

Not every player knows baseball statistics, but they know their own. My first game was May 10, 1964. I didn't know anyone in Pittsburgh, so my wife Karen and I stayed with another rookie, Tommie Sisk, and his wife till finding an apartment. That Sunday, Tommie was knocked out in the first inning. Relieving him, his houseguest — me — pitched five shutout innings. I'm ecstatic till learning that Sisk has been demoted to Columbus, which I'd just left. We ride home in the same car we'd driven to the park: the Sisks leave their house, the Blass guests stay. Eight days later I start my first game, at Dodger Stadium. A day before I'd wandered on the field and seen my all-time actress idol, Doris Day, fifteen feet away. I have no idea what happened *that* day. I do remember *next* day, May 18, about to warm up, seeing the scoreboard: "Starting pitchers: Steve Blass, Pirates; Don Drysdale, Dodgers." The ball starts feeling like a shotput, twenty or thirty pounds, my memory as complete as the 4–2 complete game I somehow threw. Every time LA's huge Frank Howard swung I swore his bat'd hit me. Coaching third, Leo Durocher gave me a complete education in words that I'd never heard — each inning, all game. Willie Davis and Maury Wills liked to run. Knowing this, catcher Smoky Burgess called nothing but fastballs. By the fourth, I said, "I *do* have a breaking ball." Smoky still wouldn't call it.

Finally, did I tell you about my first big-league homer? Except for Billy Williams, homering and doubling twice, I pitched a September 5, 1969 no-hitter against the Cubs. As amazingly, I went four for five. I don't recall much about my homer except that it came at 2:48 p.m., the wind was out of the northwest at thirteen miles an hour, overcast, sixty-one degrees, and Ken Holtzman was the pitcher. I hit the ball, get to first, and coach Don Leppert says, "Take a left," since I was in the habit of peeling off for the dugout. That night roommate Bill Mazeroski, turning thirty-three, and I celebrated his birthday and my emergence as a slugger.

— *Steve Blass*

I never saw Edwin Donald Snider play for the Brooklyn Dodgers. His 1947–1957 there preceded my baseball awareness of baseball, and its first few years preceded me. Yet Duke stirred a lifetime memory and he wasn't even playing for the Dodgers, either in Brooklyn or LA, but for the *Giants* at the Cardinals' old Busch Stadium, aka Sportsman's Park on Grand Avenue. To a child, going there bordered on the spiritual. Especially under arc lights, colors took on a surreal quality, the perfectly manicured grass somehow greener and thicker than anywhere else on the planet. Even at eleven, I knew May 27, 1964's matchup between Bob Gibson and Juan Marichal had, as we'd say, buzz. I grew up nearby on the Illinois side of the Mississippi, loyalty to the Cardinals a requirement, almost a birthright, yet my heart rested deep in the heart of Texas, the Houston Colt .45s radio network magically reaching my bedroom after dark. I knew Marichal was good because he'd no-hit the Colts a year earlier. Another night in 1963 my dad and I had sat in Busch's leftfield bleachers — the park's cheapest — as a Cardinals fan mocked my Colts souvenir pennant slipping down its wooden stick into a half-mast position. I hoped to use that unpleasantness to get Dad to upgrade our seat location — a $3.50 lower-level box wouldn't fit his bill, but $2.50 reserved seat might — only to have him "quick pitch" me, thinking that himself.

Our new rightfield seats were near Marichal warming up, kicking high, leg fully extended and foot well above Juan's head, before his right arm came forward. Warming up across the field, Gibson drove his high-octane fastball. What a duel — until leadoff man Chuck Hiller's fly in our direction hit the roof: 1–0, Giants. Moments later another homer followed. For years I'd spent allowance on baseball cards. Knowing Hiller's, I was shocked he took Gibson deep. By contrast, my perusal of the second batter's card told me that Duke Snider might, averaging 42 home runs, 123 RBI, and .320 for the 1953–1956 Dodgers. At Ebbets Field, he was the Duke of Flatbush. In 1958, he packed number 4, headed west, and became a Dodger celebrity with Hollywood good looks sentenced to play in the vast

Coliseum—then pitcher-friendly Dodger Stadium. In 1962, Duke had five homers; '63, joined the basement Mets; '64, wore 28 with his new team, the Giants, because Mel Ott's 4 had been retired. The resume, if not player, had just homered before my cycs.

In the last of the first, Snider trotted to right, no longer Brooklyn's centerfielder. I had no idea Duke would soon retire, only that seeing him next to Willie Mays I looked at Snider more. Playing in front of me, he got loose for the second inning by talking and throwing the ball in a humpbacked arch pattern with a Giant in the bullpen: seemingly approachable. I began to contemplate an overture. Suddenly another crack of the bat announced Ken Boyer's home run to the very bleachers where my dad and I had sat last year. The Giants led, 2–1, after three homers in two innings against two future Hall of Famers. In the third, Snider returns to right, where I determine to make contact. Waving would do no good. Duke wouldn't see me, busy watching every pitch. I decide the only solution is to repeatedly yell "Duke, Duke, Duke!" My father just looked as if to say, "What's going on?" I said: "I'm yelling at Duke to see if he'll notice me."

By the fifth, Duke hadn't, despite my voice loud enough to carry four rows of seats, over the bullpen, and within earshot of my target. With two out, Marichal readied to face Gibson. I yelled one last "Duke!" He turned his head to the left, looked at me, and with right hand waist-high near his side opened his palm and waved. At eleven, I had contacted a major leaguer. When Gibson fanned, Duke ran toward the dugout. I looked not at him but the spot where the contact occurred. The score remained 2–1: Gibson, yielding five hits; Marichal, winning and fanning 11. Note: As an Astros rookie, I met Duke, then an Expos broadcaster, in 1977. His grace was even grander than his wave.

—*Dewayne Staats*

In 1967, I became baseball's first free agent. The Red Sox won the pennant *despite* me hitting .200. It helped that Carl Yastrzemski won the Triple Crown [.326, 44 homers, and 121 RBI. Teammate Rico Petrocelli credited Yaz's "being maybe the first player to have an offseason conditioning program." New Sox manager Dick Williams "played on those great Brooklyn teams in the '50s – Robinson, Snider, Hodges – but said no one was like Yaz in '67"]. Interestingly, he then became my fixation. A lot of athletes pick out one guy and say, "I'm better than he is" for motivation. All winter I worked my butt off to beat Yaz and in '68 had the best year of my life.

That fall we had dinner. Carl says, "You've had a hell of a year [35 homers and 109 RBI]." I said: "It's your fault." Yaz says, "What are you talking about?"

I laughed, "I was obsessed with you, so I tried to stick it up your behind." He starts laughing, too, because that's what teammates do: egg each other on.

'Sixty-eight did something else. Fans wanted a character, so I gave 'em love beads, bell bottoms, a cowboy hat—The "Hawk"—my persona. You know how it is. A gentleman meets a lady. Suddenly, sparks fly. That's '68. I had 150 pairs of pants. I bought fifteen Nehru suits; before wearing five, they're out of style. In 1969 I get traded, cry, try golf, quit, do Red Sox, then White Sox, TV. In 1986, I try being GM, Mama having said, "Son, you're a good kid and I love you, but you ain't the smartest thing I ever saw." The exception is when I went after Yaz.

—*Ken Harrelson*

Like Yaz, Harrelson was a very good hitter. "I played nine years with fear," he said. "Everyone has it. I can't remember 100 at-bats when I didn't have fear. I almost quit my second year in the big leagues because I was so afraid. One day in Kansas City, Al Kaline, one of my idols, walked past me. He saw my fear. He said, 'We all have fear at the plate,' and kept on walking. That helped. In forty-five years in baseball, I've known maybe five guys who were fearless. The only one who was totally fearless was [Boston's] Tony Conigliaro [who was severely hurt in 1967]." Before or after his beaning? "*Both*," Ken said.

—*Tim Kurkjian*

To me, *Strat-O-Matic* was like life, only more important. Today it has a computer version. My game had a new game each year based on last year's statistics, every player represented with a card. You rolled some dice. They had charts. The idea was simple: If we played the entire season, everything would end like life. My chart said that if Willie Mays hit fifty-two homers in 1965, he'd hit fifty-two on *Strat-O-Matic '66*. Actually, at thirty-five, he hit thirty-seven, meaning he was still Willie Mays.

—*Jon Miller*

Talk about building confidence. I'd look around and see Willie Stargell at first, Mazeroski at second, and Roberto in right: three Hall of Famers helping you. How many pitchers can say *that*? My attitude was: "Hit the ball in their direction, and I'm going to get a sandwich. When I come back, you'll be out." Each year at a team party Willie got a huge tub, poured in every kind of liquor, added grape juice to hide the taste—didn't work, it was awful—and stirred it with a bat. When we removed the bat, booze had bleached the trademark. Today it'd be Home Depot paint thinner. Maz gave advice: "You're in the big leagues now, so no excuses. People don't want to know why you didn't do something. They want to know why you did." Roberto didn't need excuses. Once I said, "If I ever get traded, I'm gonna' pitch you inside because every pitcher throws you away and you hit .350." Roberto eyed me: "Blass, I tell you one thing. You pitch me inside, *I hit the f—ing ball to Harrisburg!*" That took care of that.

—*Steve Blass*

I did Cardinals Channel 5 St. Louis in the 1970s and '80s. Then, few clubs televised daily, so you might miss an event. Bob Gibson was the most competitive player I covered. I'd kid him, "Why don't you pitch a no-hitter when I'm on the air?" Year after year: no no-hitter. In August 1971, we're in Pittsburgh, televising Friday and Sunday but not Saturday night. The great Steelers owner, Art Rooney, loved baseball. Saturday he invites me, *St. Louis Globe Democrat* writer Jack Herman, and Art's brother, a priest, to a harness track outside Pittsburgh. At 9 o'clock, a maître d' told us: "Gibson has a no-hitter in the seventh inning." The *Globe* didn't publish Sunday, but now Jack has to make the park for Monday coverage. He arrives in time, and Gibson no-hits the Pirates, 11–0. "Gees, Bob," I still say, "the least you could have done is save it for Channel 5."

—*Jay Randolph*

In 1971, we made the Series. I won a couple games, but it was Roberto's stage, showing the world what Pittsburgh'd seen the past seventeen years.

He averaged .414, hit in every game, and homered. He threw guys out, and was even memorable when he didn't. Clemente caught one ball at the rightfield line, did a 360-degree turn, and threw a one-hop strike to Richie Hebner at third, almost getting the Orioles runner. Another time, the ball rattled near the warning track, like a hockey puck in the corner. Roberto picked it up, threw a strike to Manny Sanguillen, and the runner wisely held at third. Clemente was an MVP, got 3,000 hits, won four batting titles, five times led outfielders in assists, and had twelve Gold Gloves, but forty years later, two *non*-outs tower. No wonder that each at-bat the Three Rivers Stadium organist played *Jesus Christ Superstar*.

— *Steve Blass*

Luckily, my one-year broadcasting baseball coincided with "The Bird," named after the *Sesame Street* character, Big Bird. For weeks America had heard about Mark Fidrych. On June 28, 1976, he faced the Yankees at Tiger Stadium on ABC's *Monday Night Baseball* — everyone seeing how he talked to the ball, danced around, and patted the mound like a gardener. Fidrych won, 5–1, then acknowledged the first nationally televised sports curtain call. "Folks," I marveled, "they're not going to stop clapping until The Bird comes from the dugout. . . . Fantastic! Mark Fidrych is born tonight on coast-to-coast television." Mark became Rookie of the Year, later dying in a tragic farm accident, but the legend still lives.

— *Warner Wolf*

The '70s Orioles had terrific guys. Gordon Beard, a sportswriter in Baltimore, made a speech at a retirement function for Brooks Robinson. "In New York," Beard said, "they named a candy bar after Reggie Jackson. Here in Baltimore, we name our *children* after Brooks Robinson." Pitcher Mike Flanagan had been caught by his seventy-two-year-old grandfather in the back yard. "If I threw too far inside or too far outside, he couldn't reach it," Flanagan said. "And if he missed it, he would have to chase it. So, I had to learn how to hit the target."

— *Tim Kurkjian*

Amos Otis was a great base stealer because he studied pitchers, especially lefty Vida Blue, who relied on rhythm. To break it, Amos stepped out

of the box a lot or asked the umpire to check the ball, which so frustrated Vida that he'd throw the ball directly *at* him. Blue faced first base in the stretch, yet Amos took the biggest lead I've ever seen. Kauffman Stadium's then-artificial turf had dirt around the bases. Amos often had both feet on the carpet—about an eighteen-foot lead! He'd tell U. L. Washington, "See that wrinkle?" What wrinkle? U. L. said. "That wrinkle in his pants," A. O. said. "When that's there, he's going home."
— *Denny Matthews*

I don't think Dale Murphy ever got due credit. A great Braves teammate. Two-time [1982–1983] MVP. Played every game for four straight years. Once night we faced Doc Gooden with nine stitches in his hand. Dale'd stuck his hand through the Plexiglas a night earlier. Now, for you hockey players, nine stitches are no big deal. For a baseball player, you're talking two weeks off. Dale pinch-hits a home run off Gooden. He shoots! He scores!
— *Billy Sample*

Some of our [Astros] guys could bring it. Nolan Ryan's live four-seam fastball maintained its elevation from the mound to the plate. J. R. Richard's two-seamer was just as fast, with a lot of downward motion. Mike Scott had a heater, too. But the guy with the most heat was probably a pitcher I caught later as bullpen coach, Billy Wagner, throwing a hundred-plus. The hardest guy to catch was Joe Niekro and that ridiculous knuckleball. No defense. If he didn't know where the ball was going, how could you be there to catch it?
— *Alan Ashby*

[In 2010, *Sports Illustrated* called rookie Jason Heyward "the 6-foot-4, 245-pound man-child whose talent manager Bobby Cox compares with Hank Aaron's."] Before Heyward, I'd never seen anyone do what Bo Jackson did. In 1985, I aired Georgia college baseball. On April 2, Foley Field had its first night game, *v.* Auburn, Bo luring a huge crowd. First inning: ground out. Fourth: solo homer with the aluminum bat used in college.

Sixth: another solo blast. Seventh: walk. Eighth: Bo hits a monstrous blast going *up* when it smashes left-center's new light standard. Everyone's jaw dropped, thinking what Bo could do without having to use the majors' wooden bat. Ninth: He doubles, clearly in a slump. Auburn wins, 23–11. Aluminum was Bo's most precious metal.

—*Jim Powell*

Some think that TV and other media discriminate against Midwest baseball. If it doesn't happen in the East, it apparently doesn't happen. Frank White signed out of high school, graduated from the Royals Baseball Academy, and climbed the farm system: Cookie Rojas' backup, then a regular under Whitey Herzog. Study video, see statistics matching any middle Hall of Fame infielder's, and explain Frank not in Cooperstown [eight Gold Gloves and 2,006 hits in seventeen years with Kansas City]: in forty years of broadcasting, to me the best second baseman ever to play the game. Paul Splittorff was another farm graduate, the Royals' first pro starter, pitching for 1968 Class-A Corning, New York, a year *before* our team was born: like Frank, quiet and resolute, won twenty games, helped take three straight '70s West titles, started the 1980 LCS-winning game. Today they're terrific Royals TV analysts, overlooked by each Coast, but beloved in mid-America.

—*Fred White*

One spring training in Winter Haven, Florida, Oil Can Boyd rented several adult movies from a local video store. It was nearly time to break camp and head north when The Can was detained because he hadn't returned the movies. It became a story for the enterprising Boston writers, one of whom went to the video store to get the facts of the story, including verifying the specific titles of the porn movies. Writer: *Is "Debbie Does Dallas" on the list*? Clerk: *Yes, sir, it is*. The problem was cleared up, the movies were returned, and Boyd was allowed to leave with the team, but not before Chuck Waseleski, a statistical guy who worked for the Red Sox, came up with the funniest line ever in a sport that always has provided the funniest lines. He called it The Can Film Festival.

—*Tim Kurkjian*

By 1993–1994, the Twins were near the end of a terrific run. Kent Hrbek wasn't the player he had been. On a plane, Dave Winfield, who wasn't either, would come up to first class with the coaches and manager, spread his long legs out, and tell stories. Like them, Kirby Puckett would retire soon, yet still loved baseball. I'd be at the park at 1 o'clock for a night game and see Kirby, hitting ball after ball off the batting coach: amusing himself, gearing up. "Come on, you got nothing! Bring it! Bring it!" Whack! Whack! Then: "Come on, b____, bring it in here!" Roy Campanella said, "You gotta' be a man to play baseball for a living, but you gotta' have a lot of little boy in you, too." Whack! That was Kirby, making himself work harder, a little boy inside the man.

— *Jim Powell*

Robin Yount's maybe my all-time favorite player. Spent his whole career with one club, the Brewers. He could have gone tons of other places for a ton of better money. He just liked it here. Three thousand hits. Two-time MVP [1982 and 1989]. Started as a shortstop, moved to center, which tells you his athletic skill. He seemed to be able to do whatever he needed to win. Didn't blabber, just went out and did it. As a player, think of him as the opposite of me.

— *Bob Uecker*

On Wednesday, September 6, 1995, ESPN paid a visit to Oriole Park at Camden Yards. Baseball was just coming out of the strike, and we needed good news: Cal Ripken Jr.'s 2,131st successive game, passing Lou Gehrig. ESPN wanted me to do the game, which I respectfully declined. This was a national *game*, but a Baltimore *thing*, and I wanted to do local radio. Chris Berman did ESPN's broadcast. I was his guest, wearing a tuxedo, 'cause I was to host ceremonies on the field.

In the third inning, I ran to the restroom. President Clinton was to join me in the fourth, and I wanted to be sure I was set. Unfortunately, leaving the restroom for the booth, I was blocked by the Secret Service.

"I'm the broadcaster," I said. "I'm going to interview the president next inning."

"I don't think so," the agent said. This was not a practical joke. This huge night, me and the president, and the booth might as well be in Boise.

Thankfully, another Secret Service agent, a big Orioles fan, then appeared. "Hey, let him through!" he said. "He's going to be interviewing the president." Passing agent number one, I tried not to rub it in.

Fourth inning: the president comes on the air, the count on Cal goes to 3 and 0. I make a little funny. "This night of all nights," I said, "he [Shawn Boskie] can't be walking Cal, not in this game. Maybe you should send a presidential order down there ordering him to throw Cal a strike."

"I know one good thing," President Clinton said. "Cal wants to hit this pitch, but if it's not a strike he'll take the walk for the good of the team 'cause that's the kind of guy he is."

"That's very true," I said. "On the other hand, if he [Boskie] grooves one, even on 3 and 0 . . . "

"Oh, well," said the president, "then Cal'll hit it a long way."

At that moment Cal swings—and *boom*! Home run! I start describing it, but the president, who has his own microphone—I can't just take it away—starts going, "Go! Go! Yes! Ah-ha!" He's clapping his hands, shouting into the microphone, and all I am—I hear it later—is some disembodied background Voice.

It kinda' put me off, 'cause this was a major moment in baseball history. Then I thought, "No, he's the president of the United States. The First Fan. He's reflecting the excitement of the night better than any broadcaster could." Plus, I could now put on my resume, "Worked with President Bill Clinton, a very close friend."

P.S. The Angels were retired in the fifth, the game now official. Applause rocks the adjacent warehouse, Cal repeatedly tips his cap, and Rafael Palmeiro and Bobby Bonilla finally pull him from the dugout. Ripken circles the ballpark, high-fiving and hand-shaking. The warehouse banner changes from "2-1-3-0." People forget how hard that era was for baseball. To the rescue: perfect player, imperfect time.

—*Jon Miller*

In 1995, I debut in the big leagues after ten years in the minors, so the year is already special. That spring I check the schedule: Angels at Baltimore September 4, 5, and 6. If Ripken keeps his streak intact, he'll break Lou's record. By September we're nearing history, like other [history] I'd rather forget: having led the AL West by thirteen games in early August, the Halos' lead is shrinking. In Baltimore, we spoil Monday's party, 5–3. Next day Cal ties Gehrig. A month before I'd taped an interview, but had a cold, which made me worry. What if it's contagious? What a way to end Cal's streak! Instead, Wednesday we're in the fifth inning, which ordinarily I handle. Tonight wasn't ordinary —nor was Bob Starr, in his twenty-fourth big-league year. Engineer Kirk Daniels and I asked him to handle the occasion. As Jon Miller notes, Cal toured the track, Bob talking for ten minutes, ad-libbing brilliantly. I look on, stunned. Finally, he hits the cough button, saying, "Well, young man, are you going to say anything?" I said, truthfully, "I don't want to ruin this. Keep talking," and Bob did. Ultimately, the Angels blew the West, losing a playoff. Memory compensates: one, a record that won't be broken; two, an artist behind the mike.

—_Mario Impemba_

As The Streak mounted, Camden Yards and the road selling out each day, an amazing thing occurred. Each day, around the seventh, you'd see hundreds of empty seats: not people leaving, but getting in line so Cal could sign a post-game autograph, hat, bat, whatever, till the last fan left. In Kansas City, one game ended at 10:15 p.m. Cal stayed till almost 1 o'clock, talking with each person, asking a young kid what position he played, whether he's a Little Leaguer, making him feel like a million dollars. More players could use Cal's class.

—_Fred Manfra_

I was twenty-nine when the Brewers hired me for 1997 TV. A surreal aspect of my rookie big-league year was the chance to chat up people whom I had watched, read about, and cheered for as a kid. Dave Parker was Cardinals' hitting coach, and I was determined to get "the Cobra" for our pre-game interview. Stonewalled before the series opener, I doggedly approached the cage next day. "Dave, I'm the Brewers TV guy and we'd love to have you on today's pre-game show." Parker looked me up and down a couple times as he processed my request. "Hold on a minute. Let me check our BP [batting practice] schedule," he said, glancing at a clip-

board on the other side of the cage and looking me over again. Finally, the Cobra spoke: "Sorry, we hit for another hour. And boy, zip up your fly."
— *Matt Vasgersian*

May 6, 1998, Cubs-Astros at Wrigley Field. Kerry Wood, twenty, in his fifth big-league start, is amazing right away. First inning: Wood strikes out the side, his second pitch a belt-high fastball, eluding catcher Sandy Martinez, who couldn't get his glove up. Umpire Jerry Meals gets hit in the mask, like a wakeup call. Later I asked Jerry and Sandy if they'd been crossed up. Nope: The pitch got there before either could react. If memory serves, the batter, Craig Biggio, didn't swing, since he wasn't going to hit it. Remember as a kid throwing a wiffle ball, especially one without holes, into the wind? Your brothers and friends wouldn't come *close* to hitting it. That's how Kerry's curveball looked to the Astros, wiffling all day. Winning, 2–0, Wood had a one-hitter, didn't walk a man, and fanned 20 to tie Roger Clemens' single-game mark, break the NL's, and shatter the Cubs'. I've aired 4,500 games, including no-hitters by Juan Nieves, Scott Erickson, and Carlos Zambrano, but none like this: easily the best-pitched game I've seen.
— *Pat Hughes*

[In 2001, Arizona's Luis Gonzalez had fifty-seven homers, won the All-Star Game Home Run Derby, and hit a World Series–winning ninth-inning Game 7 single. He played for six teams, including Houston twice.] If Luis isn't the nicest guy in the game, he's 1A. Early with the Astros, he played leftfield one day at Wrigley Field. During a pitching change, he saw a man walk to the bleacher railing, dump the contents of a small box onto the warning track and grass, and quickly be surrounded by security. As Gonzalez told me, "I moved closer to hear and learned the man's father had recently died and that his last request was to have his ashes scattered here." The security people huddled. Then the chief said, "All right. You have to go, but your father can stay!"
— *Jeff Kingery*

Before 2008, Tampa Bay was called the *Devil Rays*, even the *Woeful Rays*. Still, Wade Boggs will always have August 7, 1999: the twenty-third man to reach 3,000 hits. Many Voices say they wouldn't script such a moment, and to a point I agree. Yet hearing other 3,000th hit calls, most shouting "There it is!," I thought Boggs deserved more, writing descriptive phrases including, "The hit that makes history is ——." Needing three hits, Wade already had two — typically, singles — as he faced Chris Haney at Tropicana Field, near his boyhood Tampa home. Before the 2–2 pitch, I tell TV analyst Joe Magrane that this great two-strike hitter could now make two-strike history. Haney hung a changeup. "And there's a drive, deep rightfield," I said. "It is gone!" The crowd took over. Then: "The hit that makes history is a two-run home run!" Wade pumped his fists, pointed upward, and blew a kiss for his late mother. After another pause: "Three thousand base hits for Wade Boggs and he hits a home run to do it!" Finally, a research fact I'd found: "The first man ever to hit a home run to get base hit number 3,000!" Boggs likened being first to homer for that hit to being first to step on the moon: his Neil Armstrong moment. I'll remember *my* moment for script, ad-lib, and a five-time batting champion.

    — Paul Olden

After a while, games blur. Two exceptions: one guy. In 2007, Mark Buerhle no-hits the Rangers, only Sammy Sosa reaching on a walk. Mark then picked him off, facing a minimum twenty-seven batters. Most pitchers'd be in the dugout corner — superstitious, "leave me alone." Mark's waving, laughing: "Guys, come on down." Two years later he pitches a perfect game against Tampa Bay, ironically having better stuff against Texas. We remember the amazing ninth: defensive specialist Dewayne Wise, just inserted, races back, fly ball, deep left-center, a likely homer till Wise scales the wall! — given the circumstance, the best catch I'd ever seen. The last batter grounds to short: perfecto! Here's what *I* remember: the Rays, standing, applauding in the dugout, doffing their caps.

    — Darrin Jackson

After each year's Yankees first-round draft, they do a summer show-and-tell at The Stadium. In 1992, one stop they made with the "next big thing," Derek Jeter, was the radio booth where John Sterling and I interviewed him between pitches. We looked at each other as Derek seemed totally unremarkable. You expect a first-round draft pick to be a physical specimen. He looked like any high school senior, tall, painfully thin, shy. We asked questions and Derek gave his answers, short, clipped, not much oomph. I figured he was a kid awed by his surroundings. Looking back, Derek was laying the foundation for his dealings with the media: my first time knocking on Derek's door and having him talk to you through the screen but never really asking you inside.

Little did I know that this afternoon Derek was on training wheels, not shy at all but showing he was not going to give you much: in retrospect, like Picasso learning to finger paint before going to brushes. Next day I went down to the office of Buck Showalter, the Yankees manager, who also had met Jeter. I wanted to get Buck's impression of the kid and find out the organization's scouting report on his potential.

"What did you think," I asked.

"Didn't talk to him that long," Showalter said. "Seemed like a nice kid."

"What's the report say?"

"Got all the tools. Tall, rangy, his body is going to fill out. Never going to be a big home run hitter but supposedly is a gamer who's not afraid of anything."

"Doesn't sound bad," I said.

"All the reports make these kids out to be future superstars. Why else would you take him in the first round?" Buck said. "Honestly, you have no idea how it's going to turn out. You hope for the best, hope he fills out, hope he becomes a player. But I'll tell you this, Michael: *He will never embarrass the Yankees.*"

That sort of struck me. "How can you say that?"

"Did you meet his parents?" Buck said.

"No. They brought him to the booth without them."

"They are outstanding people. I don't know what type of player he'll be, but he'll be a good man. You can always tell how a kid turns out by meeting his parents, and these two are off the charts. If he makes it on the field he will make it big because he'll never say the wrong thing or act the wrong way, able to handle everything because his parents brought him up right."

"And you got that all from his parents?" I said, amazed.

"All you need to do is meet the parents, for they're a window into their kid's future. He will never want to disappoint them."

All these years later, Showalter's words resonate because he could not have been more right. Dorothy and Dr. Charles have been a constant presence in their son's life and he has never embarrassed them, nor the organization. Oh, yeah, he turned out to be a pretty good player, too.

— *Michael Kay*

Derek's the lineal heir to DiMag, the Iron Horse, Yogi, and Mick. Begin at the beginning: He can play. Two, like all superstars, he does great things in big moments: the back-handed flip in the 2000 LCS, a game-winning 2001 Series blast. Three, as Michael Kay says above, he is really smart, able to say stuff without being remotely controversial. We're in Boston for the 2003 or '04 playoff, about twenty-five reporters surrounding him in that microscopic visitors' clubhouse and Derek's answering perfunctory questions. When it's over and the writers have moved on, I move in and tell him: "You are the best I have ever seen." He looked at me quizzically: "At what?" I said, "At saying absolutely nothing and keeping everybody happy." He had such a belly-laugh, knowing that it's true. Derek is cosmically and cosmetically good at servicing reporters' needs without stepping on his tongue or any other body part. He is also well-balanced and intelligent, with leadership skills that most of us wish we could even flirt with. By the way, did I mention that he can play, is almost never injured, and if he is, is still in the lineup. There's the old story, "If it sounds too good to be true, it probably is." Jeter *is* that good.

—*Charley Steiner*

[Dave Niehaus aired 5,284 of the 1977–2010 Mariners' 5,385 games.] My favorite player to broadcast came up at nineteen, electrifying everybody. Ran like a deer, played defense, crashed into walls [making thirteen All-Star Games, hitting 630 homers, and more than anyone keeping baseball in Seattle]. You could see the joy of playing in his eyes. April 10, 1989, was Ken Griffey Jr.'s Kingdome debut, giving dad Ken, turning thirty-nine, a birthday present: He hit the first pitch for a homer. You know the rest: 1997 MVP, ten Gold Gloves, moving on, returning, the Prodigal Son.

In 2009, he played an interleague game: not the same player, but still electric. "Fans hoping to catch a little bit of the old-time religion, baby," I said. Then Jr. swung. "Fly away! The old-time religion lives!" Retiring a year later, Jr. kept the faith in an age of drugs, excuse, and whine.

— Dave Niehaus

Mid-January 2005: not ordinarily baseball season, except in New York, where baseball is king. That winter the Yankees traded for Randy Johnson, everybody trying for his first interview. He's walking down the street when I ask for a moment of the Big Unit's time. Next thing you know, Randy, 6-foot-11, puts his hand over the camera: I'm 6-2, the cameraman 6-5, but we're pygmies next to him. It made a big splash, not an especially warm howdy to New York. Johnson won seventeen games that year and the next [retiring in January 2010 with a 303-166 record and second-best 4,875 Ks] and was great when I interviewed him in '05 for ESPN. Yet he was uncomfortable in the Apple, its baseball obsession making some withdraw. Forget a Kodak Moment. This is a moment that could only happen in New York.

— Duke Castiglione

In 1998, Randy briefly pitched in Houston, where I began broadcasting in 2006. Next year Barry Bonds came trying to top Hank Aaron's all-time 755 career home run record: "sitting on 714," as Milo Hamilton prefaced Hank's number 715. People wanted to know if partner Dave Raymond and I would call Bonds' at-bats or defer to Milo. We deferred. Bonds didn't homer, and everybody moved on. Starting a 2007 home stand, Craig Biggio was five hits shy of 3,000. Again we decided to defer if Craig batted in our inning with his odometer at 2,999, not expecting it to happen in the opener. By the seventh, Biggio already had four hits — one away. I gave the mike to Milo, who calls 3,000: Craig, typically hustling, out trying to stretch his single into a uniform-gets-dirty double. Only George Brett and Tony Gwynn Sr., had reached 3,000 in a four-hit game. Biggio's five made history, Minute Maid Park roaring for maybe Houston's all-time most popular athlete. In the eleventh, Carlos Lee hit a walkoff grand slam to beat the Rockies, later complaining to owner Drayton McLane, tongue-in-cheek, that even a homer hadn't made him player of the game.

 — *Brett Dolan*

On August 7, 2007, Bonds hit 756 against the Nationals in San Francisco. It was strange, many not wanting him to top Aaron, mostly due to Barry's steroid cloud. The night's classiest moment was Henry's post-756 taped scoreboard salute, which no one knew was coming. Ironically, Bonds' victim, Mike Bacsik, showed class, too, applauding Barry as he toured the bases, a minor-league journeyman who wasn't afraid of an infamous "stigma": your next-door neighbor who didn't act, strut, or dress like a player. The Nats make you wear a jacket on the road. Bless him, Mike wore the same tan slacks and blue blazer, probably off the rack. Hailing Bonds came naturally and modestly, Mike having baseball history in his blood. Incredibly, thirty-one years earlier Mike Bacsik Sr. had faced Aaron at 755. "If dad had given up a homer," Mike said, "I wouldn't have been part of history." Instead, dad got Hank to fly out, saving history for his son.

 — *Dave Jageler*

Dreams make you overcome circumstance and adversity. A dream can carry you when nothing else can. Many years ago a young boy believed he could be a professional baseball player. I know that dream because I shared it. This boy was born in the Dominican Republic. A loving grandmother raised him, nearly a dozen relatives living in their tiny home. The young boy learned to share, but was selfish about his dream. At sixteen, he moved with his grandmother and other relatives to Independence, Missouri, dreaming of a better life. To the young boy, that meant baseball. No one could tell him differently in Spanish or English, the latter of which he didn't speak a word. As a high school freshman, he had an English-speaking cousin who, on a visit to the principal, said the now-young man hoped to play ball. The principal said that would require a thirteen-pitch tryout with its varsity coach. The young man bombed twelve over the fence, starting a great high school career. By community college, scouts said he'd be a June 1999 first-round big-league draft pick: coupled with his upcoming New Year's Day marriage to a local girl, monumental fortune. Instead, the young man met monumental disappointment. His first three rounds ended without being called. Finally, he was picked in the thirteenth round, behind 400 other amateur players. Stunned, he sobbed, just as his now-fiancée arrived at his apartment. She expected a celebration, but found a dejected man who said he was going to quit: "No way that many players are better than me!" Pivoting his career, she flung a challenge: "What does quitting mean for *us*? I'll be in your corner, but you are *not* going to quit! If you feel the same in a year, I'll support you. Baseball thinks that 400 players are better. *Why don't you prove them wrong?*" Those words never left the young man's ears or heart as he signed for a far smaller bonus than any first-rounder. Making the bigs in a year and a half, his numbers passed *every* Hall of Famer's in their first ten years: Ruth, Aaron, Mays! On that June day his dream took a hit, the young man almost quitting. Instead, his fiancée saved it, and him. What a shame it would have been to never see the great Albert Pujols bat.

—*Wayne Hagin*

In 2007, I was in Chicago for Angels' Spanish radio. My partner Jose Mota was on their English TV network, so as usual when working solo I tried to get an announcer, reporter, or ex-player to sit with me for an inning. As a boy, I'd seen my idol, Orestes (Minnie) Minoso, play in Cuba and the bigs. Today, Minnie was at U.S. Cellular Field. Julio Franco was with his eighth team in one of those careers that seemingly never end. On air I ask: "Franco's still playing, don't you feel that you can, too?" Minnie says: "Yes, but my Social Security check is probably smaller than his pension'll be if he ever retires." [That fall Julio, forty-nine, did.] Then eighty-two, Minoso had played in five major-league decades [1949–1980, making seven All-Star teams and hitting .298]. Next to him, Julio was a pup.

—*Amaury Pi-Gonzalez*

In 2008, Josh Hamilton became a one-man wrecking crew. By June, he led the majors with sixty-three RBI. Since this was Yankee Stadium's last year, it hosted the All-Star Game, by which time Josh had ninety-five. A night earlier Josh owned Home Run Derby: twenty-eight homers in the first round, going deep thirteen straight swings, three over 500 feet. Babe

Ruth couldn't have done better. All year people scheduled their bathroom break or refrigerator run around Hamilton: Every at-bat had meaning. Try focusing equally on each player with the nation focused on a swing. [Earlier in his career Josh had tried drugs and alcohol. In 2010, clean and sober, he braved a sore knee and two fractured ribs to wed thirty-two homers and 100 RBI, top the American League in hitting (.359) and slugging percentage (.633), and become its Most Valuable Player. Texas took the franchise's first postseason tourney (Division Series *v.* Tampa Bay), then first pennant (*v.* New York in the LCS, helped by Hamilton's four home runs). His mates celebrated on the field with ginger ale.]

— *Josh Lewin*

July 30, 2009, was a getaway day for the Red Sox at Fenway Park: a steamy day perfect for Cape Cod. You think of those things broadcasting the Red Sox, wondering what fans are doing while listening. Are they on beach blankets on the sand in Hampton, New Hampshire, sailing by Martha's Vineyard, or in the dunes at Rexton Beach in Marshfield, outside Boston? Since 2003, David Ortiz had been a giant part of the Red Sox success: one clutch hit after another, legendary blasts to win unforgettable games; such a big bear of a man, always smiling, hugging little kids, mobbed everywhere: "Big Papi." Yet in 2009 he had an awful start, the magic gone, like David'd forgot how to hit, in one game leaving twelve men on base, not homering till almost June. When we found on July 30 that in '03 Ortiz had tested positive for performance-enhancing drugs, it was like someone erased the sun. Later, his rationale for being on the drug list with then-teammate Manny Ramirez was, in my view, plausible, but on this day the news hit like a hammer. David said he was surprised about the list because of the way he lived, all of us wanting to think maybe that meant he was innocent: as the Twins' Torii Hunter said, this hurt because Big Papi's "always going to be my brother." Many people in Boston felt that way. Manny told reporters, "You want more information, *go ask the players' union.*" By contrast, Papi promised to address details, doing so a week later. When he batted for the first time — awkward for me, trying to insert and explain the news — he got a typical warm reception, which made me think some people didn't know. As Papi hit in the seventh, two on, you felt it. When the

Sox needed him, he'd always delivered. Now, in a day of great embarrassment, huge mistakes, and so many questions, I still recall seconds before he swung, thinking, "Well, this is what he does. He's going to hit one just like you most expect him to do." And damned if he didn't crush a monstrous three-run homer to right-center to put Boston ahead for good. I said, "What a way to cap an absolutely fascinating day for David Ortiz, to say the least," not feeling I had to detail more. By now, in late afternoon, everyone knew the story. It *had* been a fascinating day. I hope my voice and delivery expressed how even in these conditions, the baseball gods were still in play.
    — *Dave O'Brien*

In my seventeenth year with the A's, I appreciate more than ever the *people* of baseball: front office, cup-of-coffee careerers, Hall of Famers, scouts, and broadcasters. Hosting the post-game show even helped me meet the eventual mother of my kids. Still, one thing worries me: a sense of entitlement. On April 22, 2010, Oakland hosted the Yankees. With Alex Rodriguez at first base, Robinson Cano hit a foul off A's pitcher Dallas Braden. A-Rod then cut across the infield returning to the bag. This became the infamous "A-Rod over the mound" moment. I'm sure Braden would have liked to send Alex over the moon. Post-game, A-Rod pretended not to grasp Dallas's anger over Alex's mocking "this guy's . . . handful of wins." I'm not sure why that was relevant. Certainly it wasn't accurate, since next week Braden threw a perfect game. Baseball is too great a game to be spoiled by its players.
    — *Robert Buan*

A pitching duel doesn't always live up to hype. May 29, 2010, did: the Phillies' Roy Halladay at Marlins' Josh Johnson, evocative of Tom Seaver *v.* Steve Carlton. In 1969, Lou DiMuro called Jim Palmer's no-hitter. Tonight, son Mike, the home plate umpire, had a favorable and consistent zone. After the fifth I said, "Roy Halladay has faced fifteen and retired fifteen," not thinking a perfect, just complete, game, especially if the Phils could increase their 1–0 lead. Two great plays helped, guys loving working behind a quick and economical pitcher: Chase Utley's at second base and Juan Castro's at third. By the seventh, my hands shook as I debated saying "perfect game." Remembering Vin Scully with [1965's] Sandy Koufax, I said, "After seven

[then eight], Roy Halladay has a no-hitter." When Kevin Millwood threw a 2003 no-hitter, then–assistant producer Jeff Halikman, building tension, axed a ninth-inning commercial to stay at the park. Now a producer, Jeff did the same. Florida's Mike Lamb flew to center. Next, Wes Helms fanned. Ronny Paulino then tapped a nubber on one hop to Castro, who fielded, spun, and in his body language said, "I've got this. I've done this a million times. I'm going to make the throw," and he did: 2010's second perfect game, after Dallas Braden; the Phillies' second, after Jim Bunning; and just baseball's twentieth, unbelievable given its history. Noting this, I tried not to say much, not needing to, since Roy's smile and catcher Carlos Ruiz's embrace said it all. [Not content to leave well enough alone, Halladay no-hit Cincinnati, 4–0, in the 2010 Division Series: postseason's second no-no, after Don Larsen; fifth pitcher with two in a year; and fifth Cy Younger in each league. Then–Blue Jay Halladay won the 2003 AL award.]
     — *Tom McCarthy*

[In 2009, the Nationals gave San Diego State University's Stephen Strasburg a record $15.1 million contract. The draft's top choice proceeded to treat minor-league batters "like Little Leaguers," said *USA Today*. On June 8, 2010, Strasburg had a cosmic major-league debut, a sellout crowd of 40,315 feasting on St. Stephen: seven innings, zero walks, and fourteen Ks. Strasburg beat Pittsburgh, 5–2. The radar gun routinely hit 100 miles-per-hour. The town of Strasburg, Virginia, considered temporarily adding "Stephen" to its name.] Till now, constant losing had dimmed even the bright days since DC's 2005 return to baseball. This night showed the effect of twenty-first-century hype: media coverage like the World Series and crowd noise to rival any I'd ever heard. From the ovation Strasburg got walking in from the bullpen, to his curtain call after finishing the seventh inning with his seventh straight strikeout, the crowd was as spectacular as his fastball and curve. In his second start, baseball's worst-drawing team, Cleveland, easily had its best crowd since Opening Day, their Team Store kiosk peddling only Strasburg game jerseys and t-shirts. [By early August the Phenom had a 2.91 ERA and ninety-two Ks in sixty-eight innings.] Even Joe Hardy never created such buzz.
     — *Charlie Slowes*

Credit blogging, Twitter, and Facebook for letting us know Strasburg. He fanned twenty-three in a game in college. In the minors, each start was an event, MLB showing his last Triple-A game. This helped him handle June 8's pressure: every fan hanging on every pitch; stratospheric expectations, which he *surpassed*; dropping an early curveball strike on the Bucs' Lastings Milledge, who fell out of the box like it was going to hit him in the head. Strasburg Ks six in the first three innings; five in the fifth and sixth. In the seventh, he pitches like a man possessed. Garrett Jones strikes out swinging. Delwyn Young and Andy LaRoche each fans on three pitches, only a ninety-four pitch count exiting "Strasmus" from the game. On Nats TV, Bob Carpenter told analyst Rob Dibble, "If I closed my eyes right now and heard this crowd in the nation's capital, I would think that Walter Johnson just walked out of the cornfield, took the mound, and struck out the side." You kept thinking, if he stays healthy, twenty years from now Strasburg'll be inducted at Cooperstown. [In August 2010, the Nats said that he had torn a collateral ligament in his throwing elbow, would need Tommy John Surgery to replace it, and would miss at least a year.]

— *Dave Jageler*

Chapter Four

Dugout Man

In 2005, Bob Costas critiqued PBS Television's Charlie Rose. "He's doing what he was born to do. Perfect guy, in his perfect job" — late-night talk. FDR was born to be president; Ethel Merman, break chandeliers; Frank Sinatra, wow. Some are born to manage. Tom Lasorda mixed The Strip and South Philadelphia. Sparky Anderson was baseball's Norman Vincent Peale. Joe Torre was "perfect guy, perfect job."

As a player, Torre won a batting title, was named 1971 MVP, and got 2,342 hits. Later he managed the Braves, Mets, and Cardinals; did Angels TV; and joined the Yanks. A fine batter hits .300. Joe's 1996–2007 Stripes hit 1,000, making each postseason. Skippers once went directly from a flag to the Fall Classic. Today's must win three series: a steeper climb. Torre won six flags and four World Series: "perfect guy, perfect job."

Numbers judge between the lines. Torre went beyond to get the keys to New York City, light Rockefeller Center's Christmas tree, beat prostate cancer, and remain "the person I needed to be" — becoming baseball's Saint Joe. Above all, he killed the old cliché: "Rooting for the Yankees is like rooting for U.S. Steel," except that it was no cliché.

A writer once noted Tom Landry "never mocking a writer's question, no matter how absurd." Similarly, Torre put a human, even warm, face on a once disliked, even hated, team. He mastered 24/7 Big Apple media, massaged owner George Steinbrenner, and was the ultimate players' manager, insulating the clubhouse from probers and paparazzi. Such amalgams are hard to find.

The 2007 Yanks fired him, like they had Casey Stengel forty-seven years ear-
lier. In November, the Dodgers hired Flatbush Joe, who followed them to Tinsel-
town. It would have less surprised if Madonna had become a nun. "Perfect guy"
braved Manny Ramirez, helped pack Chavez Ravine, and won the NL Western
division twice before leaving in 2010. In 2011, Torre became the big leagues' execu-
tive vice president for baseball operations.

Merman was asked if Broadway had been good to her. "Yes," she said, "but
I've been good to Broadway." Baseball's Charlie Rose and other skippers have often
been good to The Game.

In 1958, CBS TV gave future Tigers Voice George Kell the *Game of the*
Week's pre-game show. George snagged Casey Stengel, hoping to ask about
the Bombers batting order. Someone later asked Kell how it went. "Fine,"
he said. "But in our fifteen minutes, Casey didn't get past the leadoff hitter."
—*Dan Dickerson*

In 1962, I did a limited number of telecasts for the International League
Syracuse Chiefs. The Chiefs had a dual working agreement with the Senators and expansion Mets. When I wasn't doing games I would occasionally
go to New York. One afternoon I was at the Polo Grounds before a game
and noticed Stengel sitting alone in the dugout. I walked over and uttered
the rather innocuous question, "How you doing, Casey?" He replied, "You
know it's an amazing thing you ask me that because I had the Toledo ball-
club in 1930 and a guy come up to me and he asks me how I was doin', and
we went out there that day and we won ourselves a doubleheader and I
just figure anytime someone asks me how I'm doing we might go out there
and win ourselves a couple a ballgames." Needless to say, I had no follow-
up question.
—*Hank Greenwald*

When the MLB Network opened [on January 1, 2009], it showed Don
Larsen's perfect game. The people who were there seem to multiply each
year. I was in the dugout as Don mowed the Dodgers down. Come the
eighth inning, players start talking to each other: "You know, a no-hitter . . .
man, a perfect game." Then they start advising the manager, "Play this guy
here, move an outfielder there." Stengel didn't like it. Finally he explodes:

"G—damn it, *I'll* tell you where to play!"—as usual, having the final word. It must have worked. Casey positioned Yogi Berra perfectly behind the plate to catch Larsen's final strike.

—*Jerry Coleman*

My first full year was 1965. Three years later Harry Walker became Houston's manager. There's no question Harry knew how to hit. [He was the 1947 NL batting champion.] Managing was something else. Harry called me a troublemaker. Anyone was a troublemaker who was smarter than Harry, and that didn't take much. It was a pleasure to be traded [in late 1971] to Cincinnati. After I finished playing in '84, I thought about managing. I took one job, then revisited it in the morning. I woke up thinking, "You're hired to be fired." I learned that from Harry.

—*Joe Morgan*

The Expos' first game was April 8, 1969—Montreal 11, Mets 10, at Shea Stadium. For the first time baseball expanded beyond America, two national anthems were played, and the Canadian flag flew next to ours. Naturally, the Expos celebrated afterward. One writer, crammed into manager Gene Mauch's office after leaving the Mets clubhouse, noted New York starter Tom Seaver calling the Expos tri-colored red, white, and blue cap "funny." Not blinking, Mauch snapped, "Tell Tom I remember the time, not too long ago, when everyone laughed at the *entire* Mets uniform!" Mauch was barbed, quick-witted, and old school. He loathed facial hair. When pitcher Steve Renko grew sideburns, Gene said, "Steve, I see the sideburns are down and the ERA is up." They disappeared, like the 'Spos.

—*Dave Van Horne*

Before 1969, Ted Williams turned down countless offers to manage, but new Senators owner Bob Short convinced him to save baseball in Washington: ironic, since Short was already scheming to move to Texas. The term "larger than life" was made for Ted: tall, handsome, with a booming voice. As a kid I saw minor-leaguer Bob Lemon homer twice to win a game. Turns out Williams played against him in World War II: "He'd pitch, play at third, was wasted in the field." After the war Ted told Indians skipper Lou Boudreau that Bob should only pitch, which he did, "and I oughta' know because his slider made me look silly. Williams told me his famed near-trade for Joe DiMaggio "was considered by both teams until [Red Sox owner] Mr. [Tom] Yawkey reconsidered." Wistful, he wondered if "we both might have thrived: Joe, swinging at the [Fenway leftfield] Wall and me at the [Stadium's rightfield] porch." A quarter-century later, "I still wonder." Talking to Ted was like touring baseball history.

— *Ron Menchine*

In 1970, my Padres are behind, 1–0, on an error, in our bottom of the eighth inning. San Diego manager Preston Gomez pinch-hits Cito Gaston for Clay Kirby, who's throwing a no-hitter. Cito makes out, Kirby loses his no-no, and [Padres president] Buzzie Bavasi and a lot of people blame Preston for taking him out. In 1974, I'm an Astro managed by Gomez, both of us feeling déjà vu. Like 1970, we're behind on an error, 2–0, despite Don Wilson's no-hitter. Unlike then, I'm in the dugout, not at second base. In the sixth, Preston's pacing when suddenly he looks at me: "Does this look familiar?" I said, "Sure does." He said: "And you know what I'm going to do, don't you?" I said: "Absolutely." What are the odds? In the bottom of the *eighth* Preston pinch-hits for *Wilson!* We lose. One manager takes two guys out with a no-hitter in the eighth because we're behind on an error.

— *Dave Campbell*

I broadcast the Angels for a decade starting in 1969: a team in need of an identity, and often a manager. My first manager was Lefty Phillips, for whom English was a second language. Once the Angels led by a run in the ninth inning, two out, bases full. The batter grounded between shortstop Jim Fregosi's legs. Next day Lefty leaned against the cage, saying, "That's water *over* the bridge." The first Angels manager was [1961–1969's] Bill Rigney. Succeeding him, Phillips preceded Del Rice, Bobby Winkles, Whitey Herzog, Dick Williams, Norm Sherry, and Dave Garcia. In 1978, Fregosi became the Halos' eighth skipper in a decade. Owner Gene Autry said, "We'll just keep changing till we get it right."

— *Dick Enberg*

In 1978, I first visited my dad on the field when he managed a Dodgers team in Alberta. I was seven and a rookie batboy. Two things stand out. First, dad was ejected from the game after an animated talk with the home plate umpire. I got to hear what was said: even in summer, a vocabulary lesson. Second, watching games on TV had whet my appetite to run to the plate, collect bats, and run along the screen behind home plate to get a foul. As I'm processing dad's language, I see a ball roll to the screen. My chance! I race to the ball, getting there just before the catcher. Only it wasn't a foul but wild pitch, and I officially interfered. Luckily, the catcher was on my dad's team, not about to say anything inappropriate to the manager's kid; especially a now-*enraged* manager's kid. That catcher, Dann Bilardello, eventually made it to the bigs. That summer he also took me to the movie *Grease.*

— *Ryan Lefebvre*

The Royals' greatest comeback happened at Milwaukee, Friday evening, June 15, 1979. We had a day game scheduled for Saturday, so when we got down by nine runs, 11–2, in the fourth inning, Whitey Herzog took his starters out and told them to go back to the hotel for a good night's sleep. Incredibly, the subs rally, winning, 14–11. Our hotel, the Pfister, had a lounge off the main lobby. Around 11 p.m., the guys who'd left the game to get some sleep were still there, telling stories and having a few cool ones. The team bus arrives, one sub saying, "We don't need you guys, we won!" The regulars roared: "Sure you did! Real funny." It took a few more drinks to convince them.

— *Denny Matthews*

[Sparky Anderson died in 2010, at seventy-six, having led the 1970–1978 Reds to five division titles, four pennants, and a 1975–1976 world title. In June 1979, he succeeded Les Moss at Detroit, 57-102 as recently as 1975.] This had been Moss's big league managing debut, and as bad as you felt for him, a Tigers fan was thrilled by Sparky's hiring. I was a youngster [twenty-one], and it's hard to describe the jolt when I heard the news from dad. We'd been down so long, just trying to compete, and Sparky says, "We'll win a World Series in five years" — which he did in 1984 [starting

35-5, taking the AL East and LCS, then beating San Diego: the first manager to win a Series in each league]. If you talk to players who grew up with him—Jack Morris, Lance Parrish, or Kirk Gibson, still marveling at Sparky whipping him into shape—they'll say how completely they bought into his message: dedication and total work, winning, not prizing stats. Such a love of the game, a knack for bold pronouncements, so good at interacting with people: a great human being. Plus, that language, which could obscure his brilliance as a baseball man. ["Me carrying a briefcase is like a hot dog wearing earrings." "I've got my faults, but living in the past is not one of them. There's no future in it." "I only had a high school education, and, believe me, I had to cheat to get that."] What a conversation he must be having with Casey Stengel.

—*Dan Dickerson*

"In baseball," Yogi Berra said, "you don't know nothin'." He would have loved 1979. Going by the book means hitting a right-swinging batter against a left-handed pitcher. On August 5 at Pittsburgh, right-handed hitting Steve Nicosia goes four for four against the Phils. In the ninth, Pirates skipper Chuck Tanner pinch-hits John Milner against Tug McGraw: each a lefty. Milner grand slams: Bucs, 12–8. Six days later McGraw, on the mound again in Philly, faces lefty catcher Ed Ott, whom Tanner lets hit. Boom: another slam. Two months later we win the Series, led by lefty Willie Stargell, who hit guys throwing right, left, or both. Or as Yogi said of Mickey Mantle, "He can hit left or right. I think you'd call him *amphibious*."

—*Lanny Frattare*

In winter 1982, I was traded with a couple other players from Philadelphia to San Francisco for reliever Al Holland and Joe Morgan. Giants manager Frank Robinson, calling Morgan "my assistant manager," fought GM Tom Haller about the deal. I didn't want to be there, either, so '83 was a rough spring training. Still, I'm opening day pitcher as actor Yul Brynner comes out to throw the first pitch. Ironically, I'd seen *The King and I* the night before. Yul comes out, sort of a bad dude, a little guy, winds up, and throws the worst pitch I've ever seen, bouncing three times before the plate. I'm not even sure it *reached* the plate. I take the mound, not telling anyone I've had a hot spot in my arm, and give up four runs in the first two innings. Frank comes out, having given up on *me*. He puts his hand out. I put the ball in it. He tells me: "Yul Brynner had better s— than you have."

— *Mike Krukow*

Hello to Mr. Jello. The 1982 Mariners have just arrived in Chicago, and beat writer Tracy Ringolsby is in the bar trying to distract manager Rene Lachemann. Co-conspirator Richie Zisk gets Rene's suite key from traveling secretary Lee Pelekoudas. He, Larry Andersen, and I go upstairs, put cherry Jello with buckets of ice in the toilet, and put suite furniture, including bed, in the bathroom. The dresser won't fit, so we unpack Rene's suitcase and store his clothes. When the phone rings, we remove the speakers, jimmy the suite door, write disparaging remarks on the mirrors and TV screens with soap, and leave. Rene enters, is trapped, nowhere to sit, no way to call, Jello everywhere, the bathroom so jammed the hotel had to take off the door. Next day, arriving at Comiskey Park, we see on the blackboard: "$500 reward for information on Mr. Jello." Lachemann tried to smoke us out by saying his friend, White Sox skipper Tony La Russa, had security people dusting for fingerprints. Next, the hotel was going to charge us for room damages. Scared, we didn't buckle. In Milwaukee, we put balloons in Rene's office holding up a box of Jello. He calls area balloon shops to find who placed an order — all but hired a private eye. Finally, at the year-end team party, Mr. Jello's culprits confessed. It didn't make us better — 76-86 — but made the season shorter.

— *Joe Simpson*

My major league debut was opening day, Twins-Tigers, April 1983, at the Metrodome. I'm twenty-seven, doing TV, excited till Detroit scores six runs in the first, young starter Brad Havens giving a three-run homer to Larry Herndon to the football press box in right-centerfield. Later, I'm having a beer in the press lounge when Twins skipper Billy Gardner sits down and starts sipping. I say, "Havens left after only two-thirds of an inning. One good thing, Billy, is that he threw only thirty pitches. You could probably bring him back in a couple days to pitch again." He took a sip, smiled, and said: "You're right, I could." Pause. "But why in the world would I *want* to?"

— *Pat Hughes*

Giants manager Bruce Bochy has a size 8 head. He caught for three big-league teams, bringing his helmet with him to each because it was baseball's only one that fit. His new equipment manager would spray-paint it to match the new team's colors. "One night, Boch hit a walk-off home run," said former Padre Terry Kennedy. "We ran a red carpet from the door of the clubhouse to his locker, where we put a six-pack of beer, with ice, *in his helmet*. You might be able to get a six-pack in some other guy's helmet, but only in Boch's could you add the ice."
— *Tim Kurkjian*

In Game 6 of the 1986 World Series, I was in the Boston clubhouse looking at the World Series trophy when Mookie Wilson's grounder went under Bill Buckner's glove. Three days later, I entered manager John McNamara's office after what was to have been a downtown "victory" parade. Looking up from his chair was a broken man. "Why me, Joe? I go to church," the lifetime Catholic congregant said. "I don't understand why this had to happen." Red Sox fans haven't either, and they've wondered for a while.
— *Joe Castiglione*

As you get older, you identify with the manager. Jimmy Leyland joined the awful Pirates in 1986, the two of us becoming friends. My favorite all-time game was September 30, 1990, at Busch Stadium, the Bucs holding a 2–0 late-inning lead. In the ninth, Denny Walling grounds to Jose Lind, who throws to first baseman Sid Bream for the final out: the Pirates' first of three straight division titles and first since 1979. Beneath me Jim and his coaches—Ray Miller, Gene Lamont, Rich Donnelly, and Tommy Sandt—celebrate Doug Drabek's clinching three-hit shutout and league-high twenty-second win. Outsiders don't grasp how friendships get you through missed flights, early morning arrivals, clubhouse politics. If you're not a people person, find another field.
— *Lanny Frattare*

In 1987, I became Mets pre- and post-game radio host, taping a daily segment with then-skipper Davey Johnson. It ran six or seven minutes, but

the education stayed. Barely knowing Davey, I had to earn his trust. The Mets were world champions, so he could have tried to intimidate this neo-phyte into softball questions but didn't, spending enormous time before and after the segment explaining every nuance of the team. Davey was a rebel, only getting mad when I tried to help. Frank Cashen was Mets GM and if Johnson didn't like a roster move he'd say, "Frank Cashen did a dumb thing today." When we finished, I said that if he were uncomfortable with what he'd said we could tape again. He almost bit my head off for suggesting it, and that's how it aired. Maybe he figured his insight would make me sympathetic. Usually, it did. Post-game callers second-guessed every decision Davey made, including breakfast. I defended him because I understood how and why he utilized his personnel. Lots of fans didn't care, wanting to rip him, and did. One night he happened by our booth, and like a fisherman, I reeled him in, Davey agreeing to take calls on the air. Instead of ripping Johnson to a third party, fans could hammer him by phone! Big expectations. Bigger letdown. One after another caller said, "Davey, we love you!" "Oh, Davey, you're the best." I couldn't believe it. The same folks wanting to ship this guy to Siberia were suddenly all kissy face. Big critics become bigger marshmallows, in person or on the air.
    — *Howie Rose*

Joe Morgan's surely the most colorful-ever Red Sox manager: the origi-nal Honest Abe. In 1989, we're at Comiskey Park, Boston platooning catch-ers: lefty Rich Gedman, a great guy, and righty Rick Cerone, not a great guy. Chicago was pitching right-handed Shawn Hillegas. That night, after our daily pre-game show, I said, "Maybe I should have asked this on air, but why is Cerone, not Gedman, catching?"
    "Hillegas is left-handed," Joe said. "Therefore, Cerone's going to catch."
    "Joe," I said, "Hillegas is *right-handed*."
    "Oh, gees, I screwed up," said Morgan, his language more colorful, but you get the point. "What am I going to tell Gedman?" He then went to Rich, confessing.
    Improbably, Cerone homered off Hillegas to win the game. I'm think-ing, should I give the background, or not? No, Joe's my friend. What good would it do to say, "Here's why Cerone's playing"? I let it go, we'll see what happens later.

Joe loved to play the track. After the game, writers ask, "Did you have a hunch, like a horse, playing Cerone?" Honest Joe said, "No, I screwed up. I thought Hillegas was a lefty. That's why Cerone played, and why I apologized to Gedman." On second thought, maybe Morgan is George Washington, who never told a lie.

— *Joe Castiglione*

Forget the book's cover. Even truly nice managers want to win. For a long time I worked for the Orioles' regional TV network, Home Team Sports. After Camden Yards opened in 1992, every day I'd sit in my in-game well. One night Brewers catcher B. J. Surhoff, not seeing it, dives to catch a ball near the dugout. He's about to crush me and the cameraman, so I put two hands on his shoulder, steadying him. Johnny Oates was then the wonderful [1991–1994] Orioles manager, later died of a brain tumor [in 2004, at fifty-eight], just the kindest guy in the world. He tells me: "You should have let him fall."

— *Tom Davis*

I became Mariners radio network weekend post-game host in 1993 as Lou Piniella arrived from Cincinnati to become manager, hoping to breathe fire in the franchise. As I found, anything could light his match. My first week producer Kevin Cremin gave me a tape deck and microphone, asking me to "just get Lou in his office," after, as it happened, the Mariners kicked away a game. I navigate the Kingdome, Lou awaiting our first post-game interview. In his office, twenty-five journalists are at one end, faces cast in fear. Fifteen feet away Lou sat behind a desk, with a lighted cigarette and can of Budweiser, in underwear and undershirt, drawing long draws on his smoke and chasing it down with beer. The media group looked fright-ened to draw a breath. Quickly, I try to comprehend why nobody is talk-ing to Lou. How come everyone is sitting so far from his desk? Why is Lou in underwear? Like many fans, I'd witnessed Piniella's base-throwing, umpire-berating, and psycho blowups. But to see that same tortured soul in his underwear seemed bizarre. Plus, why was everyone looking at *me*, especially when Lou's icy stare joined theirs? Smartly, I figure that since nobody is talking and Lou is just sitting there he and the other journalists are waiting for me to record his post-game show.

I approach the desk, turn on the tape deck, and see Lou's face turn from disdain to disbelief. "You got a good effort from your starter," I began. "Can you tell us about Erik Hanson's night?" Lou eyed my microphone. "Hanson gave us a good start, but this club's got bigger problems," he said. "I got an infield that can't seem to play catch, I got a bullpen that can't hold a lead, and some of our hitters look like they belong back in Calgary." Lou drew the cigarette, chased a Bud, and stared. "Looks like the Indians are a hot club," I resumed, to which he said, "Son, we've got bigger problems than the Indians." Lou stood, my mike following him, needing everything for the post-game show. "I, I, I'll tell you what," he said, now pacing. Kevin didn't tell me about this, I realized. Still, I need it all. Be an athlete! Keep up with Lou!

"This is a club that lost ninety-eight games last year and I'll be damned if I'm spending all year watching this crap night after night!" he blurted, voice rising. "I'm gonna' f—ing tell you I'm not putting up with this s— anymore. If these hitters don't understand what it takes to hit in the big leagues we'll find some that do . . . and my bullpen . . . I mean, am I right or am I right?" Wow! Incredible! A ranting, raving, cursing Lou Piniella is cutting loose . . . in his underwear! What a post-game show!

"If these young men can't throw f—ing strikes I'm gonna'," Lou said, then froze, and cocked his head. "Wait a minute . . . get the f— out of here!" he screamed, then swung, knocking beer and notebooks in the air. "All of you sons of a b— get the f— outa' here," whereupon they complied. I dashed to the radio booth to give Cremin the post-game tape. "What'd ya' get?" Kevin said, putting it in the deck. "The first part is pretty good," I said, "but Lou starts swearing about halfway through." Trying to leave the booth unnoticed, I met an engineer.

"How did it go?" he said.

"Lou was okay to start with," I said, "but he got annoyed at my second question."

"Oh," said the engineer, "*you're* not supposed to ask questions—just put the mike on Lou's desk and let *reporters* ask the questions." Whoever said that what you don't know can't hurt you?

—*Rich Waltz*

By 1994, the Twins weren't the same team that won the 1987 and 1991 Series: fourteen games out, next-to-last, Tom Kelly trying somehow to keep them loose. In a game at Tiger Stadium, Cecil Fielder hit a monstrous 500-foot shot off Rick Aguilera. Afterward, we board the team bus. As it starts, Tom leaves his first-row seat, walks toward the back, peering everywhere, looking out the window, like searching for a plane. Finally, he points and says, "There it goes!" — the homer. The whole bus broke up. I'm not sure if Rick joined in.

— *Jim Powell*

In 1994, I began to host the Mariners pre-game show, which included the *Lou Piniella Show*. After topping .500 in '93, the Mariners had reverted, their bullpen a toxic waste. Before meeting me, Lou met about twenty media members behind the batting cage. "Here comes Lou," one of our crew said, suddenly. Looking up, I saw Lou was steaming, those dark eyes aflame. The last time I saw him like this he was half-dressed: This couldn't end well. Mariners PR man Dave Aust led Piniella to our third-baseline remote. "G—damn media only wants to talk about the f—ing bullpen," Lou blurted, sitting next to me. "What the hell am I supposed to do? I can't throw the f—ing ball for them. Who do they want me to bring in? Hell, I've used everyone down there and they keep asking me to use someone else. Damn it, they should go ask the GM." Piniella then glared.

"Skip," I said, "I promise I won't ask you about the bullpen."

A calm came over him. "Son, I appreciate that. I don't want to talk about my bullpen anymore," patting me on the back.

Exhaling, I began to speak. "Lou, another tough loss last night, but it was good to see Edgar [Martinez] back in the lineup and he's hot."

"Edgar is Edgar." Lou responded, "He's a professional hitter, and we need him in the middle of our lineup around Junior, Tino [Martinez], and Jay [Buhner]. We got a good hitting club. Look," he paused, "scoring runs isn't our problem . . . our problem is, ah . . . our problem is . . . look, let's be honest, our problem is our—*bullpen!*" Lou began a three-minute rant on his bullpen's inability to throw strikes: perfect for our three-minute interview. "Thanks, Lou," I finally said, "and good luck tonight." He hadn't cursed, and I'd barely said a word.

— *Rich Waltz*

Jim Fregosi was Phillies 1991–1996 skipper, a good feel for Philadelphia, knew that baseball in our city is a way of life—but not how ubiquitous the media had become. Fregosi liked back-and-forth with people covering him: lots of one-liners and baseball talk in his office pre-game session. Many beat writers take vacation time Saturday, replaced by substitutes. One Saturday the subject of WIP Radio came up, sports talk becoming big and veterans like Fregosi trying to grasp its place. WIP had knocked him, so Jim begins his best chest-out reply by saying only "guys from South Philadelphia who [bleeped] their sisters listen to it anyway." Normally, no big deal: outrageous Jimmy being Jimmy, regulars knowing what was off the record. In this case, a backup reporter called a station host and repeated what Fregosi said. The host didn't like Fregosi and waited till drive-time Monday to air it, when more people listen. It produced a firestorm. Jimmy apologized, even led that fall's Columbus Day parade in South Philadelphia, but the damage was done. Fregosi was fired after the 1996 season. No one is immune to 24/7 media.

— *Chris Wheeler*

The Diamondbacks' first game in 1998 was my first in the big leagues. Fans came early to watch the retractable roof open, and left once it closed. Unsurprisingly, we lost to Colorado. *Quite* surprisingly, we lost less than 100 games [ninety-seven]. One game we won was up the coast at Candlestick Park. The D'backs had a two-run ninth-inning lead, bases full, Barry Bonds up, and closer Gregg Olson, the crowd, and yours truly doing a double-take: Manager Buck Showalter was ordering an intentional walk. It was a gamble, but rational, since Bonds was the Giants' best hitter. Walk him, yield a run, but maybe win the game. Bonds walks. Olson went 3–2 on the next batter, Brent Mayne, then got him. Skippers count for worse or, here, better.

— *Greg Schulte*

In 2000, Phillies manager Terry "Tito" Francona was fired before the last game of a 65–97 season. Arriving at the park, all of us knew what had happened. I had a manager's radio show to tape and wondered how we'd fill the time, assuming there was no way Francona would want to do it.

As usual, Tito was behind a desk, his normally playful eyes red from tears shed that morning. Surprisingly, he said, "Guess we have a show to do." I suggested it wasn't necessary, but he insisted, "No, let's do it." Halfway through the first segment, he began to talk about people who'd been special to him and how much he'd appreciated their help. Then Tito lost it, and that ended the show. I still have the disc of what we were able to air. Remarkably, a half-hour later he did our pre-game TV show, which went off without a hitch. In 2004, Tito ended the Red Sox' eighty-six-year championship drought. Managers can be a hero in one place, a what-if in another.

— *Chris Wheeler*

Many extol the "good old days" when each player knew how to bunt to advance a runner. You know, "Why can't guys *bunt* anymore?" A good manager believes in bunting a runner over only when he's got a guy who can *bunt!* Power hitters and RBI men *can't*—in the old days, or now. Roberto Clemente played eighteen years, had 3,000 hits, and successfully sacrificed thirty-six times: twelve in his first two years, before being thought an RBI threat, and only *twice* in his last *six*. Willie Stargell, all-time Bucs home run leader [475], was asked to bunt nine times in twenty-one years, none in his last fourteen. Dave Parker bunted once in nineteen—as a rookie. In the "good old days," run producers weren't asked to bunt. Guys who could handle the bat and bunt *were*. Nothing's changed! Tim Foli of the Bucs' '79 champions sacrifice-bunted 169 times in sixteen seasons. Following him at short, Jay Bell had 159 in eighteen. Famed for 1960 and wizardry at second base, Bill Mazeroski added eighty-seven in seventeen. To many, Ralph Kiner still means Pittsburgh. In ten years, eight as a Pirate, he bunted nine times, five with the '54 Cubs. Look at today's winning managers. They ask guys to do what they can, not can't. As a '70s song went, when it comes to bunting, "*These* are the good old days."

— *Greg Brown*

Before managing, Tito pinch-hit in 1986 at Wrigley Field: shadows past the mound, a lousy time to see. Worse, Nolan Ryan is in his prime, a titanic curve and fastball. Unbowed, Tito decides to look for a first-pitch fastball. Ryan starts that big, high leg kick followed by a grunt as he released. On cue—hit the fastball!—Tito swings mightily as the ball leaves Nolan's hand. Alas, since it's a curve with a 12-to-6 rotation that hit the dirt, Francona misses by at least a foot. Usually Ryan never changed expression. Now, though, like the crowd, he couldn't help turning his back to the plate, shoulders shaking, his stone face split into an ear-to-ear-grin. Ryan turns back, strikes Tito out. Francona slumps to the dugout, where his *teammates* are laughing at his swing. It's typical of Tito that he loves this story: the only player on a baseball diamond to make Nolan Ryan laugh.

— *Chris Wheeler*

Miller Park opened in 2001, great optimism, the long lost Brewers seemingly getting better. Any new park has snafus, as we saw on Father's Day, the end of a home stand, my wife and our three young daughters coming to see me off. After the game, twenty-three people, including us, get in an elevator, close the door, and get stuck, trapped between floors. I call security and traveling secretary Dan Larrea and wait for help, except that nobody can move the elevator. Finally, rescuers climb on top, open the roof, and hoist us out one by one. My family drives home as I head for the airport and Brewers charter to Cincinnati. Driving like a banshee, I call Dan, who says, "We're on the plane. How far are you away?" I say four, five minutes, hearing Dan inform manager Davey Lopes, seated across the aisle. Lopes says, "Leave him," and our plane does. I go home, have an unexpected Father's Day meal, and next morning fly commercial to Cincy. Next week the Brewers hit Chicago. Some players buy garish and obnoxious clothes, deciding if they sweep the series they'll wear their "sweep suits" on the plane to Pittsburgh. The 38–34 Brewers lose four straight to the lowly Bucs, ending the season 68–94. Like optimism, the sweep suits went away.

— *Jim Powell*

Through 2002, Lou and I did what he called the daily *Best Three Minutes in TV*, my partner funny, honest, and reflective. That year he left to manage Tampa Bay, closer to family, though some felt Lou and Mariners brass hadn't always seen eye-to-eye. In 2003, Fox Sports Northwest had me interview Lou on the field at Oakland before he returned to Seattle. Approaching, Lou had a big smile, greeted me with a hug, and said, "I miss the *Best Three Minutes in TV.*" I asked about Tampa Bay. Piniella praised getting to see his family. Next, I asked about revisiting the franchise he took from ineptitude to cultdom. Lou mentioned Griffey, Buhner, Ichiro, The Big Unit, and then it happened: Baseball's toughest manager broke down. He looked away, tried to resume, but couldn't, tearing about the Northwest's love affair, three LCS, and saving baseball in Seattle. I asked about 2001's 116-victory Mariners. Lou asked for time to compose himself, *again* broke down, then spent eight emotional minutes on how he'd feel stepping onto Safeco Field. Lou rose, patted me on the back, said "Thank you, sorry I got a little emotional," and turned toward the dugout, his game face again on. I moved to Marlins TV; Lou, the Cubs, retiring in 2010. Once I spoke to a former Piniella player. "Lou quickly separates the weak ones," he said, "finding out which players are strong enough to play for him." I knew what he meant.

— *Rich Waltz*

Joe Torre handled the media, New York's chaos, his tempestuous Yankees owner, and needing to take three playoff series to win the World Series, to become, well, Joe Torre. A lot of components come into play. One, he's very bright. Two, he grew up in New York, has street smarts and common sense. Three, he has a metronomical personality. Remember that TV ad, "Never let 'em see you sweat"? That's Joe. Torre received his Doctorate in Cool from the University of Steinbrenner. It took more than a decade to earn his degree. As a result, what's ever going to faze him? It didn't hurt that his boss had a bottomless pit of cash for roster renovations when needed as opposed to managing in St. Louis, Atlanta, and at Shea. Throw in how he managed two of sports' most storied franchises: the Yankees and Dodgers. All in all, not a bad resume, is it?

— *Charley Steiner*

As a lifelong Dodgers fan, I was around the bend in 2004 anticipating my first broadcast at Dodger Stadium. Then-manager Jim Tracy learned about that, telling me, "I hear you grew up with us, this is your first game here, and I know it's a big moment. I hope you have a good broadcast, and remember this day for the rest of your life." I'm never rooting against that man, no matter *what* his uniform.

    — *Jeff Munn*

Moving to LA, I was immediately asked about working for the Yankees and what pressures there might have been. Not that many, really. But I grew up in a mindset that if you won, the prevailing reaction would and should be elation, jubilation, and satisfaction. With the Yankees, there were often unreasonable expectations because if you didn't win the World Series, you failed, even though twenty-nine other teams were trying to do the same. Joe bore that burden for twelve years, won four Series in five years, and when he didn't win he'd failed! Something's wrong there. It was always, always interesting announcing the Yankees. It wasn't always, always fun. After a while, the expectations wore me out, and I only announced there from 2002–2004. When Joe arrived in Los Angeles in 2008, we talked about it: You don't try less, you don't play less hard, but if you don't succeed you come back another day, do your best, and again have at it. That's the beauty of baseball's 162-game season. I often wondered if the Yankees understood the difference between a baseball and a football state of mind.

    — *Charley Steiner*

Of the managers I've covered, Jack McKeon made the most bizarre moves that worked out fine: luck or insight, who knows? In 2003, Trader Jack twice inserted Mike Mordecai as a tie-game pinch-runner for clean-up hitter Mike Lowell, Florida failing to score. With Lowell's spot up in extra innings I said how nice it would be if he were still in the game and not light-hitting Mordecai, who promptly cranks his only homers of the year, each a game-winner. In postseason, Jack used every starter but Mark Redman in relief at least once, not worrying about the future. In Game 6 of the Series, Jack starts Josh Beckett on short rest, unconcerned about tomorrow. Beckett, clinching, hurls a five-hit shutout. Yet Jack's most unorthodox maneuver was in 2004: Marlins up, 10–8, in the eighth at Philly, Billy Koch loading the bases as Jack gets Armando Benitez up in the pen. On a 2–1 pitch to Jason Michaels, he's out of the dugout almost before the ball hits the catcher's glove, Jack using his closer with the bases full and a 3–1 count. If you've been following me, you know what happens. Benitez strikes out Michaels, gets Mike Lieberthal to end the inning, then works a scoreless ninth to pick up what I called a "double save." Brilliant or fortunate, who cares when you win?

— *Len Kasper*

Davey Lopes was fired late in 2001. I didn't shed a tear. Seven years later, I met an old school embodiment, Bobby Cox, the only manager to wear steel spikes all the time, despite multiple operations, knee replacements, and trouble walking. Bobby tried to do the right thing, teaching guys the right way. In 2010, the Braves were in Milwaukee, hitting and bullpen coach Terry Pendleton and Eddie Perez, respectively, helping Cox act out of character. They go to Johnnie Walker's, really a pimp suit store which closed that June, to be fitted, get suits, and decide to wear them on the get-away flight if they sweep the series, which Atlanta does. Out Bobby comes: orange suit with orange and white wide stripe, cap. Terry: lavender suit, purple cap, shoes, vest. Roger McDowell: gray, black, and white patterned jacket, a Fedora. Each has matching shoes and handkerchiefs in pockets. Bobby and his coaches sneak into first class. Players file on, see them, and are convulsed. The Braves win sixteen of their next twenty games to take first place: unlike Lopes', Cox's "sweep suits" worked. That fall the Braves lost the Division Series [injuries and Brooks Conrad's DS record three single-game errors too Sisyphean a boulder for even the retiring Cox to push]. After the last game, fans chanted "Bobby!", Cox leaving the dugout to tip his cap. The Giants stopped partying, faced Atlanta's dugout, and tipped *their* caps to *him*. "He's a legend in this sport," said the Giants' Freddy Sanchez. "We had to show our respect. First things first. Then we could go celebrate." Players would walk through walls for this genius at motivating and relaxing. Once *Sports Illustrated* asked big leaguers for whom they'd most like to play. Bobby won, hands down.

— *Jim Powell*

In 2005, my first year with the Rays, Lou Piniella introduced me to broadcaster/manager relations. The team stunk, ownership changing, yet Lou was almost always calm taping my daily show. One day at Yankee

Stadium, his famous temper showed. The Rays led, 10–2, before giving up thirteen eighth-inning runs, Lou's pen so spent he let Travis Harper take a beating, including back-to-back-to-back homers by Gary Sheffield, Alex Rodriguez, and Hideki Matsui. Afterward, writers repeatedly asked about leaving Harper in. Next day Lou met them in his office before our show, always easy to tell when he wasn't in a sunshiny mood, like now. The first question asked if overnight Lou'd rethought his decision. "*What?!*" he said, volume like a T-Rex, standing up behind a desk, complexion turning from pale to magenta. "Are you telling me I don't care about or protect my *players?!*" A salty tirade went on and on. Eventually, Lou, breathing heavily, ended the session, entered a bathroom behind his desk, and flipped a chair that hit the glass shower door. I stood stone still, having not blinked in the last five minutes, finally remembering to breathe. Lou reappeared, sinking into his chair, as I asked if he needed a few minutes. Staring straight ahead, he said no. "Lou, I know it's a tough topic," I began, fearing this question might get me disemboweled, "but I need to ask you about Travis Harper and the pen. It's what people are talking about, ya' know." I feigned confidence and forged a half-smile. Lou turned, winked, and said, "You can ask me anything you want." We proceeded to do the same pre-game chat we did 161 other times that year. Lou could be tough, unpredictable. But for how he helped me, the things he taught, and the way he was patient with a rookie, he will always be "Sweet Lou."

— *Andy Freed*

The 2007 Rockies wild card playoff victory over San Diego capped a story far beyond the field. Manager Clint Hurdle was the franchise's 2002–2009 public "face," tying stability and charity. Clint's daughter, Madison, has Prader-Willi Syndrome, a rare genetic disorder, their relationship so beautiful it prompted his tireless work with kids, including Kyle Blakeman, a Denver-area teenager diagnosed in 2005 with a rare kidney cancer. Through a neighbor, Clint befriended Kyle as he went through remission before the cancer recurred. In August 2007, the Rockies were at .500 as Hurdle stopped at the hospital, Kyle's condition worsening, and asked his lucky number. Kyle said "*64!*" — his football uniform number. That night Clint put and circled it on his lineup card before the Rockies, down, 5–1, in the ninth, rallied for a 6–5 victory: The Power of *64* had begun. From that point, Clint daily placed a circled *64* atop his card, even when Kyle passed away five days after telling it and before Colorado's 12–1 finish forced a playoff. By LCS Game 4, the local media had chronicled the story. Kyle's little sister, Macie, threw out the first pitch, everywhere tears and cheers. In the fourth, trailing, 1–0, we exploded. At break I eyed the scoreboard, disbelieving. "Look!" I told partner Jeff Kingery. "We scored six runs in the fourth inning! 6–4!" Irony heightened when Arizona scored three runs, on the final out Coors Field exploding; the Rockies' ticket to the Fall Classic punched by a 6–4 final score. The lucky number had come through. After the celebration, Clint and the Blakeman family walked toward the parking lot, Kyle's mother, Joanna, saying her son's baseball number had been 21. That night's Rockies victory was their *21st* in the last 22 games.

— *Jack Corrigan*

In seventeen years doing baseball, the most unique manager I've known is Joe Maddon, conversation shifting from pitch counts to fifteenth-century European culture to Akinori Iwamura's groundball batting average. More than anything, Joe keeps perspective, learned since being ejected seven times in his rookie seventy-game minor-league year: even-tempered, self-critical, and profoundly literate. My favorite 2008 moment came before LCS Game 7. Having endured the Red Sox kicking sand in Tampa Bay's face for the last decade, a fatalistic fan base felt fear. Meeting Joe was my pre-game norm. That night he's eating a sandwich, music playing on his laptop, coulda' been June in Kansas City. "Joe," I said, "I'm amazed at how calm you are." He smiled. "Sure, it's intense. But I think about all we've accomplished in such a short time. Think of the good people who've worked so long for this franchise. Think of how proud they must be now to come to work. Think of the joy we've brought to this area. It's changed, and changed forever." *Perspective*. "Do I think we're going to win tonight? Yes. But even if we don't, we've *already* won." I was stunned by his leadership: no act, just belief in what you do. The Rays won the flag. Back in Joe's office, I noted what he'd said before the game. "The perfect way to approach the night," I said. "And congratulations. You're next year's American League's All-Star manager!"

— *Andy Freed*

Chapter Five

Unordinary Joes

Each sport has stars. Baseball has characters, too. Doug Rader, driving his golf cart into a lake. Jim Piersall, running his hundredth homer backward around the bases. Mickey Hatcher, painting his body green for St. Patrick's Day. Mitch Williams becoming "Wild Thing." No character is like The Yog.

Born to Italian immigrants, the jug-eared Larry Berra and a teen friend one day saw a 1930s theater travelogue about India. It starred a yogi, whom his pal compared to Berra. Like gold, the nickname stuck. Yogi "thought funny and said what he thought," said another boyhood friend, Joe Garagiola. Always go to other people's funerals, Berra later warned: "Otherwise they won't come to yours."

Like Garagiola, Yogi grew up in a hurry. At nineteen, he survived D-Day — June 6, 1944. Back home, Berra hit 358 homers, had catching's most runs batted in, and became three-time MVP. "Baseball is 90 percent mental and the other half is physical," he explained. "If you can't imitate him, don't copy him." Yogi never did, admitting only that Yankees coach Bill Dickey "had learned me his experience."

In 1956, Berra caught Don Larsen's World Series perfect game, then spotted the team publicist. "Hi. What's new?" he said. Yogi coined, "When you come to a fork in the road, take it." His fork led to most all-time Fall Classic games (seventy-five), hits (seventy-one), played (fourteen), and won (ten): to biographer Allen Barra, "becoming the greatest winner in American professional sports."

Yogi married wife Carmen in 1949. Son Dale made the bigs. Dad's bowling alley rolled 300. By any measure, Berra's 2002 insurance ad — number 8, in barber chair; barber and duck, agape — merits TV's Lourdes. At his Montclair University Museum and Learning Center, "I like to be there, teaching kids things like sportsmanship and work." If Yogi were a film, it would be The Quiet Man *meets* Mr. Lucky.

In 2008, Berra was introduced at Yankee Stadium's finale. The din swelled, rose above the outfield, and crashed against the tiers. Garagiola was once asked how far Yogi went in high school. "Nine blocks," he jibed. By any name, few lives have gone further.

I can't remember not knowing Yogi. I'd ask him, "What time is it?" He says: "Now?" Once, lost going to his home, I called him. "Where are you?" he says. I tell him. He says, "You're not far away. You come this way. Don't go that way." Even when Yogi doesn't make sense, he does. In 1960, Herbert Hoover and India's Prime Minister [Jawaharlal Nehru] were introduced before Game 3 of the World Series. The next day I saw my old pal. "You amaze me, Yog," I said. "You've now become such a world figure that you draw more applause than either a prime minister or former president. Can you explain it?" Yogi paused. "Certainly. I'm a better hitter."
— *Joe Garagiola*

At a 2007 Induction Weekend party at Cooperstown, I told Yogi Berra that Stroud's, the famous chicken restaurant in Kansas City, had closed its location. Yogi was devastated. When he coached and managed the Yankees, he went to Stroud's at least a couple times in any trip to Kansas City, the restaurant even staying open for him late after a game. I told Yogi they were trying to find a new location, to which he said, "If they don't, I'm not coming back to Kansas City." I thought of another Yogism: "If they don't want to come, who's going to stop 'em?"
— *Denny Matthews*

In 1985, Yogi was our Yankees manager for sixteen games, till Mr. Steinbrenner fired him. What a sweetheart of a guy. Yogi'd come over, "How you doing, little guy?" I'd say, "Yogi, you're smaller than I am." Somehow he survived.
— *Billy Sample*

Catcher Clint Courtney — "Scrap Iron" — loved to fight but hated to fly, taking sedation from a bottle. Behind the plate, Clint drew marks in the dirt for each called ball he thought a strike. After a fifth "blown call" he drew a slash, the umpire ejecting him. Clint: "I haven't said a word."

Ump: "Doesn't matter."

Once Clint told me that with a runner on third he was afraid to throw the ball back to the pitcher because "a bad throw scores a run." His solution: practice an hour each day to regain self-confidence. I tell him to "regard me as the pitcher. Look at my chest. Throw it there." In a couple days, Clint thinks he's OK: "I'm starting tomorrow." Tomorrow he has a final worry: "How tall are you?" A shade under six feet, I said. "What if the pitcher's 6-2 or 6-3?" he pleaded. Clint, I said, "A chest is a chest."

— *Bob Wolff*

In 1959, Dick Howser gave me the name "The Hawk." It wasn't hard, my nose broken in six places. In time, it became my alter ego. I'd be in the on-deck circle, runner on third, and say, "Kenny, get out of the way and let Hawk take charge." I'm quiet and introverted, as my wife can attest. Hawk was my antithesis. He wants to wear loud clothes, have hair flowing to your fanny. I think this helps on TV. A broadcaster has to have personality. I love listening to Jon Miller: great humor, mimicry, doesn't seem that he knows it all, draws word-pictures, so natural. The stuff I came up with—Frank Thomas as "The Big Hurt," Jack McDowell "Black Jack," "Put it on the board," things like that—was natural, too. I'd be in rightfield, Killebrew up, guy on third, and Jim Lonborg'd strike him out: "He gone," I'd say, or "grab some bench. Get that next SOB up there." That's me. Talking as often as we do, you better be yourself, 'cause people spot a phony fast.

— *Ken Harrelson*

Lou Piniella was a character before he was a Yankee. The early Royals wore button-down jersey tops. Once in a while, Lou got so frustrated making an out that he'd grab his jersey by the collar and pull on it as hard as he could, ripping the buttons off. It's a wonder he didn't put out someone's eye. One sunny Saturday at old Municipal Stadium, Lou hit into an inning-ending double play, cussing and kicking the dirt and grass. Shortstop Freddie Patek brings out Lou's glove, with sunglasses inside. Lou grabs them, throws glasses and glove on the ground, and heads to leftfield. He gets there, picks everything up, and puts the glasses on — still steamed. The inning's second batter flies to left. Flipping down his glasses, Lou finds that a lens had popped out hitting the ground: He's blinded in one eye by the sun, starts spinning like a top to get an angle, yet amazingly made the catch. Thankfully, managing, sunglasses were no longer a concern.

— *Denny Matthews*

Pat Zachry, a smart guy, got confused one afternoon pitching for the Mets. They've been in existence since 1962 and no Met has thrown a no-hitter, but on April 10, 1982, at Wrigley, Zachry had one going with two outs in the eighth when it was broken up by Bob Molinaro. After the game, he told Marty Noble of *Newsday*, "You can't write this, but I'm kind of glad that it was broken up." "Why?" Noble asked. "Because I thought the eighth inning was the ninth inning," Zachry said. Which means, if he had gotten the last out of the eighth, he might have leapt into the arms of the catcher. How embarrassing would that have been? Many years later, when another Met nearly threw a no-hitter, Noble called Zachry for permission to write the story. "It's OK to tell it now," he said.

— *Tim Kurkjian*

Jim Wohlford was easy to pick on, a nice guy who platooned in left-field. One spring he hadn't made the Royals roster despite telling me, "Denny, Jim Wohlford can hit." I'd say: "I know, Wolfy, you can hit." Taking batting practice, he had eight to ten guys in his group, getting only five or six swings and maybe a bunt. Not the best place to get good work. Wolfy gets his hacks, comes out, and I could tell he was steamed. Keep in mind, I never heard Jim say a bad thing about anyone — till now. "I can't wait until we get some of the deadwood out of here," he said, meaning minor leaguers, "so we can get some more swings." Sure enough, the "deadwood" on next day's bus headed to the minor-league camp at Sarasota included — Jim Wohlford.

— *Denny Matthews*

Nineteen eighty-two, my second year with the A's, was a good time to cover Rickey Henderson, since he stole a record 130 bases. I also saw an unknown side of arguably baseball's greatest leadoff hitter. In Kansas City, most teams stayed in a hotel with a bar, Quincy's, downstairs, which, being single at the time, I would frequent before at closing time climbing stairs to the lobby. This night, starting pitcher Brian Kingman left when I did, infamous for losing twenty games in 1980. The cerebral Kingman and manager Billy Martin had constant friction. At the top of the stairs stood Billy and his four coaches. I whispered, "What's *this* about?" Near the top, Kingman whispered, "Billy's waiting for me." Having knocked heads about his pitching style and effort, Martin now wanted to knock heads *literally*. When we reached Billy's vultures, words started spewing. Soon he said, "We're going outside to rumble." I pleaded not to, whereupon Martin said, "You're just a broadcaster." In short, step aside. Billy walked into the KC night, stooge coaches following. So did Brian, by *himself*. Several A's players in the lobby turned away. By contrast, Henderson went racing to the door, which one coach tried to block, Rickey saying that if Martin had help outside, he would help his teammate. Billy and Brian did scrap, trading punches. A miserable 1982 ended with Billy being fired. As for Rickey, he'll be remembered for some things comical, others historical. I'll recall the personal: his courage and fairness. The only player not to turn his head—in essence, *back*—on Kingman was the team's star.

—*Wayne Hagin*

Pitcher Dennis Eckersley went four years between pickoffs: amazingly, the *last* guy he picked off in 1982 was the *first* guy he picked off in 1978, Kenny Williams. In 1983, the Orioles' Tippy Martinez picked three runners off first base in the same inning. His catcher was Lenn Sakata, an infielder who'd never caught but had to that night because manager Joe Altobelli had used up the bench trying to tie the score in the ninth. With a second baseman behind the plate, three Blue Jays were a little too anxious leading off first, and Martinez nailed them all—a baseball first, and surely last. "Tippy had the worst pick-off move of any left-hander I've ever seen," teammate Mike Flanagan said. "I bet he never picked off another runner before or after that." Sakata hit the game-winning home run, later voted by Oriole fans the greatest game in club history. When Memorial Stadium closed in 1991, many former Orioles came back to say good-bye, going to the positions that they'd played. Sakata didn't go to second base, he went behind the plate. And every fan in the ballpark got it.

— *Tim Kurkjian*

In 1965, the Cardinals gave out 1964 World Series rings. They threw mine into the outfield grass, and between innings I'd go out and look around. Finally, in the fifth inning I find it, people screaming and cheering. I put it on over two fingers. It wasn't made for me but it was the one they gave me: probably the highlight of my baseball career. Or maybe that came two years later. I hit a grand slam off Ron Herbel—and as I get back into the dugout, you know, guys were slapping me on the back and stepping on me and everything else. I was lying on the floor. I got up to look at the field. There's Giants manager Herman Franks going to the mound to take Herbel out of the game, and he's got Herbel's suitcase packed.

— *Bob Uecker*

I joined Bob in 1984, finding a perfectionist who'd read commercial spots over and over to ensure they were right. He suggested we share a scorebook, so the guy away from the mike would find it updated when he got back. If he made any announcing mistake, he wanted me to correct him off-air so that he could correct himself. I did post-game, each day Bob not leaving till he made me lose it. He'd make an animal sound—wounded dog, baby seal—imitate somebody we knew, or had just seen in the booth. Bob used props—pencils, hot dogs, coming in with pretzels sticking out of each ear—anything so he could say, "I knew I was gonna' get you." And you know, he did, every time.

— *Pat Hughes*

Whenever the Brewers went into Montreal, Uke, goofing around, would imitate the accent of a fictional French-Canadian character: "Monsieur, I warn you." Ultimately, I got Bob to let me interview his character by inventing a French journalist of dubious credentials, Mr. Jean Jacques Smythe. I start by asking him why Canadians prefer hockey to baseball. "Well, because it doesn't take too long to make a puck," Uke, as Mr. Smythe, began. "Baseball, you've got to have a small ball to put inside. Then they wrap yarn around the baseball. And then you got to kill a cow or a horse to put a cover on it. Hockey, you get a rubber tree, and you let the rubber flow out of the tree till it gets round. And then you put it out in the cold weather and it gets hard. You got hard stuff like that and you hit it with a stick." For six-and-a-half minutes Bob ad-libbed wonderfully, sounding like he was from Quebec. I asked if we could air it. "Oh, I don't think so," Bob says. I say, "Gee, it's funny." He reluctantly agrees. We play it, phone calls stream in, who *is* this guy? I interview Mr. Smythe a few more times, always at Olympic Stadium, whose French signage translated into broken English. Uke didn't know what it meant, but, hey, neither did a listener. Nobody knew it was the legend, Bob Uecker, just that some jerk was *insulting* the legend. Only with the Uke.

—*Jim Powell*

The musician Al Hirt helped start Bob's career, leading to, among other things, nearly a hundred gigs on Johnny Carson's *Tonight Show*. After Uke's first appearance Carson asked, "Did that guy *really* play baseball?" His timing was that good. Johnny asked if he'd ever been asked to endorse a product. Bob answered that he "had a unique and lucrative contract with a sporting goods company, Rawlings, *not* to use any of their products." Once Carson asked about fans. "Of a hundred people," Bob said, "fifty are going to say he [Uke] stunk and he was a disgrace to his uniform. And the other fifty are going to tell you he was garbage. So you have two schools of thought."

—*Pat Hughes*

Tim Ireland's playing career included a "cup of coffee" as an early 1980s Royals infielder and outfielder—despite or because of wearing a garlic necklace under his minor-league uniform for nine innings, then opting not to shower. No one sat next to Tim on long bus trips. As a baseball strategist, he had no peer. In 1993, his El Paso Diablos were struggling to make the playoffs. Tim wanted a relief pitcher to spot start, but knew if given too much time to think the reliever might mentally self-destruct. So he gave a concession worker $50 to pose as a player the parent Brewers had just signed out of Mexico: 5-foot-6, a face older than his size, speaking little English. The only other person in on the joke was pitching coach Rob Derksen, who told the team that "Jose was a stud in Mexico and the Brewers signed him to help us win." Especially confused were two catchers who couldn't communicate with the mysterious phenom to find what he threw. One pitcher was so sure the new addition spelled his release that he had his wife begin to pack and head home. Ireland even told the equipment manager that "Jose" needed spikes and a glove because his gear bag had been stolen. Forty-five minutes before the game, the Diablos about to snap, Tim told them the truth— just in time for his *real* starter to warm up without worrying himself to death.

—*Matt Vasgersian*

The Giants' Mike Krukow was a character. When a baseball lodged in the webbing of pitcher Terry Mulholland's glove, he threw the glove to first baseman Bob Brenly for the out. "You blew it," teammate Krukow told Brenly. "You should have whipped it around the infield."

Then there was first baseman Kent Hrbek, the only player who showed up for World Series parties in 1987 and '91 because the food and beer were free. In 1990, he met White Sox rookie Craig Grebeck, who wore the same number, 14, and was roughly half his size: 140 pounds to 280 pounds. "You're too small to wear that number," Hrbek told him. "Put a slash between the one and the four and be one-fourth."

—*Tim Kurkjian*

My most memorable character was Jimmy Piersall. Everyone knew from Jimmy's 1950s depression problems how he was certifiably nuts. As Cubs farm system outfield instructor, he had an enormous influence on how I played the game, observing that if you hustle, nobody'll question your effort, only skill. "Throw the ball into the cutoff man as hard as you can!" he'd say. "Throw it, get rid of it *now!*" — subtle as a hammer. He taught hitting, base running, loyalty, above all. Jimmy was at 1985 spring training, my first with the Cubs. I hit with Billy Hatcher and Dave Owen *after* stars like Gary Matthews, Ryne Sandberg, and Leon Durham finished. They're hitting bombs, a tough act to follow. Behind the fence a guy all over us calls us "Chop-Chop," so that's what we call him. "Come on, Chop-Chop, you can't hit the fence. No power. You stink!" It's tough enough to hit as a kid without being ridiculed. One day Piersall approaches him dropping some expletives. "Shut the f— up. Get the hell out of here, you f—ing crazy bastard! I'll come over and knock you on your a—." Usually you can't get away with this language. "I can," Jimmy told me, "'cause I'm crazy." His message: Chop-Chop, get off *my* guys! Soon fans are saying, "You're right, Jimmy. Give these kids a break."

—*Darrin Jackson*

Growing up a White Sox fan, I thought that Harry Caray and Piersall were often more interesting than the game. In 1982, Harry joined the Cubs. In 1991, finding that Jimmy would be at a game to observe their Peoria Chiefs, I asked if he'd join me. Would he? Piersall always had a lot to say. Before the game I got good news: Jimmy'd heard me the night before. And bad: I'd worn him out, calling every play like the ninth. He said Harry told him to ease into a game, build momentum. Everyone knows Piersall's mind doesn't have a politically correct filter. He'll rip players and managers, use salty language in breaks, then stop swearing when the light comes on. This night I didn't know how such an old-schooler would like the San Diego Chicken stealing his thunder. To my shock, he loved it, doing Chicken play-by-play. In one inning the Chicken, coaching first, tried to distract the pitcher with female posters: Farrah Fawcett, making Jimmy chuckle; then, a plus-sized woman, making Jimmy blurt, "Look, he's got a poster of a big fat broad." I'm an adult, and he's *still* more interesting.

—*Dave Wills*

In my fourth year as a minor-leaguer, the Cubs have to judge: Should Jackson make the team? If I go down again, I probably won't be back. One spring training day Piersall walks up: "Kid, I went to bat for you. I told 'em you were ready for the major leagues. Don't f— it up, or I'm fired!" I make the team, have a good season, retire years later, and become a Sox broadcaster. We're in spring training, and he starts mentoring me again. "Tell it like it is, don't hold back," speaking with authority, from one old to another young player and now announcer. Jimmy couldn't control what left his mouth, we all know that. This meant that everything that did leave it was true.

—*Darrin Jackson*

In 1991, I got my first baseball radio job at Cubs Class-A Huntington, West Virginia, a wide-eyed fan meeting former big-leaguers-turned-coaches and instructors who traveled in and out of the Appalachian League. Jimmy was still unpredictable, reputed to bite your head off if he didn't like you, so haltingly, I ask him to join me for an inning. To my delight, he agrees, patronizing me with amusement and obligation. Jimmy sensed he could use my questions to tell old standbys without repercussion. "One day we were playing in Cleveland," he says. "I was warming up in the outfield when I noticed a young mother holding her baby in the first row above the fence. I happened to be looking at her when I noticed she was about to drop the baby. Luckily my instincts as an outfielder were so good I sprinted toward the fence and as the young lady dropped the child I was there to catch it."

Unwittingly his straight man, I say, "Wow . . . then what happened?"

Jimmy responds, "Young man, unfortunately my instincts were so good I turned and threw the little son-of-a-bitch to second!"

Jimmy stayed another inning till loud crackling pierced our headsets. I noted that lightning storms weren't uncommon around game time—all Piersall needed to hear. Eyes big as silver dollars, Jimmy's next broadcast words were his last—"Young man, you do a fine job"—beelining for the door without taking off his headset, pulling our modest mixing board from its connection, and knocking us off the air. Thunder and lightning and Jimmy Piersall *v.* me. If it had been a fight, it would have been stopped *before* the first round.

—*Matt Vasgersian*

Dan Plesac was a late-1990s Blue Jays reliever who loved playing ball and loved to have fun. In Toronto, "the world's fastest grounds crew" comes out at the end of the fifth inning to clean dirt and change bases. One day Plesac, knowing he won't pitch till later, takes the uniform of a taller grounds guy and joins the crew. He heads to third base, where coincidentally teammate Otis Nixon has just been stranded to end the inning. Otis is waiting for someone to bring his glove and hat when Plesac lays into him about the Jays' stranding too many runners. To Dan's surprise, Nixon stared at him without a word. Plesac finished sweeping, changed back into

uniform, and went about his business for the rest of the game. Afterward, the first player who approaches him in the clubhouse is Nixon. "Damn, Sac," he says, "we've got a guy on the grounds crew who looks *just like you!*"
—*Dan Shulman*

My first year in the bigs, I carried books containing quotes and anecdotes: "rain delay material." Once I read on the air about ex-Brewers great Gorman Thomas having been unavailable for a game after wrenching his back while getting out of a cab in Cleveland. Next day I'm in the booth when a baseball hits the tin press box facing. A few seconds later a ball hit the window, then another. On the field a ranting Thomas armed with a bucket of balls and a fungo bat is peppering my booth with drives. When the game began my partner Bill Schroeder says solemnly, "Gorman's outside. He wants to talk to you." I left the booth, felt a firm grip on my right shoulder, and turned to see the former home run champ peering down at me like an executioner about to inject his prey. I show the book's offending passage only to find Gorman's not mad, just getting a laugh, insisting Jamie Easterly's back, not his, had given way. A few years later my ex-tormentor filled in as our TV commentator on a three-game series. Gorman's creative expletives could make the biggest potty-mouth blush, worrying Brewers president Wendy Selig-Prieb, whose fondness for Gorman as a player made her cautiously approve his debut. Sadly, she and other brass made such a point of not cursing that Thomas was frightened into not speaking, for two games not saying boo. Before the final, we loosened him up to where he described a bloop single as a "flaming duck fart." Almost immediately, a phone call came into the truck telling us to keep Gorman clean. Not surprisingly, the rest of the telecast went from potentially brilliant to a colossal bore.
—*Matt Vasgersian*

Baseball Voices can work other sports, too, as I did with Al McGuire for five years, including Marquette TV basketball. After a day game in Louisville I said, "Let's get a cab to the airport." Al's response made me do a double-take: "No, Pat, *let's hitchhike.* Someone will recognize me, they'll pick us up, and we'll save money on the cab." Soon I have my thumb sticking up as, sure enough, a van recognizes Al. "Hey, that you, Al McGuire? You need a ride?" Al said, "Yeah, me and my partner, Pat, trying to get to the airport." The guy says: "Get in." I'm in the back seat of a total stranger's vehicle, and Al's telling kids about coaching against John Wooden, winning NCAAs, arguing with refs: hilarious. At the airport I say, "That was amazing. You're probably still going to turn in that expense for the cab, aren't you?" Al said, "I don't keep the small stuff. I got enough big scams going." Another time we do Marquette at Charlotte. I fly in Monday night, next morning calling home. "Everything's fine," my wife said, "except I just got a strange call from Al McGuire starting, 'Where's Pat?'" She said, "Charlotte, North Carolina." Al goes, "*Charlotte*? *That's* where I'm supposed to be." Al arrives from Milwaukee ninety minutes before tipoff: hasn't shaved in five days, sweat suit on, suit and tie in a garment bag, and says, "Fellahs, how you doing?" We say, "Great, we're ready to go on." Al says, "I'll be fine," grabs a Charlotte coach, takes him aside, and in twenty minutes learns everything he needs to know. Al goes in, showers, and comes out a minute before airtime. "Hi, everybody, along with Al McGuire, this is Pat Hughes," I begin. "Al, tell us about this team." Al acts like he's done homework for weeks. "Oh, wait till you see this shooter. Oh, can he shoot." I'm smiling, thinking, "Al, this morning you didn't even know where you were supposed to be for the game." He is beautiful. "*Charlotte*? *That's* where I'm supposed to be."

    — *Pat Hughes*

Sportscasting's unwritten rule is to be "professional" — no profanity, be fair, use proper grammar, don't get personal. I agree, yet sometimes your personality or "inner fan" comes out. In August 2006, Chicago beat the Astros, 8–6, taking eighteen innings and five hours and thirty-six minutes to finish, ending after 12:30 a.m. The Cubs' pen was so empty that next afternoon's scheduled starter, Rich Hill, worked the last two innings. Between 2:00 and 4:00 a.m., they find a new starter: Ryan O'Malley of AAA Iowa, a few hours away in Round Rock, Texas, racing to get to Houston for his big-league debut. I'm running, too, on fumes, with little sleep, caffeine fueling my energy. As it happened, O'Malley energized partner Bob Brenly and me, beating Andy Pettitte, 1–0. Afterward, we interviewed Ryan, who got a shaving-cream pie in the face from mates, then went to commercial as Ryan embraced his father near the dugout. Dad's face wore cream, too, and the proudest look a pop could have. Leaving break, emotion high and mental gas tank empty after twenty-seven innings in twenty hours, we showed the shot—and suddenly neither Bob nor I could speak, mumbling through our final segment, admitting we were choked up by the incredible moment between a father and son. I never thought I'd cry on the air doing baseball, and I know some announcers deem it a sin, but I beg to differ. First, you ill serve your audience if you can't or won't react naturally to what you see. Also, at that moment I didn't care much about being a broadcaster. Being part of that experience mattered more: a proud dad embracing his son after the greatest achievement of his life.

— *Len Kasper*

Baseball has the best nicknames. Catcher Doug Gwosdz was "Eye Chart." G-W-O-S-D-Z. Rockies pitcher David Lee was "Diesel." Something happened to the bus driver in spring training 1999, so Lee had to drive the team bus. He pulled into a gas station and pronounced, "We need some diesel!" And there was minor-leaguer "Pork Chop" Pough. "When I was eight, my nickname was 'Pokie,'" he said. "We had another kid on our team named 'Pokie,' but I was much bigger than him, so everyone started calling me 'Pork Chop.' Teachers in high school called me that. They didn't even know my name was Clyde."

— *Tim Kurkjian*

Chapter Six

The Sum of Its Parts

Actor *Desi Arnaz was once asked how TV's* I Love Lucy *had changed his life. "That's a silly question," he said. "Ask what it hasn't changed." What hasn't changed is the union of special team and special year.*

Brooklyn's nirvana remains 1955. Pittsburgh still oozes a 1960 World Series that puzzled Ripley. The 1980 Phillies exorcised defeat, while 2005 means the Pale Hose leaving the Black Sox behind. At the other pole, the 1962 Metropolitan Baseball Club of New York was so bad it became chic in the ephemera capital of the world.

In 1957, the Dodgers and Giants confirmed California's elephant in the room. Grudgingly, the 1962 National League expanded to Houston and New York. Mets skipper Casey Stengel vowed to "work on the little finesses. Runners at first and second, and the first baseman holding a runner, breaking in and back to take a pick-off throw." Losing his first exhibition, 17–1, the Perfessor saw the light, not liking what he saw. "The little finesses ain't gonna be our problem."

The Mets' regular-season debut was Metsian, Roger Craig's first-inning balk helping St. Louis score twice. Their home opener was Friday, April 13, the Amazin's soon the hero of every dog that was under. Acronym Marvin Eugene Throneberry aped Alfonse at the plate and Gaston in the field, umpire Dusty Boggess calling him out for missing first base on a triple. Coach Cookie Lavagetto intercepted an angry Stengel: "Don't argue too long – he missed second, too."

Casey never asked "how we lost 120. I asked how we won 40." The season ended with Joe Pignatano hitting into a triple play. Richie Ashburn then took his team MVP prize – a boat – out on the Delaware River, where it sank. By con-

trast, the 1969 Metropolitans rose like Saint Bernadette. On October 16, "Let's Go Mets!" morphed into "We're Number One!" In the year men walked in space, baseball's new aristoi walked on air.

Today, a coach will cry, "You're worse than the '62 Mets!" or antipodally, "Remember the Miracle Mets!" In Casablanca, *Bogart tells Bergman, "We'll always have Paris." Many Voices will always have special team/special year.*

In 1940, the Cardinals traded Ducky Medwick to the Dodgers, at which time I said I was now a Dodgers fan. Right away my dad, Milo, taught me a great lesson in team loyalty. "You may be a *Ducky* fan. But you're first a *Cardinals* fan."
— *Milo Hamilton*

For the Senators, early 1949 was an exception to misery's rule. Somehow they win nine straight games, hailed by a parade down Pennsylvania Avenue. Signs read: "We'll Win Plenty with Sam Dente" and "Drink a Toast with Eddie Yost." Mostly I aired records — against my team. In 1953, Mickey Mantle's drive off Chuck Stobbs stopped 565 feet away: the first "tape-measure" homer. Later Stobbs threw a ball that bounced, cleared the backstop, and stuck in mustard at a concession stand: baseball's longest wild pitch. In May 1956, Mantle's blast off Pedro Ramos headed straight up, struck the façade, now called frieze, after clearing the third deck at Yankee Stadium. Otherwise it would have become the first fair ball to leave that ballpark. Every year was special — when you played the Senators.
— *Bob Wolff*

In 1953 the Boston Braves left for Milwaukee. We're in spring training at Bradenton when the shift was announced. We go up north, where Milwaukee had a huge downtown parade. Inside the Schroeder Hotel, people put up a *Christmas* tree — in *April* — saying that since we'd missed Christmas, they wanted to celebrate it with us now: hundreds of presents under the tree — radios, appliances, shaving kits — gaga from day one. Folks brought lunches to the park, gave us free gas, milk, and beer. Each year the Braves got cars from dealers rent-free. Warren Spahn, who won 363 games — more than any lefty, all but seven for the Braves — already *had* a car, so fans gave

him another—for his family. You talk about Brooklyn, Cubs fans, today's Red Sox. In '50s Milwaukee, *every* day was Christmas.
  — *Ernie Johnson*

I grew up in solid Cardinals Country, south-central Missouri, within earshot at night of blowtorch KMOX Radio. However, days or nights, we listened to the hometown station for which I first worked: Lebanon's KLWT, which we called "Keep Listening, We're Trying." It loved the Redbirds, too, since until the late '50s the big leagues were confined to the country's northeast quadrant. Anything south and west belonged to them: among others, Stan Musial, whom my father saw hit a homer out of the park and across a street; Bob Gibson, so intense he wouldn't let his own little girl beat him at tic-tac-toe; Curt Flood, the slick centerfielder who fueled free agency but wound up a bartender; and Lou Brock, the speedy ex-Cub whose 1964 trade provided the final piece of a Cardinals dynasty. To this day, whenever I interview Cubs fan George Will, I wear my red Cardinals' warm-up jacket. Each year he gets a Christmas card from a "friend" with a picture of Brock in a Cubs' uniform, prompting George to write, and I paraphrase, that should the Nazis take power they could recruit brownshirts among Cardinals' fans. They are special, showing expansion's dilution of the true baseball audience. Where but St. Louis could you see a fine hit-and-run applauded?—by the *opposing* team. This may explain why it took so hard Mark McGwire's revelation of better living through chemistry. The Missouri State Senate renamed a part of I-70 called Mark McGwire highway. I thought it made more sense just to keep the name and widen it to sixteen lanes.

Being a radio fan, I fondly recall Harry Caray, who in World War II announced sports at a Michigan station whose news director was Paul Harvey. Later Harry called games in his undershirt, snagged fouls with a fishing net, and interacted with Jack Buck. Once they kept an endlessly rain-delayed game at the park, not returning to local stations, Harry and Jack debating the pennant race, rookies, and MVP candidates before finally in desperation—perhaps also fueled by Budweiser—noting that it was grab bag day. They emptied one grab bag, musing what the next might hold. A suggestion was "a lock of hair from Branch Rickey's eyebrows." In 1971–

1981, Harry broadcast the White Sox with first team All-Flake Jimmy Piersall, who on occasion could lose control. In the booth, I saw a little signal Harry and Jimmy worked out when Piersall's medication wore thin. Harry would reach over, squeeze Jimmy's forearm, and help Piersall downshift into normal gear. Baseball is a wonderful game. Even with Stephen Strasburg, I can't wait for Washington to get a major league team.

— *Jim Bohannon*

[By 1955, Brooklyn had lost seven straight World Series, five against the Yankees. Not surprisingly, it feared the worst, even when the Bums led Game 7, 2–0.] In New Jersey, my mother, listening at home, started walking the family dog. Named Blackie. She began in the sixth. In the seventh, same thing, more pressure, she's anxious, she walked Blackie. Then, in the ninth, the Dodgers are three outs away from winning their first world championship, she feels the pressure, she gets the leash, but she can't find Blackie! The dog's hiding. [At 3:45 p.m. the Dodgers won. "Ladies and gentlemen," Vin Scully said on NBC, "the Brooklyn Dodgers are the champions of the world."] All winter, people asked how I remained so calm. I was from New York, the Dodgers had lost so many times, and then finally to win against the Yankees. That's why I shut up when Pee Wee [Reese] threw to [Gil] Hodges [for Brooklyn's final out]. If I'd said another word at that very instant, I'd have broken down and cried."

— *Vin Scully*

I was born in 1965, the Braves moving to my home, Atlanta, as Bud Selig sued to keep them in Milwaukee. In Georgia, they were bad, but I found ways to love them: great training for a career. By 1996, I'd done post-game radio, wanting play-by-play. Where do I get it? *Milwaukee!* As a kid, I'd read about its 1950s glory years, arriving now to find many still traumatized by the move. An early job was to emcee Miller Park's groundbreaking: Hank Aaron, Selig, Robin Yount putting shovels in the dirt; Bob Uecker attending, a Milwaukee native who'd played there in the '60s. At Miller, they've built a Braves Wall of Honor to salute ex-players: Warren Spahn inducted posthumously, 2005; Andy Pafko, '06; Aaron back about every year, honored baseball, even when it didn't honor him. In 1996, I interviewed with the Brewers on a thirty-five-degrees-below-zero-wind-chill day. Outside, I bump into Braves shortstop Johnny Logan, whom I later asked to compare Milwaukee now as a baseball town as opposed to the '50s. "The biggest difference," he said, "is that most of those fans have passed on." In 2009, I returned to Atlanta, broadcasting in the Pete Van Wieren radio booth, having grown up on WTBS's him, Skip Caray, and Ernie Johnson. Two cities: one thread.

— *Jim Powell*

My favorite year was '69, because of Ted Williams. He had an opinion on everything, usually well informed, meshing with our club, where nearly every Senator had a college background: in baseball, then rare. The team brains had master's degrees: Jim Hannan, Dave Baldwin, and Jim French, our funniest guy and easily loudest dresser. One night Jim and Ted got to bantering over Frenchie's sports shirts of every design and color. "Where'd you get *that* thing?" Williams asked. "Sure beats those threads you wear," said Jim. Even Ted laughed, his road wardrobe a white golf shirt, blue blazer, and gray pants—clean and pressed but always the same. I gave Ted the nickname "Ted Threads." One night on the plane he sat near *Washington Post* baseball writer George Minot and me, feet resting on the seat in front. I nudged George: "Look at Ted's shoes – one black and one brown." It wasn't true, but might have been, and Minot broke up. Hitting .400, you wear what you want.

— *Ron Menchine*

I caught the baseball bug at six, in my first game in 1962, seeing a WOR-TV sign on the Mets' Polo Grounds press box. I heard the 1963 World Series in Miss Holliday's second-grade class, and Jim Bunning's Father's Day 1964 perfect game in the family car. But 1969 was special: Lindsey Nelson, Bob Murphy, and Ralph Kiner broadcast *my* Boys of Summer to dad and me. I remember July 9, sweltering. We didn't have downstairs air conditioning but did have color TV: priorities that seemed natural, as spellbound I watched Tom Seaver's "Imperfect Game." (I still curse Jimmy Qualls.) Two months later Steve Carlton struck out nineteen Mets on Rosh Hashanah, the Jewish New Year, meaning we were in temple. Dad did what I did next month in the Series, using a tiny transistor radio and earpiece to track the Mets. Driving home, we heard Ron Swoboda hit the night's second two-run blast, Murph so excited I was sure he'd fall out of the booth. Only the '69 Mets could strike out nineteen times—and win! (Years later, meeting Carlton, I recalled the game. He was not amused.) Lindsey, Ralph and Murph helped a thirteen-year-old learn that champagne wasn't just for drinking. A locker room celebration followed the Mets' division-clinching, *Kiner's Korner* post-game show starring a couch full of giddy players, the giddiest Tug McGraw. Back then, local-team Series coverage was barred, Ralph and Lindsey blessedly joining Jim Simpson and Curt Gowdy, respectively, on NBC Radio/TV. I listened to the daytime games by transistor, snaking the earpiece inside my shirt. Our poor French teacher Madame Riche must have wondered at this eighth-grade buzz. We had a system. I'd whisper, "[Tommie] Agee just homered—pass it on!" Really sophisticated. In Game 5, the Mets needed a win to clinch. When the last bell rang, I ran home at full speed hoping to get there before the ninth! Turning on a TV then meant waiting for the set to "warm up." Finally, it did, the inning just starting, Gowdy behind the mike. Where, I ask, is *Lindsey*? In the clubhouse, preparing to interview the Mets in the ultimate champagne bath. My baseball bug never felt so good.

—*Peter King*

Let us relive the Greatest New York Sports Story ever told—and the effect it had on my life, maybe yours. I begin with geometry, never a strength, especially when, distracted by the 1969 Mets, I had a better chance of being Cy Young than of proving a required theorem. Each day I failed a test in Michael Banner's high school class. Catch-up allegedly began October 17, the day after the Mets beat Baltimore, except that Mr. Banner kept testing and I kept failing. By June 1970, he said I'd have to pass the Regents exam or take geometry again next fall or worse—in *summer school*. Like the Mets, Vegas made me a 100–1 underdog. Even with a tutor, I flunked one practice Regents after another, discouraged but not disconsolate, for I began to channel—the Mets! This sounds corny, but however frustrated I became, I told myself that if I believed and worked hard I could do the impossible, like them. As Regents day approached, I'd go to sleep replaying the Amazin's. Gradually, things began to make sense, and when I took the test, skipper Gil Hodges, his coaches, and twenty-five players took it, too. Believe it or not, I got an 87! My entire year of pre-Regents test scores hadn't hit 87! A passing grade was 65! My geometry textbook had become the '69 Orioles! Mine's not the only such story, and that's the point. I tell my children that nothing is beyond their reach, just as I hope they tell *their* kids. Cleon Jones' Game 5 choreography, kneeling to punctuate the final out, was perfect, like the delirium in class. Our English teacher, Paul Freda, let us hear the end with a stipulation that we'd turn our radios off and return to Samuel Taylor Coleridge's "The Rime of the Ancient Mariner," an epic then as welcome as the plague. Mr. Freda read for several moments, then added, "The game is done, I've won, I've won." Throwing the book over his shoulder, he ordered radios back on for the post-game show: a day that shaped much of my life, never mind career. The '69 Mets are the gift that keeps on *teaching*.

— *Howie Rose*

[Sparky Anderson's mid-1970s Big Red Machine was driven by an All-Star batting order: Pete Rose, Ken Griffey, Joe Morgan, Johnny Bench, Tony Perez, George Foster, Dave Concepcion, and Cesar Geronimo. Gary Nolan, Jack Billingham, and Don Gullett started. Rawly Eastwick, Clay Carroll, and Pedro Borbon spelled relief. The '75ers clinched the NL West September 7, finished 108–54, swept the LCS, and won an out-of-this-World Series. Next year five regulars hit more than .300. Cincinnati led in *every* league offensive category, then swept postseason.] Byrum Saam had done Philly's games since the 1930s. One day he said to me, "Young man, do you realize how lucky you are?" "Yeah," I said, rather flippantly. Then: "What do you mean?" "This is your third year with the club and you have two World Series rings," Saam told me. "I've been with the Phillies thirty-six years, and I've never gotten one."

— *Marty Brennaman*

I debuted as a batboy June 27, 1980, my father's first year as Giants batting coach. A year earlier Dad had punched manager Tommy Lasorda in the nose while still a Dodger. Or maybe he took the Giants job first and *then* punched Tommy in the nose, I'm not sure. I was nine and schizophrenic:

wearing my new Giants uniform, but my favorite team still the Dodgers! Then, each team braced to play the other, especially in San Francisco: fights in the stands, fans on the field, full beer cups launched on people's heads. What a night to become a batboy, in the middle of a riot disguised as a baseball game, not to mention LA's Jerry Reuss throwing a no-no, fans hoisting all they could on the field. Dad had been Rookie of the Year, won a World Series, and was a Dodger when Reuss and Ken Brett gave me a new glove the year before. Now, though, we *Giants* would never root for LA again. The more I thought, the more upset I got: How dare Reuss no-hit *us* at *Candlestick*?

— *Ryan Lefebvre*

In 1982, Harvey Kuenn became Brewers manager. The name "Harvey's Wallbangers" said it all. They led the league in runs scored, homers, and wins. Robin Yount was league MVP. What a lineup: Robin, Paulie [Paul Molitor], Cecil Cooper, Ted Simmons, Ben Oglivie, and Gorman Thomas. I probably hung around those guys after games more than I did as a *player*. Molitor, Yount, and Cooper each had over 200 hits. Robin and Paulie scored 265 runs. Cooper, Oglivie, and Stormin' Gorman had more than 30 homers and 100 RBI. They win a last-day division title, a great five-game LCS, almost win the Series. This is a memory thing, but I guess that team is my favorite. Each day was get up and get out of here—gone.

— *Bob Uecker*

Except for managing the 1980 Padres, I've broadcast them since 1972. We're still looking for that world title. Our closest came in 1984, and Cubs fans won't forget it. We breeze in the NL West, Tony Gwynn taking his first batting title. The LCS was then best-of-five, Cubs win the first two, and we're deader than the dodo bird. The Padres take the next two and by Game 5 our fans are throwing babies out of the upper deck. The Cubs grab a 3–0 lead, we score two in the sixth, and then Leon Durham lets a grounder through his legs: 3-all. Gwynn doubles. Steve Garvey singles. Like Harry Caray boomed, "Cubs win!" — only now it's the Padres, 6–3. Cinderella hits midnight in our World Series against Detroit. As Jack Brickhouse liked to say, "Hey, anyone can have a bad century." I hope this one's better.

— *Jerry Coleman*

I've done baseball since 1977, and no year was as amazing as my first in Baltimore. The 1988 Orioles started the season a historic 0 and 21. Only the 1904 Senators and 1920 Tigers lost even their first thirteen games. Some clubs are lucky to find one storyline. This team had a bunch. Amid the streak, the Orioles return home, wondering at the response. The Orioles decide to market the first game back as "Fantastic Fans Night," with their great past, stars like Jim Palmer, Boog Powell, Frank, and Brooks, and a Series title as recently as '83. The game sells out, showing the O's hold on Baltimore. That night they finalize a new stadium by Inner Harbor, which becomes Camden Yards, which inspires all the new parks since. Sadly, the '88 team lost 107 games, but next year is 87–75, losing the AL East the final weekend in Toronto. *More* storylines. After awhile, you run out of ink.

— *Joe Angel*

"Ain't nothing easy," Andy Griffith as TV's *Matlock* said. On October 2, 1991, Billy Swift saved the game guaranteeing that the Mariners would finish .500 for the first time. "And at seven minutes after ten down here in Texas," I said, "the M's get a fifteen-year-old simian off their back, a gorilla, a monkey, that is gone. . . . Flying home mighty happy, I guarantee you. My, oh, my, it's finally over," incredible as it seemed. Baseball surprises you. After losing some great players in the late '90s, the 2001 Mariners sign Ichiro Suzuki and finish 116–46. Ichiro wins a Gold Glove, takes a batting title, and becomes AL Rookie of the Year and MVP. In 2004, he gets 262 hits, breaking George Sisler's 1920 big-league record 257. The Hall of Fame says he's been there more than any other current player, loves baseball history, on the fast track to be inducted. A final note on 2001: Our 116 victories tied for most-ever with the '06 Cubs. Like Ichiro's 2004, it may last a while.

— *Dave Niehaus*

For a long time you could literally count a Braves crowd. Finally, in 1991, we contend a year after finishing last. I'd come to Atlanta-Fulton County Stadium early each day to circle its club level. I didn't want to miss a thing, because it might not happen again. The last day was unforgettable. We led the Dodgers by a game. ["Stretch by Smoltz. The pitch to Cedeno. A high fly ball to rightfield! It's fairly deep! Back goes Justice! He's got it! And the magic number for Atlanta is down to one! The Braves have clinched a tie for (NL West) first!"] The Giants then beat LA. That started our great streak, making postseason through 2005. Win or lose, it's the same: You broadcast when they tell you. And you'd better be ready when they do.

— *Pete Van Wieren*

In 1993, big-league baseball came to Denver. When our first workout ended, reporters from the region gathered around Don Baylor. The first questioner said, "Coach, how did it go?"—so typical of a local media caring only for Broncos football. Baylor did a slow burn. "Let's get one thing straight," he said. "I'm the manager." The education of a baseball-mad area had begun. After two road losses, we opened April 9 at Mile High Stadium, our pad till Coors Field was ready in 1995. TV's Charlie Jones had called Wimbledon, the Super Bowl, 1986 World Cup final, and many Olympics. He said, "The Rockies opener was as big as them combined," drawing a league regular season record 80,227. Our first batter, Eric Young, homered. Cried Charlie: "You could hear the roar in *California!*" In centerfield, Montreal's Marquis Grissom said he felt the ground shake when the ball went out. Leftfielder John Vander Wal yelled to him, "This is not our day." Later my partner, Wayne Hagin, and I joked it was an off night if we had 65,000. We drew 4,483,350 for the year, more than any team had or, because parks are smaller now, will.

— *Jeff Kingery*

On August 24, 1995, we trail the Angels by eleven-and-a-half games. Junior Griffey, with never a walkoff homer, smacks a two-out, two-run ninth inning blast to beat the Yanks. ["Swung on, belted! Fly away!" M's, 9–7.] On September 1, we're seven-and-a-half behind, still a lot, but win twenty of the next twenty-nine, including a last-week grand-slam in Texas. ["Waving that black beauty. . . . What a shot by Junior, and he has never hit a bigger one."] We tie the Angels. Randy Johnson takes a 9–1 playoff. In the ninth I remember saying, "left-hander ready, branding iron hot," as he Ks the last guy: after nineteen years of frustration, our first title, Randy looking "to the sky." In a dome, you could see the sun.

— *Dave Niehaus*

A no-hitter and walkoff homer are baseball's yin and yang. On July 12, 1997, the Bucs' Francisco Cordova and Ricardo Rincon yield no hits in nine innings at Three Rivers Stadium, yet no game is a no-hitter until it *ends* with no hits. Rincon sets down the side in the tenth, then Mark Smith pinch-hits a three-run blast in the bottom half to win the National League's first-ever combined extra-inning no-no. "He got it all!" I said. "Home run! No-hitter! And the Pirates win by the final score of 3 to 0!" Even a no-no needs a run.

— *Lanny Frattare*

In 1992, I'd never made postseason. Prophetically, my new Orioles contract specified that I could leave after a year if offered the '93 expansion Marlins lead job — exactly what occurred. After more losing, GM Dave Dombrowski signed 1997 free agents, raised salaries, and *still* the Marlins struggle. At the All-Star break, ownership decides to blow up the team. A funny thing then happens: Out of nowhere, the Marlins meld — the first wild card to win a World Series in coincidentally the first year I aired a winner. I'd left Colombia at eight, spoke no English till ten, but in Chicago fell in love with baseball: every Cubs game daytime and on TV. In the '97 World Series, the Marlins' Craig Counsell's Game 7 ninth-inning sacrifice fly ties Cleveland, each pitch meaning everything: the highlight of my career. In the eleventh, Edgar Renteria singles past Indians pitcher Charles Nagy's glove. One Colombian, Renteria, wins the Series, another calling it in English: nirvana, in any tongue.

— *Joe Angel*

Baseball lost a lot of fans in the strike of 1994–1995. Retrieving them was 1998's home run race, the Cardinals' Mark McGwire and Cubs' Sammy Sosa breaking Roger Maris's single-season home record of sixty-one in '61. Sosa had sixty-six, McGwire, a cosmic seventy. Working every day, I was at the vortex of a once-in-a-lifetime thrill. Cubs fan cheered when Sosa went deep in St. Louis. Wrigley went bananas when McGwire found Waveland Avenue. To some, Yankees–Red Sox is baseball's greatest rivalry; others, Dodgers-Giants; many think it's ours. The Great Race would have wowed. Cubs-Cardinals made it throb. The year began tragically, with Harry Caray's death before spring training. Six months later Jack Brickhouse died, too. How each would have loved '98: the Cubs in a wild card tussle; the assault on Maris trumping all. When Mac and Sammy topped sixty, I wondered how I could salute these two legendary Voices. In Milwaukee, Sosa goes deep. I say, "Gone, home run, number sixty-five, and he's tied with Mark McGwire again! 'Holy Cow!' and 'Hey-hey!' for Harry and Jack," using each's trademark call. I then go back to play-by-play. Did I plan the call? Of course. Do I regret it? No way.

— *Pat Hughes*

Having done baseball since 1950, I long ago came to the view that it is the world's most unpredictable game. I've witnessed eleven no-hitters, and could spin a tale about each, all being different. Instead, let's focus on 2003. The Astros were at the old Yankee Stadium. Houston started young Roy Oswalt, who, warming up for the second inning, suffered a chronic groin injury, leaving the game. In come relievers Pete Munro, Kirk Saarloos, Brad Lidge, Octavio Dotel, and Billy Wagner: Amazingly, like Oswalt, none of 'em gave a hit! Skipper Jimy Williams was too busy to note the unfolding story: his Astros no-hitting the Yankees, 8–0! The scorecard showed the totals, but in the dugout and bullpen Jimy and the relievers couldn't understand why some veterans weren't talking. Tradition says you don't jinx a no-no in progress. Later Jimy and others told me they didn't know one was happening: six pitchers throwing a combined no-hitter. It never happened before, and I bet it'll never happens again.

— *Milo Hamilton*

Under postseason's microscope, casual fans become super-fans, especially in a Series. The 2003 Marlins were again the NL wild card. In Miami, over 65,000 saw Mr. Marlin, outfielder Jeff Conine, throw out the Giants' J. T. Snow at the plate to win the Division Series, Pudge Rodriguez raising the ball in triumph: the first postseason game ending with the tying run tossed out at home! In the LCS, the Cubs lead in games, 3–2, and Game Six, 3–0, five outs from their first World Series since 1945. Luis Castillo then hits down Wrigley's leftfield line. Moises Alou leaps in the stands, but a fan, Steve Bartman, grabs the ball. Four straight Marlins reach base. The Cubs miss a double play. Mike Mordecai's base-clearing double keys an *eight-run inning*, my partner, Jon "Boog" Sciambi, and I saying "*Mike Mordecai! Are you kidding?*" Next night both teams blow leads, Marlins winning, 9–6, to make the Series against – whom? – Boston or New York, meeting a night later in *their* LCS Game 7. All day we wait to see where we'd fly, the score 5-all as buses finally left for the airport. Riding, we argue preference: Boston's famed Fenway Park, or iconic Yankee Stadium. (The Stadium won.) At the gate, we're boarding as the Yankees' Aaron Boone homers to win the game, our traveling party roaring. Born in New York, Boog exults, "I'm going *home* to broadcast the World Series!" I'm as thrilled for him as happy for myself: in my then-thirty-fifth big-league season, my first Fall Classic. It, too, ended happily: the Marlins' second title in just eleven years.

— *Dave Van Horne*

Before 2004, asked my favorite call, I said: "It hasn't happened yet." That year it did, starting with the LCS. The Yankees took Games 1–3, the last, 19–8. I remember thinking: "The Red Sox are better than this." Still, I never thought they'd be the first team ever to rally from 0–3 postseason. David Ortiz wins the next two games with a walkoff homer and extra-inning single. In Game 6, Boston leads, Alex Rodriguez grounds to the mound, pitcher Bronson Arroyo goes to first, and A-Rod knocks the ball from his glove, prompting a mental "Not another Red Sox tragic moment!" as the ball rolls down the line. Fortunately, umpire-in-chief Joe West called A-Rod out for obstruction—amazingly, the LCS now tied. Before, I hadn't thought about a winning call. Why *would* I? The Yankees, way ahead, had history on their side. The last time the Red Sox had beaten them in a game that *mattered* was 1904, then–New York Highlander Jack Chesbro's wild pitch scoring Boston's pennant-clinching run. Exactly *one hundred years before*! Since then, if it counted, the Yankees won: 1949, Joe McCarthy relieving Ellis Kinder; '78, Bucky Dent; 2003, Aaron Boone: always *someone*! Game Seven, a blowout, gave me a chance to think, two things in my mind: My call had to stress this unparalleled comeback, and how it beat the *Yankees*. Sox up, 10–3, Ruben Sierra grounds to second. "Pokey Reese has it!" I said. "He throws to first! And the Red Sox have won the American League pennant; the Red Sox have won the most significant game in their history!

Of all the victories, and all the games that they ever played, this is the most *important!*" An editorial, to be sure, but looking back, irrefutable, for without it, what happened next doesn't happen.
— *Joe Castiglione*

Before Mr. Strasburg, the Nationals' best moment was baseball's regular-season return after deserting DC. A 2005 season-opening nine-game road trip gave RFK Stadium time to prepare for a massive opening day security check with President Bush on hand. Brian Schneider played catch preparing him for the first pitch, Bush later greeting each player. Bob Wolff, for whom Nationals Park's TV booth is named, took the train from New York, ecstatic. Many players found it deliverance, remembering 2004 Expos home games moved to Puerto Rico. For me, adults racing into the park when gates opened was magical: kids when the '71 Senators left, now overcome, crying during batting practice. On pre-game XM Radio, I told that to host Phil Wood, a native Washingtonian hosting area baseball shows for more than thirty years—and *Phil's* eyes began to tear. Livan Hernandez pitched eight and one-third shutout innings. Vinny Castilla had a double, triple, and homer, still calling it his career highlight. Livan agrees: to him, bigger than Florida winning the 1997 World Series. In 2010, he returned to the Nationals, still awaiting *their* October.
— *Charlie Slowes*

Contrary to opinion, the 2004 World Series was not anticlimactic, since beating the Yankees would have meant less if the Sox had lost the Classic—another near-miss. Instead, unlike the LCS, I had several days to contemplate Game 4's final out at Busch Stadium, finally deciding that you couldn't script it. I just hoped the final out would be definitive, no checked swing, trapped ball, did he or didn't he? Johnny Damon led off by homering. Later, Trot Nixon had a bases-loaded double. In the seventh, anticipating a champagne shower, I went to change, running into an old friend, Bruce Manno, Cardinals farm director. I told him what I was doing, then thought, "Hey, he's with the Cardinals, about ready to be swept." Thankfully, he understood. By the ninth, partner Jerry Trupiano was in the clubhouse, so I'm alone, total concentration. I wouldn't have heard a firecracker go off under me. The first two outs were quick. Edgar Renteria then hit against Keith Foulke. "The 1–0 pitch. Swing and a ground ball, stabbed by Foulke! He has it! He underhands to first! And the Red Sox have won baseball's world championship for the first time in eighty-six years! The Red Sox have won baseball's world championship! *Can you believe it*?" I shut up, let the crowd roar, and then talked of family and friends, remembering Ken Coleman and Ned Martin, who never won a Series in twenty-four and thirty-two years, respectively, with the Sox. In 1967, Ned's "And there's pandemonium on the field!" immortalized their last-day pennant. I repeated it: Saluting another person never felt so good. Each year, I sign off by quoting Bart Giamatti's great piece, *The Green Fields of the Mind*: baseball "breaks your heart. It is designed to break your heart," except that this time it hadn't for people waiting an eternity. We went on a Series trophy tour throughout New England, my signature, I guess, now *Can you believe it?* In New Haven, my hometown, Red Sox president Larry Lucchino, having gone to law school there at Yale, asked me to repeat it, the crowd going nuts. Hard to believe, even now.

— *Joe Castiglione*

I don't know about the Astros' greatest year, but their greatest game was in the 2005 Division Series, beating Atlanta, 7–6, in eighteen innings, postseason's longest in innings and length of time — five hours and fifty minutes. A night before Houston took a 2–1 game lead. Next afternoon Adam LaRoche grand slams: Atlanta, 4–0. By the fifth, down, 5–1, 'Stros skipper Phil Garner calls the bullpen, unaware six more calls would follow. In the eighth, the *Braves'* worn-out pen yields the game's second slam — *another* record — Lance Berkman's homer caught by a fan who will revisit our narrative. Astros trail, 6–5. Pitcher Kyle Farnsworth stays in, pleasing Brad Ausmus, who hits maybe the team's biggest-ever homer an inch above the left-centerfield wall: 6-all. For the next seven innings Houston can't buy a hit. Meanwhile, a Rocket prepares his launch. Earlier, needing to throw between starts, Roger Clemens had called son Koby to the clubhouse, Garner learning later that Rocket threw thirty minutes in an indoor batting cage. "My favorite all-time managing vision," he said, "is looking at the stands going crazy and then looking at the pen and the only guy I see is Clem-

ens." Roger pinch-hit in the fifteenth. "Well, here comes Clemens," pitching coach Jim Hickey told Phil. "He's gonna' hit a home run, win the game, then save a small country." Clemens sacrifice bunted, no one complaining since he proceeds to pitch three scoreless innings. Roger led off our eighteenth after the 'Stros used all their position players, striking out, but his bat wasn't needed. Chris Burke smacked a 2–0 pitch—the game's *553rd*—into the Crawford [bleacher] Boxes to send the fans into ecstasy. Incredibly, the same fan who caught Berkman's homer grabbed Burke's: Shaun Dean.
    —*Bill Brown*

Special year? How about the first White Sox title since 1917? We had a parade after the 2005 Series, more than 2 million people on our route. I'm riding in the last bus with [manager] Ozzie Guillen, [owner] Jerry Reinsdorf, Mayor Daley, and one of the security guys. I ask him, "What about the Bears in '86, after the Super Bowl?"
    He says, "Hawk, that was nothing compared to this!"
    "Nothing?" I said.
    He shook his head. "Absolutely nothing." People were crying, chanting *Ozzie! Ozzie!*—the face of the White Sox.
    That fall a *Chicago Tribune* poll looked at exposure, radio/TV ratings, coverage, attendance, and found that the Sox had caught the Cubs in area popularity. Before Ozzie, you could walk down Michigan Avenue. Of a hundred pieces of apparel—T-shirts, caps—ninety-eight were Cubs. Now it's a hundred Sox. Ozzie's brought a breath of fresh air, changed our culture. Before Ozzie, even our interns were doom and gloom. Now, a little p and vinegar to their step. Just ask the Cubs.
    —*Ken Harrelson*

The final days of the NL West's 2006 season were similar to the prior few years'. A close race was misrepresented by the national media as a battle of underachievers. Actually, all year the Dodgers and Padres played spirited and competitive baseball—each taking turns atop the division, hoping to play deep into fall. Entering September 18, the Padres had dominated the season series, thirteen games to four. That night, before a Monday record 55,831 at Dodger Stadium, they seemed about to beat the Blue again. Ahead, 9–5, in the ninth, manager Bruce Bochy inserted a rookie, the reliable Jon Adkins. Following is a transcript of what happened: not my play-by-play but my own internal monologue.

First batter, LA's Jeff Kent: home run, 9–6. *Not a big deal. Let's just get this thing done because I've got to drive back to San Diego tonight for a homestand that begins tomorrow.*

Second batter, J. D. Drew: Home run, 9–7. *S—, they've just gone back-to-back here and now Trevor's gonna get a save.*

The Padres then inserted Hall of Fame closer Trevor Hoffman. Russell Martin promptly cleared the left-centerfield fence, 9–8. *Three straight bombs, are you f—ing kidding me?*

At this point, I caught the strangest sight on camera: Fans who'd exited early—a Southern California birthright—were seen turning around in the parking lot and running back inside.

Fourth batter, Marion Anderson, home run to right-center: 9-all. I'm not exactly sure what I said on air—I seem to remember a loud, amateurish moan—but I know what I thought: *There is no chance this has just happened.*

Unbelievably, the Dodgers had just hit four consecutive home runs on eleven pitches. Only three previous times had this occurred in major league history, none in a pennant race with the home team trailing by exactly four runs in the ninth. After San Diego manufactured a go-ahead run in the top of the tenth, LA responded with—you guessed it—a two-run homer by Nomar Garciaparra in the bottom half: 11–10. You can look it up.

Airing the Padres, you feared they might not recover from such a brutal, bizarre beating. Instead, they won the West a few weeks later. In this rivalry's final 2006 act, the Dodgers won the NL wild card the final weekend. There is still no chance that any of this happened.

—*Matt Vasgersian*

Myth says that in 2008 everything for Tampa Bay fell wondrously into place. Actually, unpredictability, injury, and unlikelihood fused. Reliever Grant Balfour didn't make the club in March. David Price began his first pro season in Single-A. Evan Longoria rejoined the club only when Willy Aybar's hamstring tore. Pitchers Scott Kazmir, Matt Garza, and Troy Percival were out a month or more. Dioner Navarro lacerated his right hand.

Rocco Baldelli's Mitochondrial Disease threatened to end his career. [It did in January 2011.] What a revolving door for the cash-strapped Rays, battling financial skyscrapers New York and Boston. To the rescue: Journeyman Nathan Haynes' hit beat the Red Sox. Balancing a daily experimental cocktail of medicines, Baldelli returned to beat Baltimore. One of Gabe Gross's three walkoff hits beat Mariano Rivera. Assuming his scrapbook already bulged, I asked if Gabe wanted my paper chronicling his latest thriller. "Sure," he said. "I've never experienced anything like this." The most improbable plot changer was career minor leaguer Dan Johnson, joining us September 9 in Boston, our lead one-half game. Joe Maddon planned to start Johnson — till stuck in traffic he missed the game's first pitch. Behind a run, Jonathan Papelbon pitching, the Rays seemed about to lose first place — till Johnson pinch-hit a ninety-five-mile-per-hour fastball over the Sox bullpen, Rays winning, 5–4. Later Maddon said Johnson wouldn't have batted if Joe knew he was a 0-for-15 career pinch hitter. The Rays won again next night in fourteen innings, later clinching their first playoff berth. For unsung heroes, years of lousy food, overnight bus rides, and minor league anonymity were rewarded. The Little Engine That Could, Had.

— *Andy Freed*

As Andy describes, the '08 Rays beat the "Big Boys" to amazingly win the AL East. At one point Boston beat us nine straight at Fenway. Now, we lead there in the LCS, 7–0, seventh inning, Game 5, about to clinch. I look to the ninth, thinking of tidbits I can use to close the game, since the Rays can't lose. When they do, 8–7, I felt closer than in any game to literally being sick. The previous year Cleveland collapsed in the LCS against — the Red Sox. Remembering, Andy thought this might cost us a World Series. I said I didn't think this is how the Rays' tale was supposed to end. The Red Sox won Game 6: momentum against our destiny. Next night David Price faced Jed Lowrie in the ninth. "Swing and a ground ball to second, this should do it!" I said. "Aki [Akinori Iwamura] has it, takes it to second himself, this improbable season has another chapter to it! The Rays are going to the World Series! Rays beat the Red Sox, 3 to 1!" Recalling the prior two games, clearly we didn't want to peak too soon.

— *Dave Wills*

I did the Yankees, now the Dodgers, and they reflect Northeastern baseball *v.* the rest of the country: New York, Philly, and Boston having a primal passion for their clubs, cities close geographically and socially, constant burning and churning, hustling and bustling. Until 2004, Boston felt jealousy and resentment: "Here come the big bad Yankees." When the Sox knocked them off, then won the Series, a vast burden lifted. Each city's tabloids love to incite with provocative headlines, talk radio, blogs, the Internet feeding off one another. Out West it's different. The Dodgers-Giants rivalry, for instance, is nowhere what it was in New York a half-century ago, with neighbor kids cheering different teams. In LA they might argue who's more talented, [Angels] Torii Hunter *v.* [Dodgers] Andre Ethier, but not with anywhere near the passion of Willie, Mickey, and the Duke: The last time I checked they haven't written a song about Torii and Andre, have they? Geographically, LA and Anaheim are forty miles apart. Sociologically? They are a world apart. The Dodgers and Angels meet a half-dozen times a season in the Freeway Series. The Yankees and Red Sox met *twenty-six* times in 2003! Then twenty-six *more* times in 2004! A minimum of eighteen times a year! Each year, Northeastern baseball feels like a second Hundred Years War. Either way, what a story for 24/7 media: 162 games, 30 in preseason, if you're lucky, 19 more in October—200 chapters in one season's book.

—*Charley Steiner*

[Ending a fifty-six-year world title drought, the 2010 Giants won the NL West, downed Atlanta in the DS and Philly in the LCS, then beat the similarly fifty-year World Series–challenged Rangers *nee* Senators, "cobbling pieces together like an Erector Set," wrote Tom Verducci, "assembling random veteran parts around a core of four factory-ordered, homegrown starting pitchers"—Madison Bumgarner, Matt Cain, Tim Lincecum, and Jonathan Sanchez. Aubrey Huff hit twenty-six homers. Cut by Florida in August, Cody Ross became LCS Most Valuable Player. In 1997, then-Marlin Edgar Renteria's single won the Series. The now-Giants shortstop became Fall Classic MVP. Brian Wilson was a bearded *uber*reliever. Rookie of the Year Buster Posey, twenty-three, caught far beyond his age. Said pitcher Jeremy Affeldt: "We're all the people nobody wanted"—except Gaga by the Bay.] With apologies to Charles Dickens, I've seen the San Francisco Giants through the best and worst of times. I broadcast their back-to-back years of 96 and 100 losses. I saw them lose the World Series in 1962, 1989, and 2002, despite a parade of stars. In 2010, I saw them win a Series for the first time since they left New York: different not just because they won, but because unlike any other Giants team they were totally reflective of the city. They called themselves a bunch of misfits and ordinary Joes. Some were bald, some wore beards, and one [Huff] wore a thong—no wonder the city embraced them. I'm happiest for those who suffered through the Candlestick Park era and whose loyalty and perseverance were finally rewarded. [It wasn't always easy. One night a foul landed in a sea of empty seats. Hank (Greenwald) gave the section number, adding, "Anyone coming to tomorrow's game might want to stop and pick it up."]

    — Hank Greenwald

Chapter Seven

The Wonder of Being Ernie

Listing much, biography can tell too little: 1948–2002 Voice, mostly Detroit; author and lyricist; essayist, The Game for All America; *legacy, baseball's most beloved man. "Some guys do nothing, and think they're the sun, moon, and stars," the late Ned Martin said. "The wonder of being Ernie goes far beyond being great behind the mike." The musical* Peter Pan *sang, "I've got to crow." In 2010, Harwell, ninety-two, died of cancer. Having much to crow about, he didn't.*

At five, Ernie was Atlanta Crackers batboy; sixteen, The Sporting News *Atlanta correspondent; twenties, sports editor, marine magazine* Leatherneck. *Talking, you wouldn't know. He sang a duet with Pearl Bailey, invented a bottle can opener, had a racehorse named after him, wrote for Sammy Fain and Johnny Mercer, and calmed Motown in 1967 after rioting killed forty-three. You had to find it from someone else.*

Ernie was the first sports Voice to telecast coast-to-coast, be baptized in the Jordan River, or be traded for a player. A home run was "loonng gone." A called third strike batter "stood there like the house by the side of the road." Each spring he read on-air from the Song of Solomon: "For lo, the winter is past, the rain is over and gone, the flowers appear on the earth; the time of the singing of birds is come, and the voice of the turtle is heard in our land." *His voice was always there.*

In December 1990, ex-Michigan football-coach-turned-Tigers-president Bo Schembechler fired the man "who passed Joe Louis, Al Kaline, and Gordie Howe as the greatest sports legend Detroit has ever had," to quote Cubs Voice Pat Hughes. The Grinch had stolen Christmas, making Michigan pop its cork. When the club was sold, Ernie was rehired and named Voice of Sports Illustrated's *all-time dream team. How did he do all this with such magnanimity and grace?*

His wife of sixty-eight years, "Miss Lulu," was Harwell's best friend. Their four children, reading, and exercise kept him young. Raised in Washington, Georgia, he distilled a small town's rites and rhythms. Finally, Ernie believed in The Kindly Light That Led. In 1973, Harwell wrote the tune "Move Over Babe, Here Comes Henry." Each Sunday he sang songs like "Amazing Grace" and "Rock of Ages" and "Abide With Me."

Why did Ernie's death light a candle in untold houses by the road? I think that deep down all of us wanted to be him — the slight figure with glasses, beret, clear soul, and open mind. Oscar Wilde penned The Importance of Being Earnest. *"The Wonder of Being Ernie" evokes baseball's most beloved man, even now.*

A couple of years ago I was on the field at Giants spring training camp in Scottsdale, Arizona, when, looking over, I saw Ernie watching batting practice. In town for a family wedding, he'd been retired for several years. We struck up a conversation, and Ernie said he really came by because he wanted to see the Cactus League again. In 1950 to '53, Harwell aired the Giants, who, except for Florida in 1951, trained at the site we were standing on. He proceeded to recall a young Willie Mays; Bobby Thomson's 1951 home run; how there weren't many cars then in the Cactus League, but locals rode their horses to the games and tied them up on hitching posts — unbelievable oral history. Many think the secret to baseball broadcasting is to flaunt the myriad tidbits they've accumulated, or consume every minute with filler. Ernie knew better. Give the score a lot. Describe the action. Convey the game's excitement. Don't fill with clutter. Tell stories in a context. Seems simple, but there was a reason Harwell was so beloved, and it's not just that he was a lovely man.

— *Dave Flemming*

By the '80s, I'd done basketball and football but no baseball, my favorite sport, so as time passed I thought I'd see what its play-by-play was like. When the Pontiac Silverdome opened in 1975, the Lions left Tiger Stadium, vacating the third-base-line football press box. A decade later, abandoned, it seemed perfect for a would-be baseball Voice to learn the craft: I talk into the mike, practicing a few times each year until I brilliantly think, "Maybe I should have someone listen." Our paths had crossed, so I call Ernie, who says, "Come over to my house," in suburban Farmington Hills. I do, nervous as can be, turning on my recorder at his kitchen table. Ernie starts and stops it, comments, not perfunctorily but with a practiced ear. Little things: "You don't have to say 'down low,' just 'low,' cleaner," or "not up high, it's 'high,' save a word." Plus: "Work off your scorecard. People tune in all the time. Tell 'em how we got here." Ernie used two pens for his scorecard. A red pen meant innings where runs scored on a single, walk, whatever. Blue meant pitchers dominated. That way you could instantly inform a listener. I still have my notes. I was a WWJ Detroit street reporter, not sure about tomorrow. Ernie kept me motivated till I got my break a year later: "I heard your [Michigan] football broadcast. It was terrific," his letter said. I've kept that, too.

—*Dan Dickerson*

Like some Hall of Fame players, some broadcasters aren't exactly champions of character, proving the adage that when you meet heroes and find what they are, you often wish you'd never met. That wasn't true of Ernie. I met him as the A's third announcer in 1981. Concluding, he asked for my phone number, saying he wanted to stay in touch: I especially liked our pre–spring training talks because talking to him inspired you for the year. Ernie's secret was the comfort he gave a listener, particularly when life became fierce, as increasingly it did in Michigan. Dying, he still told people not to worry and asked them not to cry, transcending a world that defines celebrity by what you *seem*, not who you *are*. Listen to Denny McLain's 1968 or Detroit's 1984 world title: play-by-play gentle, yet vivid and alive. On the road, Ernie met friends, read the Bible, took long walks in solitude, helped to cope with being away. Graduating from college, I got a thesaurus from a friend, who inscribed: "You can have piles of money stacked to the ceiling but the size of your funeral will ultimately depend on the weather!" Translation: Character is not what you gain, but what you leave. My radio may not hear Ernie's voice anymore, but my heart is still tuned in.

—*Wayne Hagin*

Ernie Harwell met more people by saying yes than anyone I've known. He said yes by meeting Tigers fans on the road who phoned the hotel, inviting him to lunch. He said yes to friends, dropping by the booth to say hello. In 1983, I was in an early Rotisserie League, now Fantasy Baseball, in Grand Rapids. At year's end we had a banquet, presenting our silly trophies. A guy in our league worked for a local store sponsoring an Ernie book-signing. Through him, we asked if Harwell could attend our duck ball season-ending soiree. Of course, he said yes. That night he went from his signing to our party, delighting in our geeky questions, telling stories. Many times Ernie'd get a ride home from a complete stranger at the park who was a Tiger fan. We worried about him, but next day he'd be back, saying yes.

—*Dan Dickerson*

In 1988, Ernie's "Welcome to the Major Leagues" letter was waiting when I arrived in Arizona for spring training. He was always low-key, ready to do the pre-game show, liking the quotable quote. You might like to know the origin of Ernie's most famous phrase: "The batter stood there like the house by the side of the road!" Harwell told me that he learned Sam Walter Foss's inspirational poem as a boy in Atlanta, trying to stop stuttering by taking elocution lessons. The 1800s poem was primarily read at graduations. Eerily, its final passage could have been written about Ernie.

"Let me live in my house by the side of the road,
Where the race of men go by
They are good, they are bad, they are weak, they are strong,
Wise, foolish, so am I.
Then why should I sit in the scorner's seat,
Or hurl the cynic's ban?
Let me live in my house by the side of the road
And be *a friend of man*."

Ernie and I last spoke about a month before his death, our friend ending a brief chat with a hearty, "Call anytime, Paul." Today I wish I could do just that.

—*Paul Olden*

1993, I'm doing college and Class-A ball. The Twins' Herb Carneal's health creates an opening beside partner John Gordon. A friend, WCCO Minneapolis' Jim Ashbery, suggests to John that I be among three minor-league guys to audition. Saturday I get a call asking if starting Monday I'd like to "announce for a week. Then we'll decide what we do." Arriving at Tiger Stadium, I meet John, read notes, then hear this familiar voice: "I'm looking for Jimmy Powell." Ernie extends his hand like I'm a twenty-year veteran, not a nobody in the first day of a seven-day deal, then tells me about the Tigers, saying come on the field tomorrow and I'll introduce you: Cecil Fielder, Travis Fryman, Lou Whitaker, Tony Phillips. No great announcer would've done what Ernie did: help a guy he'd never known, with no idea we'd meet again. Next week I got the job, later joining Atlanta, where Ernie had announced at Ponce de Leon Park, my Dad went to games, and I grew up. I once told the Twins' story at Milwaukee's charitable Diamond Dinner, where, emceeing, I introduced Ernie, its Man of the Year. "Doing things like this all the time," I said, Harwell had never told it.
— *Jim Powell*

In 1999, Detroit's stomping grounds at "the corner of Michigan and Trumbull," as Ernie said, closed: the intersection of professional baseball in Detroit for 104 years. Next spring I asked if he missed Tiger Stadium. Typically, Harwell looked back *and* ahead. "Yes, but I love this new ballpark," meaning Comerica Park. "We've got a great facility here." Its booth was well away from the field, not like Tiger Stadium where a warning sign should have been posted: "Broadcast at Your Peril." The Tigers even offered a net for protection. The upside was the chance to soak up the crowd. "We do miss that closeness, seeing players sweat and hearing 'em cuss," Ernie said. "I'd have outfielders in late September [sparse crowd, wind blowing out] tell me, 'I heard your broadcast!'" Don't expect *that* at any park today.
— *Paul Olden*

I join the Tigers in 2000: first year at Comerica, we get Juan Gonzalez, are supposed to contend. We don't. Awaiting a bus in Minnesota, I ask Ernie, "How you do stay enthused, keep energy, when the team's *9 and*

23?" He said, "Remember, someone's always tuning into the game, *despite* knowing your record. *Give them a reason to listen.*" In 1975, the Tigers lost nineteen straight, but I listened to a portion of every game hoping that they'd someday, somehow, win. Maybe it's a great game between two bad teams; a great individual performance; something you've never seen: you tune in because you love baseball. Several weeks after our talk we get runners on first and second base with no outs. The pitcher steps off the rubber, tags the runner between second and third, then runs at the guy between first and second, tagging him! I turn to Ernie: "Double pick-off by the pitcher without making a throw. Ever see that before?" Ernie smiled. "Nope."
— *Dan Dickerson*

When Tiger Stadium was vacated, Ernie wanted a piece of memorabilia from the park, so he chose one of the urinals from the visiting clubhouse. Why? I asked. "It's personal," he said. "Every great visiting player in the American League history used it. I'm going to clean it up and make it into a planter for my wife."
— *Tim Kurkjian*

I first met Ernie in 2001, the Tigers in Phoenix for an interleague game. It was "Seventies Night," everyone made to wear awful 1970s garb. They gave me a polyester shirt to wear, probably glows in the dark, and grudgingly I retreat to the men's room to put it on. It's a size too small, I can't close a button, and I'm bare-chested, trying to figure it out, when a thin man comes in. "Hello, I'm Ernie Harwell, glad to meet you," he says. My face was beet red, never so embarrassed. I wanted to crawl under the sink. Right then I wanted Ernie to get amnesia, or more deservedly, me.
— *Jeff Munn*

Ernie retired in 2002. Next year I began Tigers TV, for this Detroiter a dream come true. Another dream was to work with him, even for a game. When my Fox Sports Detroit partner, Rod Allen, had to miss a couple games, Ernie and I teamed June 1 — as luck would have it, Roger Clemens' try for his 300th victory, Comerica packed, a beautiful day. I tried to stay out of the way: so many years, so many stories, Ernie so presenting the Tigers, baseball history, and broadcasting with all the trademark things that made Ernie, Ernie, that he may be remembered as baseball's greatest Voice. I was straight man for his wonderful shtick of "so and so from such a city" got a foul. "Who caught it?" I said of one. "A man from Ypsilanti!" he replied. Clemens left after six, up, 8–6, nine outs from number 300. The Yankees won in seventeen, 10–9. Ernie stayed all five hours and ten minutes. At the end, he signed my score sheet, now more than messy. The IRS couldn't pry it away.

—*Mario Impemba*

Growing up in Shepherd, Michigan, I spent many days and nights hearing Ernie, wishing that one day I'd be in a big-league booth. Many people call their parents a hero, like me. A hero can also be a famous childhood idol, like John Lennon or Babe Ruth. That's what Ernie was, plus friend. At Marquette, I interviewed him for its radio station, Ernie saying my name a few times on air, something no young announcer forgets. He wrote when I got my first big-league TV job, called when I joined the Cubs, profiled me in his *Detroit Free Press* column, and posed for a picture with my dad, my son, and me: three generations with a legend. Ernie was as advertised, broadcasting's kindest, most generous, and most gracious person, remarkable in this cut-throat business, remembering your name a year later even if he hadn't seen you since. If anybody could have acted like a big-timer, it was him, but he didn't, no matter who you were. He had that Georgia drawl, yet if you asked anyone they'd say, "Of *course* he's from Michigan"—a deep, unmistakable, and reassuring voice. I ask what Ernie would do in a certain situation. If that's not a hero, what is?

—*Len Kasper*

My home was in western New York, geographically perfect to hear most big-league announcers. Today you pick up everyone on XM and the Internet. Back then, it was a science fiddling with the radio. I'd hear Ernie, that beautiful lilt, his homespun aphorisms. Jon Miller caught and held your attention. Chuck Thompson was an easy listen, Harry Caray so interesting. I try to bring some of each, despite knowing you need your own style. I once caught Ernie two or three nights in a row, then showed up for a three-game Buffalo-Rochester series sounding like a really bad imitation, even stealing his "standing there like a house" strike. Then, I thought it awesome. Now I'd like to burn the tapes. There's only one Harry, Vin Scully, or, of course, Ernie. The best advice is to be yourself: hard in your twenties, still trying to figure out who the hell you are.

— *Josh Lewin*

Broadcasters seek seasoned colleagues for advice. When the A's began struggling in 2007, my partner Vince Cotroneo and I developed a little code reminding us we still had a job to do. It was two words: "Ernie Harwell," stemming from what he said about announcing the [55-106] 2002 Tigers.

"How do you do it?" I said.

"Every game is its own chapter," Ernie replied. "You tell the story of the game that day."

Another time his Tigers, in the middle of a brutal trip, faced a late-night cross-country flight. "How do you deal with the travel after all these years?" I asked him, then in his eighties. His response was pure Ernie: "I've got a good book and I don't really have anything better to do." Think about that. Don't sweat it. You can't control it, anyway.

— *Ken Korach*

In 2007, I was in my room at Milwaukee's Pfister Hotel, minutes after being introduced as the Brewers TV Voice, when the phone rang. "This is Ernie Harwell calling from Michigan," said a voice I'd spent hundreds of hours listening to and mimicking down to the "*loonng* gone" my early years on radio. Now it was my first congratulatory call. Eight years earlier in Arlington, Texas, then-Tigers hitting coach Lance Parrish arranged a meet and greet with Ernie, who invited me to spend the night "shadowing" him at the park: "It might do some good if you don't mind hanging out with an old-timah'." I was at his side from pre-game prep to post-game wrap, our paths not crossing again till the phone rang at the Pfister. Ernie admitted being nervous his 1948 first year at Brooklyn, warned I'd fight "jittuhs," and said he'd always worried about not being good enough— crazy, I know! He loved Milwaukee and said I'd enjoy the Midwest despite, like him, being from the South. "Friendly people passionate about their teams. Just be honest and be yourself." Pause. "You might want to buy a heavy coat, though!" Till now I'd been unsure how to live in this fantasy world without losing family, faith, and serenity. Ernie kept it all intact. In 2007, he joined me on the air as Detroit's Justin Verlander no-hit the Brewers, laughing "That'll teach ya'!" In 2007, at eighty-nine, he told of just signing a ten-year contract with a ten-year *option* as spokesman for Blue Cross Blue Shield! As impossible as it sounds, the perfect broadcaster was a better man.

   — *Brian Anderson*

   Although we knew it was coming, Ernie's death was a loss on so many levels. When I did the Red Sox, I had the chance to spend some time with him. How's this for irony? On May 4, 2010, the Marlins were being blown away by the Giants' [2008–2009 Cy Younger] Tim Lincecum: thirteen Ks in seven innings. In the bottom of the second, Dan Uggla and John Baker took consecutive called third strikes. I'm not prone to use others' lines, but for some inexplicable reason I said, "Both are out for excessive window shopping." I chuckled to myself, because that was Ernie's phrase. Three innings later, the story broke that he'd passed away. I didn't think about it until next morning, but when I read that Ernie had died around 7:30 I went to MLB Audio and found I'd used Ernie's line at 7:28. How odd is that? I love the Mitch Albom line: "If baseball had a voice, it would sound just like Ernie Harwell."

   — *Glenn Geffner*

   It's hard to imagine Ernie and Harry Kalas gone. When Ernie died, I got thinking about the people they'd helped. I was around Harry for more than a decade and knew what he meant to Philadelphia. My first big-league home run call was Scott Rolen's blast down the line at Veterans Stadium. Ending, I saw Harry nodding, glasses down on his nose, giving a thumbs up: the greatest affirmation a broadcaster could receive. When he had a 2009 heart attack, it was a death in a family—ours. For a long time Ernie was more faraway. Then, in 1992, the Orioles' Jim Hunter, almost a mentor, invited my older brother Ray and me to a Yankees series in Toronto. Jim was there for CBS Radio with Ernie, looking exactly the same as when I last saw him in 2007. Ernie introduced Ray and me to everyone, treating us like family: a man who broadcast when the Bums owned Brooklyn, Willie Mays played, and whom *my* dad and *his* dad heard in New York now predicting I'd be a big-league announcer. At lunch, I mentioned that I couldn't figure how to simultaneously keep statistics *and* do football play-by-play. To my amazement, Ernie took out a yellow legal pad and showed me how *he'd* kept stats, a simple formula, but one that simplified my life. When I thanked him from time to time, Ernie smiled, then asked, "How is your brother Ray doing?" He wasn't just filling time that weekend, but like Harry, in tune with folks all around.

    — *Tom McCarthy*

As a Little Leaguer in Pennsylvania, I'd heard him air [1954–1959] games in Baltimore. In Detroit, I was Ernie's last broadcast partner. Anyone talking with him walked away thinking "I'm Ernie's best friend," since he treated everyone the same. I loved to get him laughing on the air. A friend, Steve Atkins, owns a big pie company and he'd bring some to the booth, where I'd eat in a game, sharing with the crew. Ernie would say, "Oh, Jim, I don't want any," then sneak back off air and have some pie. I'd look around, catch him, and Ernie'd smile that smile. "Just sampling," he said.

    — *Jim Price*

One night I got to reminiscing with Al Kaline about the first ESPN Radio game I did: 1999, in New York, with Ernie. In the fifth inning, I'd looked at George Steinbrenner's box and seen Wayne Gretzky, whom I knew from LA, waving. Naturally, I wave back and signal, "Come on over!" Ernie and I are at the mike when Wayne enters our booth. He sits behind us, saying between innings, "You know, that's one of my heroes you're working with." I nod. "Yeah, Ernie's special." Wayne says seriously, "You don't understand. Across the border [Brantford, Ontario, 150 miles from Detroit] I'd listen every day. *He was my childhood.*" Half an inning later, Ernie removed his headset, discovering the royalty to his rear. "What a pleasure to meet you," he said. "No, it's *my* pleasure," said Gretzky. Delightfully, they start to debate who's more in awe! "Ernie," Wayne continues, "I can't tell you how many nights I fell asleep to you." Harwell laughs: "I can't tell you how many people say I've put them asleep." Later, Wayne told me his greatest thrill was "finally meeting someone whom you've idolized and finding they're even neater than you'd hoped."

    — *Rick Sutcliffe*

Chapter Eight

The Office

"If the old masters had labeled their fruit, one wouldn't be so likely to mistake pears for turnips," Mark Twain wrote of painting. It is less likely to mistake one owner for another.

Horace Stoneham liked to drink alone, with strangers, and with friends. Branch Rickey called Jackie Robinson "a man whose wounds you could not feel or share." Walter O'Malley betrayed Brooklyn, bound Los Angeles, and/or was baseball's Cortez. Bill Veeck signed a midget, coined an exploding scoreboard, and staged "Disco Night." Counting in their counting house, each prized the bottom line.

Edward Bennett Williams helped plot Camden Yards, the Orioles' once-ATM. George Steinbrenner used free agency, built a YES Network cash cow, and made the Yankees again marquee. Red Sox ownership's river of black has run through a 600-plus game sellout streak. Antipodally, red colored the post-war Boston Braves, Lou Perini once paying dry cleaning for 18,000 coats, shirts, and pants. Seats painted for opening day hadn't dried.

Ray Kroc seized the public address microphone to condemn his Padres: "I've never seen such stupid ballplaying in my life." When Detroit lost a 1967 last-day pennant, its owner wrote a poignant note to himself: "John Fetzer has just died. This is his ghost speaking." Gho(a)stly: Bud Selig, hiring Bob Uecker as a scout. Uke's first report, soaked in gravy and mashed potatoes, led directly to radio/TV.

Depending on the owner, each braved or benefited from a supporting cast: farm directors, bird-dog scouts; a hitting don like Charlie Lau; an instructor like Johnny Sain, extremely making pitchers over. One coach, Frank Crosetti, cashed fifteen World Series checks. Another, Tom Lasorda, later managing, said, "I want my team to think baseball the way my wife shops – twenty-four hours a day."

Frantic Frankie Lane roiled Cleveland by dealing Rocky Colavito for Harvey Kuenn, saying, "I traded hamburger for steak." At the hotel, the Indians general manager found a dummy hanging in effigy from a lamppost. Another GM, George Weiss, upon retiring, unnerved his wife. "I married George for better or worse," she said, "but not for lunch." Baseball's front office includes "pears [and] turnips" — also lemons, roses, and an occasional thorn.

Clark Griffith meant baseball at the end of the nineteenth century and first half of the twentieth. In 1906, he pitched his 237th and last victory. Five years earlier, he and Ban Johnson formed the renegade American League. Mr. Griffith became White Sox player-manager, managed three other teams, and in 1920 became sole Senators owner till his death in 1955. Cash-poor, he rarely postponed due to weather, feeling that with people traveling to see a game it should be played whenever possible. Mr. Griffith demanded hustle. Once rain pelted Griffith Stadium, which the visiting team took advantage of, bunting a ball ten to fifteen feet into a puddle. Knuckleball pitcher Mickey Haefner came in slowly, stepping gingerly so he didn't slip, and threw to first. *Safe*! Enraged, Mr. Griffith felt that, irrespective of weather, Haefner should have raced toward the ball. He stewed for a while, then in the seventh inning sent word around the press box: Haefner could take his knuckler and ginger elsewhere, having just been released.
— *Bob Wolff*

I'm not a great negotiator. For a time, Dad was my Little League coach, not wanting me to pitch. One night he came home after work. I snuck into his car, stole the keys, and said he wasn't getting them back unless he let me pitch. That lasted a minute and a half. With the Pirates, I once held out for $2,500. Finally, I drove to spring training at Pirates City, looked through a chain link fence, and watched guys work out: not exactly a hard-line negotiating stance. Knowing he had me, general manager Joe Brown walked up and said, "Why are you fooling around? Sign this thing, now." I tried one last-gasp maneuver. "Joe, I've got a deck in my pocket. Can we cut cards for $1,000?" No, he said, sign: so I did.
— *Steve Blass*

Baseball scouts have it tougher than any sport. *You* try to imagine a player ten, five, even two years away. I was Yankees personnel director for three years in the late '50s. We'd have meetings, five, six scouts debating. One of our guys, Ray Garland, had scouted a catcher in Brooklyn. "Too fat," Ray said, "he'll never make it." I wonder what Joe Torre thinks now. Another prospect debuted in 1960. We didn't want him. The Cubs did. Ron Santo should be in Cooperstown. They vote for players, writers, and broadcasters at the Hall. Hey, how about a wing for great scouts, too?

— *Jerry Coleman*

In 1959, the Cubs signed and sent me to San Antonio. One day a minor-league scout, Rogers Hornsby, the Hall of Famer, somebody to respect, came to check us out. He tells one guy, "Find another job, because you've got no future." Another: "Go back to shining shoes because you can't hit." Billy Williams, a teammate, was next to me. I whisper, "If he says that to me, I'm going to cry." Instead, Hornsby says, "You can hit in the big leagues right now." I felt like hugging him. Next year I make the Cubs, report to Pittsburgh, and sit in the stands watching Roberto Clemente, Dick Groat, Bill Mazeroski, and Don Hoak in batting practice. I'm in awe. Later, manager Lou Boudreau says, "You're my third baseman and hitting sixth." I'm a nervous wreck: The Cubs'd lost nine straight and the Pirates are throwing Bob Friend and Vern Law. I go out, sit on the bench, and hear, "How ya' doing?" I look up to see Ernie Banks. "Look at these two guys as Triple-A pitchers," he said. I tell Ernie easier said than done. My first at-bat I lined a single off Friend, later had a three-run double, then two RBI in the second game. We swept the Pirates — that season's champion! Like Hornsby, Ernie helped the world come off my shoulders.

— *Ron Santo*

In 1963, I took my new wife Karen on a honeymoon to winter baseball in the Dominican Republic: wonderful me. Two years earlier its dictator, Rafael Trujillo, had been murdered, so natives weren't tiptoeing through the tulips. Machine gunners sat at each end of the dugout. In Santiago, taxi drivers yelled the Spanish word for prostitute at us on the street, referring, we learn, to Karen's Bermuda shorts. She went out and bought a dress.

We lost the best-of-seven playoff final, left the clubhouse, and found our bus overturned. Some honeymoon. Next year Triple-A Columbus plays at Syracuse. I get in at 7:00 a.m., go to our apartment, and fall asleep. The phone rings. "I need to speak to Steve," says the gentleman. Karen: "Steve's had a long night, he's sleeping." Gentleman: "I really need to talk to him." Karen, annoyed: "He's sleeping." Gentleman: "This is Joe Brown, general manager of the Pirates. We want to call Steve up . . ." never finishing his sentence. Instead, he and I hear, "Steve, get your a— out of bed! We're going to the big leagues!" My wife. In Pittsburgh, I meet Bucs longtime equipment manager John Hallahan, who leads me to a locker and my black and gold Bucs uniform. "Don't you want to try it on, go on the field, see how it feels?" he said. It's raining, so I say, "I don't want to get it wet." John grabs me by the arm, points to the locker, and says, "Steve, if you get it wet there are two or three more uniforms. That's why we call it the *big* leagues."

— *Steve Blass*

The 1964 world champion Cardinals were special. Once we got near the World Series, Bing Devine, the team's general manager, asked if I'd do him and the Cardinals a favor. I said sure. He said, "We'd like to bring up another player—so we need to inject you with hepatitis." I said, "Hey, anything to improve the team."

— *Bob Uecker*

Joe Brown took a chance, signing me out of high school: skinny, poorly rated. In time, he became a father figure, slipping me $20 once in a while, worried about my weight—about *me*. "Go get some milkshakes," he'd say. Somehow I can't imagine that kind of relationship now between a GM and some $4 million player. At Joe's University of Baseball, my professors were guys like Elroy Face and Bob Friend and Maz and Roberto. One night this rookie was in the clubhouse while the Pirates were taking batting practice. Jerry Lynch, maybe baseball's all-time best pinch hitter, comes in, sees me, and chews me out. "I don't ever want to see you in the clubhouse when your team is on the field, whether it's practice or a game, *ever, ever again*!" I was quaking. He never did. That was Joe.

— *Steve Blass*

Charles O. Finley was an original—orange baseballs, designated runner, Harvey the Mechanical Rabbit—who transplanted the A's from Kansas City to Oakland in 1968. On opening night, his mule mascot Charlie O. stepped from a luxury van, stopped at each base, and bowed. Tennessee Ernie Ford and a marching band got ready for the National Anthem. But Charlie couldn't negotiate a live music agreement with the union, so we played a recording. The $1 million rightfield scoreboard didn't work till summer. The pitcher's mound lay on a steel soccer shell. Empty seats previewed bad attendance. Soon an Oakland pitcher was quoted saying: "Maybe we should move back to Kansas City."
— *Monte Moore*

Some say Finley knew baseball. No. He did make Jack Benny seem generous. Charlie built a lot of things—a prime-time World Series, a great A's team, free agency by mistake. I'm asked if he belongs in Cooperstown. You're talking to the wrong guy. Most teams fly charter. In August 1967, the A's flew a regularly scheduled plane from Boston to Kansas City, Finley so cheap he spread us three across in coach. His mule went first class. En route, Lew Krausse had too much to drink, Finley wanting to suspend him. Manager Alvin Dark wouldn't consider it, so Finley fires Alvin, my mentor, and I call his actions "detrimental to baseball." Next day Finley called, cussing me, asking if I want my unconditional release. I say no, making and needing my $12,000 salary, so Charlie says he'll call back in half-an-hour. Twenty minutes later, my roomie Mike Hershberger does. "As of this moment," he said, slamming the phone, "you're no longer a member of the green and gold." When Charlie released me, I didn't know it, but suddenly I'm available. White Sox GM Ed Short offered $100,000, saying, "We don't want to get in a bidding war." You know, that term *bidding war* put a germ in Hawk's mind. I turn down a Tokyo Giants three-year contract: *three* times more than any U.S. team. Boston's Haywood Sullivan—heck, everyone—called, so I phoned mama, as I did four, five times a week. Alvin says, "Kenneth, whoever gets you will win the pennant—and I think you're going to get at least $150,000." I'm not thinking of being baseball's first free agent, but listening to him and mama I get exactly that, and away we go.
— *Ken Harrelson*

In 1978, I aired the A's on Bay Area Spanish radio, glad that Finley didn't sign a commercial station to carry games in English. Instead, students Larry Baer, now Giants president and chief operating officer, and Bob Kozberg did English play-by-play on University of California–Berkeley radio KALX, its signal limited to the campus and a few downtown blocks. This let me lure listeners by giving the score in *English* at the end of each half-inning, 1,000-watt flagship KOFY AM somehow reaching most of the area. An engineer later explained that because its tower/transmitter was installed on top of cement pillars in the bay, water became a conduit to increase power: KOFY becoming *La Milagrosa*—"The Miraculous One Thousand." Leave it to Charlie. Ironically, the A's English network stretched to Honolulu. A protester phoned the A's: "It's nice they can hear you in Hawaii. Why can't we hear you *here*?"

— *Amaury Pi-Gonzalez*

Like Hawk, I played for Mr. Yawkey: loved the Red Sox so much, spent so much money, those near-misses [losing a last-day pennant or World Series in 1946, 1948, and 1949]. That's why '67 was special. In 1966, we finished ninth. Next year we start slowly, then after the All-Star break, win ten straight road games, return to Logan Airport, and they have to divert the plane. "There are 10,000 people waiting for you," the pilot says. "They seem happy with what you've done." After a long trip you usually want to sleep. Not then. They let the fans meet us, and we shared a special thing. One day [August 20], we trail the Angels, 8–0. Yaz [Carl Yastrzemski] goes through the dugout, saying, "We're going to *win* this game!" By now we *believed*. He parks one, we tie at 8, then Jerry Adair homers in the eighth to win. There were 100,000 at Revere Beach, most tuned to Sox radio, and Ken Coleman loved to tell how Adair's homer made the beach a sound wave— one crescendo, then another. The last day we're tied for first, leading Minnesota in the ninth, 5–3. The final out is a low pop to me at shortstop. Next thing I see is my roommate, Dalton Jones, playing third, jumping up and down: "Roomie, we won!" Stunned, I said, "You're right!" Fans come on the field at Fenway, so pulling and clutching it's a miracle I'm here. To win the pennant, we still needed Detroit to lose game two of a doubleheader. No ESPN, Internet, no iPod, just a clubhouse radio from Tiger Stadium.

Angels win. Mr. Yawkey had tears in his eyes, drinking champagne, more fan than owner. I think of him when somebody thanks me for '67, which happens every day.

— *Rico Petrocelli*

In one of my early years with the Giants we were in Tucson for a spring training game with the Indians. We'd made the two-hour drive from Phoenix in the rain without knowing the status of the game. Gabe Paul was Indians GM and, with a Saturday afternoon gate in mind, was reluctant to call it. We sat around the pressroom at Hy Corbett Field for a few hours as it continued to rain. Finally, someone walked over and asked: "Well, Gabe, do you think it's going to stop?" Gabe Paul responded with unarguable logic: "Always does."

— *Hank Greenwald*

In 1967, Pittsburgh traded me to Detroit, where next year we won a World Series. Gates Brown was an all-time great pinch hitter. Between at-bats, he had a lot of time to kill. One night a Tiger starter is getting bombed. Our manager, Mayo Smith, tells pitching coach Johnny Sain to get somebody warmed up. Another batter gets a hit, Mayo looking to the bullpen. What he sees disturbs him: Nobody's warming up! Smith: "What's going *on*? Johnny, I thought I told you to get somebody warmed up!" Sain: "Mayo, the phone's *busy*. I can't get through." In our dugout, Gates Brown was using the phone to talk with someone in *California*. Today he'd use a cell.

— *Jim Price*

Nellie Fox almost never K'd, won the 1959 MVP award, made Cooperstown, and died far too young at forty-seven. As a Senators coach he hated to fly, playing cards with traveling secretary Burt Hawkins till the plane landed to forget his fear. Nellie kept his jeep under the stadium on road trips, taking the coaches and me home, driving to his home in Pennsylvania, and griping that my suitcase, loaded with baseball books I bought from used bookstores on the trip, broke its springs. George Minot wrote: "Ron Menchine's suitcase, loaded with books, terrifies bell hops throughout the league when they try to lift it." I can see Nellie nodding.

— *Ron Menchine*

As the expansion Royals new owner, Ewing Kauffman turned from a casual to great fan trying to improve his product, as he had in pharmaceuticals. Ewing wanted to train good athletes with little baseball experience and make them good ballplayers. Athletic ability mattered, even in another sport. The result was the Royals Baseball Academy, founded in Sarasota, Florida, a year after their 1969 birth. The Academy had a two-year program, including Manatee Junior College, players attending daily Ewing-mandated courses in personal finance and public speaking. After school, they studied baseball fundamentals for the rest of the day. The Academy closed in 1974, but the last laugh was Ewing's, graduates Frank White and U. L. Washington forming the Royals' late 1970s and early '80s middle infield. Moreover, each team now counsels players in public relations, speaking, and finance. Ewing's dream was unbatty, after all.

— *Denny Matthews*

The 1969 Senators were Washington's first club over .500 since *1952*. Next year Bob Short traded four key players to Detroit for mostly dead-armed Denny McLain, making this awful deal with Ted Williams away on a fishing trip! Short flew to most games in a private jet piloted by Darryl Wickie and Jim Cunningham, whom I'd introduce on air as "Honor Graduates of the Smiling Jack Aeronautical Institute" — an exclusive club. Each getaway day the man who made each flight smooth brought a bag containing miniatures of my drink of choice since college. "Let me welcome United Airlines rep Brad Eny to the booth," I'd say. "He brought our mutual friend John Daniels with him. Jack and I have spent many delightful nights together." I don't want you thinking I drank my way through games like some in our business. I never had a drop before or during the game. Back to Short, he so destroyed the Senators that the only thing worse than watching them drunk was watching them sober.

— *Ron Menchine*

Alcohol was once very much a part of the baseball culture. At the winter meetings, where many transactions happened, every general manager had a hotel headquarters suite with a well-stocked bar. One night then-Braves GM Eddie Robinson and his counterpart, the Phillies' Paul Owens, known as the "Pope," met in the latter's suite. Conversation began with cocktails, leading to a deal. Next day, Owens acquired right-hand pitcher Ron Schueler for shortstop Craig Robinson and another righty pitcher, Barry Lersch. To Atlanta, it sounded good—too good. Apparently, Robinson thought he had traded for promising left-handed pitcher Randy Lerch, *not* the veteran Lersch. Finding differently, Eddie was asked about getting the wrong guy. Nobody knows for sure, but it's thought Owens got the better of Robinson that night and early morning because the Pope could hold his Jack Daniels, as this trade proves—or 100 proofs.

—*Chris Wheeler*

Angels' owner Gene Autry told me, "David, you call a hell of a game. Not the game I'm watching, but a hell of a game." Maybe I represent the guy who adds a little whipped cream and cherry to the great game of baseball, to which I plead guilty, and proudly so.

—*Dave Niehaus*

The '70s Royals and A's specialized in bad blood. In Oakland, an A's fan, leaning over the KC bullpen railing, got whacked by a player, like putting your head through a carnival hole and meeting a water balloon. Next fan, same thing. Before long, Hal McRae grabbed a fan's umbrella and hit somebody over the head. Next morning's Oakland paper showed McRae holding this umbrella, about to strike. Charlie Lau, our hitting coach, always got on Mac because Hal's top hand dominated his swing, the top wrist rolling over too soon. At breakfast, Charlie pointed to the picture, telling Mac, "See, I keep telling you, too much top hand."

—*Denny Matthews*

On September 21, 1971, AL owners voted, 10 to 2, to let Short move the Senators to Texas. The franchise's final game was nine days later. I get to the park an emotional basket case, say good-bye to coaches and players, and go to the booth, partner Tony Roberts already there. All year we alternated the first four-and-a-half innings. Tonight is Tony's turn, DC behind, 5–1, when I take over. I begin with history—last first division, 1946; pennant, 1933; world title, 1924—before blasting the league for betraying fan loyalty. Listening at home in Minnesota, Short goes nuts, calling the booth to tell WWDC station manager Bill Sanders to "make him stop, make him stop! . . . Bill, tell him—." I leave the rest to your imagination. We ignored him. What could Short do, fire me? In the sixth, the Senators scored four runs to tie the game, fittingly keyed by Frank Howard's homer. Hondo had beseeched Short not to move to Texas. Fans roared as he crossed the plate, threw his helmet, cap, and batting glove in the stands, and acknowledged three curtain calls. "I just wish they [owners] could see this . . . [having voted] to move," I said. "The fans love Hondo as much as Hondo loves Washington." It was hard to talk. In the eighth, the Senators took a 7–5 lead. Next inning reliever Joe Grzenda got two outs before fans raced onto the field. Almost half-an-hour later, the game was forfeited to New York. "Well . . . it's a strange way to wind up major league baseball in the nation's capital," I said. "No one believed that there would not be baseball [here]. But it's sad to report—there no longer is. . . . The lights flicker here at RFK Stadium and the hopes for that long-awaited pennant die with the lights." It broke your heart. Tony and I won the Associated Press Award for excellence in broadcasting. In his *The Sporting News* column, Jerome Holtzman wrote, "For pure drama, Ron Menchine's broadcast of the Senators' last game rivals Russ Hodges' call, 'The Giants win the pennant!'" In 2005, I rejoiced when baseball returned to Washington. I wish my dream job had lasted longer, but little lasts forever. Memories, however, do.

—*Ron Menchine*

In late 1976, the winter meetings were in LA, where actor and new expansion Mariners owner Danny Kaye had heard me do the Angels. He asks about Seattle, and I said I was happy where I was. Still, I fly up to meet with Mariners' GM Dick Vertlieb. What happened then is truly weird. In Dick's office, I sit in a barber's chair, where you pump up and down. After a little schmoozing, he said, "How much money do you want?" I hadn't thought about it, wasn't that hot for the job, so I pick a number.

He says, "Well, you're not going to make more money than me."

I said, "I don't know how much money you make, and frankly, it doesn't make much difference." Back in LA, I told my wife, "I don't think we need to worry about Seattle."

Ten days later I get a call from Mr. Vertlieb, who, using profanity, starts screaming: "You *blah blah blah*, you got the job."

By now, I don't know what to think—what a nice warm welcome—so I ask my wife. She says, "It's a good deal, let's go ahead." I'm glad I did, signing a three-year contract.

—*Dick Niehaus*

Lou Gorman became a GM for Boston and Seattle after working closely with the Royals' Cedric Tallis and Joe Burke and grooming John Schuerholz and Herk Robinson. He became known for *Gormanisms*, so excited when talking his words U-turned. Ultimately, John and Herk wrote down these malapropisms and hid them inside their desks. One spring training, Lou didn't know what to do with a kid named Joel Bishop, saying, "We were faced face to face with the face of Joel Bishop." Try these: "That burns gas like it's eating peanuts," "I'll keep my ears posted," "I vaguely and vividly remember in my own mind," "We're glad to have you with you." Once Lou said, "He looked like he threw real good listening on the radio." Later, "High ceilings [were] covered with paintings and tapestries." To Lou, "The toenail on the top toe is growing into the nail." Maybe he was growing into Yogi.

—*Denny Matthews*

Your first day in the majors is supposed to be terrific. I'd just finished traveling from Wichita to my parents' home outside Pasadena when Dad meets me in the driveway to say that Cubs GM Salty Saltwell phoned. I call Salty, who says, "We want you in the big leagues." I land in Chicago at 7:00 a.m., can't fall asleep, so I get a hotel elevator, push a button, and stop at the ninth floor. Door opening, Tom Seaver sees my bags and says, "First day? Don't f— it up." I find a cab, saying two words I'd always wanted to, "Wrigley Field." Arriving, I get a locker and uniform from Cubs clubhouse manager Yosh Kawano and go running with Bill Bonham, a six-year veteran, and Bruce Sutter, a great friend I'd played with in the minors. We're near the bleachers when a guy yells, "Hey, [number] 40, what's your name, man?" I ignore him. The second time we run by he says, "Hey, 40, what's your name, man?" Third time, same thing. Bonham, the vet, says, "He does

that again, tell him to buy a program." Fourth time, the guy asks my name, I tell him to buy a program, and he says, "I did, and you ain't in it."
— *Mike Krukow*

My mentor, Bud Blattner, said not to be a bad imitation of some original. When he came up, George Brett held his bat high above his head, a bad imitation of Carl Yastrzemski. Brett had two things in his favor: a work ethic and the Royals hitting guru. In mid-1974, Charlie Lau asked George if he wanted to work on his swing. Under .200, George did, hearing Lau chant "extension through the ball and having a weight shift." It worked — permanently. People think the Royals' most important game was in the 1985 World Series. Actually, it's LCS Game 3. We'd lost the first two in Toronto. Lose the next, at home, and you're dead. Not coincidentally, it was also Brett's best-ever game. A position player, say shortstop or centerfielder, rarely dominates baseball, since you can't control what's hit your way and at most bat five times. George made huge plays at third and went four for four, homering twice. Ultimately we win the Series. Without this game, we don't make it. Somehow Charlie, an average hitter, figured how to *teach* hitting, using a wonderful teaching *tool*: his incredibly soft-spoken manner. A commercial went, "When E. F. Hutton talks, people listen." When Charlie spoke, people listened: George Brett, most of all.
— *Denny Matthews*

In 1992, I was Single-A radio Voice of the California League's High Desert Mavericks, owned by the Brett Brothers: George, Ken, Bobby and John. Often checking on our team, Ken, the Angels then-TV analyst, ultimately invited me to Anaheim to sit with him and partner Ken Wilson in the booth, the Royals in town for a four-game series. With George near 3,000 hits, we tried to avoid media, scheduling *before* the anticipated night. On September 30, four hits shy, number 5 gets two singles and a double. With each hit in this slightly-before-the-Internet age, people lined up to use payphones and hear wires spitting scores and headlines onto sheets of recycled paper. I sat right behind the leading man's brother as in the seventh George got hit four: baseball immortality! At first base, he looked into the stands to recognize his wife and mother, then to Ken, who raised a fist, sending chills down the spine of a Class-A radio hack sitting in the background. A few pitches later, George, caught up in the moment, was picked off first: Even gods can be human. Baseball players and Voices have "favorite guys." Mine was one who'd downplay his career over a few beers and mentored me on FX and Fox SportsNet. In 2003, I thought of 1992's fantastic night, which fortunately I had a chance to thank Ken for before he left us, of brain cancer, too soon, at fifty-five.

—*Matt Vasgersian*

In 2000, GM Joe Garagiola acquired right-handed pitcher Curt Schilling from Philadelphia. Some people deem Sandy Koufax and Don Drysdale baseball's best 1-2 pitching duo. Hey, give me 2001–2002's Schill and Randy Johnson. If one fired a two-hit shutout, next night the other wanted to throw a one-hit shutout. They went 90-24: Johnson, 45-11 with two Cy Young awards; Schilling, 45-13. Name two teammates doing better—*ever*. You expected both to win, since invariably they did.

—*Greg Schulte*

In 2000, the Giants entered their new home: now AT&T Park. What a change from Candlestick: a short rightfield porch; McCovey's Cove; not a bad seat. Peter Magowan made it possible, a businessman who'd run Safeway but whose real love was the Giants: growing up in New York, not in it for the bucks. I met him after he bought the team in 1992 and as the Giants almost moved because of the Stick, fans despairing of a new park *ever*. The political climate was a joke, many wanting to fix the wars in El Salvador and Nicaragua but not fix the potholes in the Mission District. No wonder they drew 10,000 a game. Magowan keeps the team there, builds a park, averages over 3 million fans. As for signing Barry Bonds, home run hero or poster child of the Steroids Age, you decide. At least Magowan was always ready to answer questions before retiring in 2008. I aired the 2003–2006 Mariners, whose owner never saw a game. It's said that leaders can be defined in one sentence: Peter Magowan kept the San Francisco Giants from being the Tampa Bay Giants.

—*Amaury Pi-Gonzalez*

I broadcast 1987–1988 in New York. Personally, I think George Steinbrenner belongs in Cooperstown: the perfect guy to buy and own the
world's flagship professional sports franchise. George's group spent $10
million to buy the Yankees in 1973, when they were nothing. [On The
Boss's 2010 death, the Yanks and their YES TV Network were worth an
estimated $4.6 *billion*.] George turned them around, like a pimp with his
girls: dressed them up, bought the best perfume, made it an event to see
the Yankees. George and I argued constantly, but it changed my view of
the Apple. I hated it before I got there full-time: too big-city for a small-
town boy. I'd tell Red Sox GM Dick O'Connell, "Subtract my pay for the
next three games in New York." Once there, I got to know the people, inner
workings, underpinnings, if you will. Plus, they love the game. Look at the
back page of the *Post* and *Daily News*: Just call it the baseball page. George
did that, more than anyone.
    — *Ken Harrelson*

Steinbrenner was without question the most influential owner in baseball in the last thirty to forty years. He lived to win, putting more money in
his team than any owner had or maybe will: not baseball's wealthiest owner, but winning was so important that George spent like he was. True, the
record was hardly spotless [two suspensions, friction with former Yanks,
and browbeat employees. Ex-aide Harvey Greene recalled "dreading a
phone call in the night. It was either Steinbrenner or a death in the family. After a while you hoped for a death in the family."]. Complex, charitable, unpredictable. The bottom line is that he brought the Yankees back to
prominence. Because of that, the good outweighed the bad.
    — *Dan Shulman*

George was The Boss. As chapter 16 notes, longtime Yankees PA.
Voice Bob Sheppard was the Voice of God. Although the former occasionally considered himself the latter, the latter never, ever considered himself
the former. In one July 2010 week baseball and the Yankees lost each icon.
On what has been a Gumpian journey (my career) I came to know both
men reasonably well. They couldn't have been more different. George was
stout, in the blazer, mock turtleneck, never a hair out of place, mercurial, a

brilliant showman as well as sportsman. Bob was long and lean, thinning white hair, professorial, an oral interpreter, who read from a script in essence provided by The Boss: the batting order of George's cast of characters. I met George in 1977, working Cleveland radio, then joined New York local and network radio and ESPN, covering him long before I worked for him. Fast-forward to August 2001. I was at Yankee Stadium for ESPN, sitting in GM Brian Cashman's office, when George walks in behind me, puts his hands on my shoulders, and says something to the effect, "I watched one of your games the other night down in Tampa," and he was very complimentary. As George left, saying that he wanted to see Brian in his lusher digs, I told "Cash" that if anything should develop with their new unnamed YES network I might be interested. That was it, or so I thought.

I head to the booth. Brian heads for the principal's office. Less than an hour later, he comes in and says, and I paraphrase here, "I've got some bad news and I've got some good news." I wasn't expecting *any* news, so the next few sentences were mind-numbing and life-changing. "The bad news is, George told me to stay the hell out of the broadcasting business and build him a Series champion." OK. What about the *good* news? "He wants to *hire* you." Next spring, my first with the Yankees, I watched YES's first game in Steinbrenner's suite with its first head, Leo Hindery, team president Randy Levine, and George. After fourteen years at ESPN, presumably they wanted to know what I thought of the telecast. As Jason Giambi batted for the first time as a Yank, George asked, "Boys, do you know why I hired him?" Note: He said hired, not signed, not brought aboard, but *hired*. After considerable silence, George said that then-Mets catcher Mike Piazza was enormously popular in the New York area's large Italian-American community. He wanted a player to trump him! To George, YES meant airing 162 blockbuster programs a year: no longer consumed just by putting "a—es in the seats," but placing eyeballs in front of TV sets.

I asked: "George, are you a sportsman, or a showman?" His response was an inhale followed by exhale: "Very good, Charles." He was a sportsman, a showman, a brilliant businessman, a Clevelander, a Tampan, and yet the quintessential New Yorker. Some shrink under the harsh glare of the big city. George lived and thrived in it.

   —*Charley Steiner*

In 2003–2005, we played Detroit in interleague, staying at the Atheneum Hotel in Detroit's Greektown, which gave "over the top" new meaning: gaudy colors, decorations everywhere, and the deepest bathtubs in the world. Diamondbacks bullpen coach Tony Dello was five feet tall. All weekend he got riffed about having his own indoor pool, big enough so that he could swim a couple laps before the game.

— *Jeff Munn*

In 2005, twenty-eight-year-old Jon Daniels was hired as Rangers general manager. Five years later they win a pennant. Early in his career at Arlington, Jon guests on the air. I start talking about how baseball has changed, GMs getting younger, comparing Jon to his Red Sox counterpart, Theo Epstein. I wanted to say that in Boston we all know how much great success young GMs can have. Instead, I said, "We all know how much great sex young general managers can have." My all-time blooper. I kept going, pretending nothing was amiss. A few batters later my partner, Jerry Remy, couldn't help himself: "Don, that was a great point you made about young general managers."

— *Don Orsillo*

Chapter Nine

The Great Deciders

"The name 'umpire' is basically theological," Eugene McCarthy wrote. "It is derived from the Old French word nom-pere, meaning 'one who is without pere,' literally 'without father or superior.' 'Refuse not,' the medieval divines warned, the umpeership and judgments of the Holy Ghoste." Bill Klem would agree. "I never made a wrong call," said the 1905–1940 arbiter, "at least in my heart."

Umpires can seem Solomonic. Lindsey Nelson worked in a gondola above second base at the Astrodome. "What if the ball hits my man Lindsey?" asked Casey Stengel. "If the ball hits the roof, it's in play," Tom Gorman said, "so I guess if it hits Lindsey, it's in play." They can also brave blood, toil, tears, and threat. In 1940, the Dodgers mocked and a parolee slugged an ump, cops hauling the con away. Later, skipper Leo Durocher was fined and suspended for abusing "one . . . without pere."

Trying to be anonymous, men in blue can err. Bill Stewart, Bruce Froemming, and Don Denkinger swung the 1948, 1977, and 1985 postseason, respectively. They can be conspicuous, not trying. 1956: Babe Pinelli's adieu was Don Larsen's perfect game. 1966: Emmett Ashford became the bigs' first black ump. 2006: John Hirschbeck called out two Dodgers runners on catcher Paul Lo Duca's same Division Series play.

Umpires can be a spectator. Klem asked Charlie Grimm why he lay down in the batter's box. "[Burleigh] Grimes is going to throw at me anyway," he said, "so I thought I'd duck early." Caretaker: In 1971, Jim Honochick forfeited the moving-to-Texas Senators' last game. Comic: In a rain delay, a streaker ran to second base, slid on the tarp, and landed in the pokey. Raising his right hand, Nestor Chylak separated his thumb and index finger by an inch.

"Presidents, like great French restaurants," wrote Douglass Cater, "have an ambiance all their own." Ibid., umps. In 1996, Jeffrey Maier, twelve, stole Derek Jeter's LCS in-play drive from Baltimore's rightfielder, Richie Garcia ruling homer. In 2009–2010, dicey calls fueled demand for better instant replay, ignoring the "theological." No one cries, "Kill the referee," McCarthy noted. "That demand is reserved for umpires. Umpires have to be dealt with absolutely, for their powers are absolute."

To quote a hymn, "Once to every man and nation comes the moment to decide."

[On June 2, 2010, Detroit's Armando Galarraga, twenty-eight, retired the first twenty-six batters *v.* visiting Cleveland: one shy of baseball's twenty-first all-time perfect game. The next batter, Jason Donald, grounded to first baseman Miguel Cabrera, who tossed to Galarraga, stepping on the bag. History!—if not in the way he expected, or hoped. Shockingly, umpire Jim Joyce, fifty-four, signals safe. At this point, Roger Clemens throws a bat. Barry Bonds cries racism. A hundred different players swear 1,000 different ways. By contrast, Galarraga calmly retook the mound, got the last out, and concluded his tour de force. Joyce left the field, watched the replay, tearfully apologized to Galarraga, and blamed not the rain in Spain but— stop the presses—*himself*. Next day, Armando gave Joyce the lineup card at home plate. Joyce, in turn, tapped the Motowner on the shoulder: nobility, in an ignoble age.] After three innings, Galarraga had nine up and down. "Perfect game!" Jim Price and I joke. After five, I say, "I don't think I've seen this in my years of doing baseball" —fifteen up and down. After seven I'm thinking, "Here we go, crunch time," except the game happened so fast, taking only an hour and forty-four minutes. After eight, I can't describe the electricity in the park, or in my veins. Nervous? I don't say a word in my last two commercial breaks.

Austin Jackson's great catch opened the Indians' ninth. In the booth, you see any ball's flight and fielder's speed and calculate a potential catch. I didn't calculate this till Jackson caught it. A rollout to short follows. Jason Donald then grounds to Cabrera's right, who guns to Galarraga, covering. From my view I can't say for sure if the batter's out, though my *impression* is that he *was*, formed by hundreds of bang-bang plays. Seeing the call, I think maybe the pitcher bobbled the ball, but a replay shows he didn't: Galarraga beat the runner. I vent a little—no perfect game— then start post-game, Tigers radio the first to interview Joyce. The anguish in his voice changed everything: "OK," I thought, "this is the human element. What do you do, stay mad at Joyce forever, when he's been so forthright about how he blew the call?"

Armando would have loved to have thrown a perfect game. For anyone interested in grace and fallibility, the end is great as is. A perfecto, and we talk inside baseball. Instead, it goes far beyond. A couple days later my wife was at our daughter's volleyball game, parents still wowed by this example for their kids. Galarraga, acting so mature. Joyce, a brave and honest symbol. Tigers manager Jim Leyland, mad on the field, but setting the right tone later: It's part of the game. Armando will be remembered longer than *had* he thrown twenty-seven up and down. I'd love someday to call a perfect game. But this was so monumentally bigger. [Notwithstanding, in early 2011 Galarraga was dealt to Arizona.]

— *Dan Dickerson*

Baseball's not showboating. Behind the plate, I felt I had more to gain by being friendly and accommodating than arguing with an umpire. I'd just say, "If you hear from me, I think you missed it." Or take the batter. I was there to work, not talk. If anything, I think the work ethic's grown since I played [1973–1989]. It used to be at the start of a series you'd go over how batters reacted to, say, bases loaded compared to no one on. Now they've got DVDs of the other team's stances, looking for weaknesses. I still think you're better off by going to your pitcher's strengths, not worrying about the batter. Here's my fastball. Hit it. Or, if you're an umpire, call it.

— *Alan Ashby*

Each September teams promote minor leaguers, swelling the roster from twenty-five to forty. Frank Howard'd take them to dinner, showing why they should bust their butts. He and Brooks Robinson are the nicest guys I met in baseball. Thankfully, I saw Hondo mad only once, against the A's, when Ron Luciano called him out on a terrible pitch. Luciano was big [6-foot-2, 240 pounds] but a Singer Midget *v.* 6–7 and 255 Howard, who reacted by jumping up and down, leaving a crater in the box. "I've never seen Hondo so mad," I said. "It looks like smoke is coming out of his ears." Frank was tossed out of the game for the only time in the three years I aired the Senators. DC has a Washington Monument of stone and steel. Our monument was the strongest man I ever saw, with better eyesight than some umpires.

— *Ron Menchine*

I've been mostly with the White Sox since 1982, when Eddie Einhorn and Jerry Reinsdorf bought them, and the only time I've been censored concerns umpires. I'll get called in: "Hey, ease up." I admit the Hawk can get on the umps pretty good. But to me one call on a 1–1 count, a blown decision at first base, can turn the whole game around. If you don't shill for players, owners, the front office, how can you shill for umps?

— *Ken Harrelson*

In 1982, I almost made major league history by being the first batboy to be thrown out of a regular-season game for arguing. The Giants and Dodgers were playing in front of a big crowd at Dodger Stadium, late in the year, contending for the West. The Giants thought starter Rich Gale was getting squeezed by the home plate umpire: "Hey! Where was *that* pitch? You've got to be *blankety-blanking* me!" After a frustrating inning, Gale came off the mound. His manager was Hall of Famer Frank Robinson, the closest thing to God I'd encountered in my eleven years on the planet. Frank pulled Gale aside and said, "You're doing fine. Just keep making pitches." Gale removed his cap, toweled his forehead, and tried soaking in Frank's advice. I remember that because I was fascinated by Robinson, especially when he got angry, and because I sat between the ump and Frank in the dugout. If tempers flared, I'd twist my head back and forth to see.

With the Giants up, the umpire starts calling close pitches strikes. More hollering. He eyes the Giants dugout and says "That's enough" — a warning. Back then, men in blue seemed to handle players better. Not taking a chance, Gale heads behind me for the tunnel, then shouts toward the plate, moves to the clubhouse, and misses how the ump removes his mask, marches to the dugout, and kicks Gale out. Dodger Stadium is a zoo, but as Robinson and the umpire meet a few feet in front of me I can hear everything being said.

Frank: "Who? Who? Who?"

Umpire: "Gale. He's gone."

"Why?"

"Frank, I warned him to cut it out."

Robinson: "Warned who? How do you know who was yelling at you?"
    Suddenly, his genius struck: "Gale's not even in the dugout. *I* was the
    one yelling."

Umpire: "I saw Gale."

Frank: "Gale isn't even in the dugout. He went to the clubhouse. You can't
    throw him out."

The umpire said he could. "Look, Frank, I've ejected *someone*, and someone
    has to go."

Frank says, "Fine, then I'm the guy."

Umpire: "Sorry, Frank, I know it didn't come from you. It came from right
    there. I saw it and heard it. *Right there*" — where only I was standing.

Frank shrugged, looked at the ump, and said, "Well, damn, if you say
so." I didn't fully understand what Mr. Robinson was doing, but the umpire did. "Oh, not him," he said, grinning slightly.

Frank said, "There's nobody else standing there." It was finally agreed
that longtime Giants trainer Joe Liscio would have to leave the game. I, by
contrast, stayed.

In the season final, Joe Morgan homered off reliever Terry Forster to
beat the Dodgers, LA losing the division by a game. I didn't lose this opportunity to greet the hero. The little kid awaiting Morgan at home plate
after he circled the bases was the almost ejected batboy, me.

— *Ryan Lefebvre*

In 2007, the Rockies won a coin flip to host a one-game NL wild card
playoff. My '90s Indians frequently made postseason. By contrast, this was
partner Jeff Kingery's second time in fifteen years. In the seventh inning,
the Rockies led, 6–5, when Garrett Atkins homered to left-center. No one
saw the ball hit a bleacher railing, so it was ruled a double, Atkins not scoring. Many say this led to replay: sadly, too late for us. In San Diego's eighth,
Matt Holliday misplayed a fly, tying the score at 6. Postseason now rode on

every pitch. The Rockies have a unique home setup to expedite clubhouse interviews, one Voice going behind the screen in the final half-inning. Each inning Jeff and I swapped places and roles as relievers slammed the door. In the thirteenth, the Padres went ahead, 8–6, Trevor Hoffman relieving. On air, I said his usually devastating changeup lacked control just as leadoffer Kaz Matsui doubled, a switch turning on the crowd. After Troy Tulowitzki's run-scoring double, Holliday drove off the rightfield wall so fiercely that the ball caromed away, scored the 8-all run, and sent Matt to third. Following an intentional walk, Jamey Carroll lined to rightfielder Brian Giles, Holliday tagging up. Jeff's description of his dash to the plate was dramatic, but umpire Tim McClelland didn't signal after Matt's collision with the catcher. From my vantage, seeing it roll away, I exclaimed, "He dropped the ball! He dropped the ball!" TV replays were inconclusive: Did Michael Barrett block Holliday from the plate, or Matt touch it first? All that mattered was McClelland's signal: safe.
    — *Jack Corrigan*

If McLelland rules the other way, maybe we play a while. A game's importance magnifies the umpire. After 162 games, whomever won moved to the Division Series. Lose, go home. As Jack says, especially in this game we knew there'd be a huge celebration if the Rockies won. Every inning he and I pass each other, one racing up, the other down to get remote gear ready to charge the field: each more winded than a cross-country runner. I don't remember doing this, but when Holliday tripled I stood up—and as he reached third, I raised my arms. The Rockies were in the playoffs for the first time since 1995, Jack getting a clubhouse champagne shower. Since then, people ask, "Where were you when . . . ?" They don't have to finish the sentence. We know.
    — *Jeff Kingery*

In 2009, Randy Johnson became baseball's twenty-fourth 300-game winner. I remember one pitch he *didn't* throw. Randy was set to pitch June 4, causing a big advance sale, but with the game rained out and next day's forecast also bad, the Nats scheduled a late-afternoon one-admission doubleheader for the Giants' last '09 visit. In the opener, Randy endured a thirty-six-minute delay, throwing his first pitch before a few thousand fans. In the sixth, his seventy-eighth and last pitch was hit for a comebacker. Johnson knocked it down, made a lunging throw, and landed on his shoulder: as precaution, taken out, up, 2–1. A generation ago 300-game guys like Nolan Ryan and Don Sutton finished. Now Tom Glavine and Roger Clemens let others finish. In the eighth, the Nats load the bases with two out. The Giants' Brian Wilson faces Adam Dunn, who works a 3–2 count. Wilson then throws a ball better hit with a seven-iron than baseball bat, but umpire Tim Timmons rings Dunn out. Next inning Wilson preserves 300. On one hand, it's history. On another, I wonder if, like the rest of us, Timmons was caught up in the moment instead of making Johnson wait.

— *Dave Jageler*

Rain delays don't happen under Houston's retractable roof. We're not as lucky on the road. Even a nice day in Pittsburgh might have a threat of rain. In a city like San Diego, other problems rear. The 2009 Astros were at Petco Park on a perfect afternoon, yet had a fifty-two-minute delay for bees swarming into leftfield with two outs in the ninth. The umpires yank the Padres off the field while the bees invade the stands, eventually congregating under the ball girl's jacket hanging over her chair in foul ground. After a delay, the beekeeper shows up to applause, takes two cans of spray, unloads everything he has under the jacket, and kills several thousand bees. Maybe it's appropriate the Astros won the game because they were once nicknamed "The Killer B's." One lesson was timing. We talked for fifty-two straight minutes without commercial—rush hour back in Houston. I heard from more people who were listening than any other game of the year. Another lesson: People focus on a call the ump blows, not the great majority they get right.

— *Brett Dolan*

In April 2010, umpire Joe West called the slow pace of the Yankees' opening series against the Red Sox "pathetic and embarrassing." Its first two games took 3:46 and 3:48—good time for a railroad schedule, bad for a game. Before game three, Joe issued his broadside, unusual for an umpire. He's right about quickening habits like unbuttoning, then buttoning, a batting glove, but ignored two things. First, since management wants to protect multi-million dollar starters, we have pitch counts, a relief parade, and complete game turned endangered species: Add half-an-hour. Second, half-inning commercial time adds another twenty minutes. Don Larsen's perfect game had a sixty-second sponsor break. Today regular season's is two minutes, the World Series' three. Keep those I's dotted, T's crossed, and gloves buttoned, but remember the big picture.

— *Bob Wolff*

My awful Senators gave me an affinity for the Cubs. Jack Brickhouse used to claim that an optimist says, "The glass is half-full." The pessimist says, "It's half-empty." The Cubs fan says, "When's the water going to spill?" In 1972, Chicago righty Milt Pappas had a perfect game with two out and two strikes in the ninth. Milt then threw two pitches he thought were strikes. Umpire Bruce Froemming disagreed, the batter walking. The next man popped out to give Pappas a no-hitter. Next day Milt still fumed: "Bruce, why didn't you call one of those a strike because that's what they were — and you'd have made history by calling a perfect game."

Froemming said, "Milt, if I did that I wouldn't have been able to live with myself."

Said Pappas: "So how do you live with yourself on all the other lousy calls you make?"

— *Ron Menchine*

One night a Triple-A umpire who shall remain unnamed had a head cold, therefore couldn't see real well, and said to me, "Jimmy, I trust you to call balls and strikes. You nod one way for a strike, the other way for a ball." I thought I was hearing things. The umpire, who later enjoyed a long big-league career, said, "I can't trust the other catcher, but I can you." Needless to say, we won the ballgame, because I was very, very honest.

— *Jim Price*

Chapter Ten

Safe Harbor

In 1950, Bronx-born Vin Scully debuted in Brooklyn. In 1957, his Dodgers left the Borough of Churches for the City of the Angels. I was born too late to hear Scully gild New York; raised too eastern to hear him in Los Angeles. For a long time I absorbed Vin from a distance: a World Series here, All-Star Game there. Necessity can become a virtue.

Like many, I met Scully on 1970s CBS Radio, then NBC TV, today Sirius XM Satellite. Distance can breed perspective. It also spurs mystique. Most Voices fall to meet an audience. Scully, eighty-three, asks his to rise. "He is day-to-day," Vin said of an injured player. "Aren't we all?" The Dodgers announcer will one day retire. His Scully school can live.

Vin's curriculum weds work, objectivity, and lilt less Pavarotti than Perry Como — language, above all. "He catches the ball gingerly, like a baby chick falling from the tree." A weak hit evokes Eugene O'Neill's "a humble thing, but thine own." Parents, nod in unison: "There's something redundant about giving noise-makers to youngsters under fourteen years of age."

Scully's score invites us to "pull up a chair." Notes include twenty-five Series, eighteen no-hitters, NBC 1983–1989 Game of the Week, Hollywood Walk of Fame, lifetime Emmy Achievement Award, and every major radio/TV Hall of Fame, tying Henry Aaron ("What a marvelous moment!") via Billy Buck ("And the Mets win it!") through Kirk Gibson as The Natural: *("In a year that has been so* improbable, *the* impossible *has happened.")*

In 1959, baseball's then-largest crowd (93,103) feted crippled Roy Campanella before an exhibition. "The lights are going out in this final tribute to Roy Cam-

panella, and everyone at the ballpark . . . are asked in silent tribute [on signal] to light a match," Vin said. "The lights are now starting to come out, like thousands and thousands of fireflies" — then, magically, "a sea of lights at the [Memorial] Coliseum." It is how millions remember him.

In the 1991 World Series, a Minnesota Twins runner reached second base. A moment later Scully referenced Death of a Salesman's *"tiny ship" (runner) seeking "safe harbor" (home plate). For announcers, a favorite port is discussing one another.*

Vin Scully spent his first four years under Red Barber, each a master of rhetoric. Red called Vin the son he never had. Vin almost looked on Red as a father. In 1950, having introduced Scully, then a rookie, to the Dodgers audience, Red said, "We've got a fellow we want you to meet in the fourth inning, too, that you're going to like. Fellow named Connie Desmond. He and I have only been together eight years. We're almost on speaking terms."

— *Pat Hughes*

Growing up in San Francisco, I'd hear Vinny from hundreds of miles away. He would say, "Let's pause for station identification on the Dodgers' radio network." This august-sounding voice then came on: "This is Clear Channel KFI, Los Angeles," then back to Scully. With luck, I might get him in our house. More often, I drove the car to meet Vin on the mountaintop, which he owns. My first response may surprise you: horror. Russ Hodges'd say of a Giants blast, "Tell it bye-bye-baby!" Goose bumps! Here's Scully's call: "Away back, and gone." I remember thinking: "No bye-bye-baby? No wonder he's working in a jerkwater town. He's terrible. He'll never get out of there to go to some good place." I was right about that. He's still there.

— *Jon Miller*

Baseball is a moveable feast. In September 1973, radio accompanied me to a high school class, football pep rally and game, and after-school job as a janitor and delivery boy as the Mets clinched the NL East and beat Cincinnati in the LCS. They weren't supposed to win that Series, and didn't. In 1986, they were, but trailed, three games to two, as Vin aired Game 6 on

NBC: two outs, one strike left, Boston up, 5–3, in the tenth. My heart sank, then jumped: "*A little roller up along first. It gets through Buckner! Here comes Knight and the Mets win it!*" said Scully, then quieting, letting pictures tell the tale: Exhilarated fans and Met players, dejected Red Sox, game-ending play replays, a sign "Now Boston Chokes" — NBC. Get it? — then Vin again: "If one picture is worth a thousand words, you've just seen a million!" Priceless. Perfect. I watch the replays and say, "I can't believe what I just saw!" — two years *before* Jack Buck said it! Happily, I'd recorded on my VCR and before I went to sleep replayed the inning twice to ensure it wasn't just a dream. Three years later, I met Vin at Dodgertown, graciously recording for a friend a new version of his call, ending "And Buckner catches the ball and the Red Sox go on to win!" They did, in 2004 and '07, baseball's feast moving on.

— *Peter King*

Everybody in our business has a Vin Scully story. Mine came my first day of work: opening day 1991. That year's Braves turnaround ended in a "worst to first" pennant and seven-game World Series: in particular, pitchers John Smoltz and Tom Glavine, acquisitions Sid Bream, Terry Pendleton, and Rafael Belliard, and new GM John Schuerholz, bringing a resume and vision. Personally, 1991 was exciting, too, at twenty-six working with legend Ernie Johnson and, occasionally, my dad. On the first day of any job you try to show you're worthy. I also had the pressure of not wanting to disappoint Dad four booths down the hall. Ernie and I alternated play-by-play and color. Additionally, I'd come back from a first commercial break, give lineups, umpires, and pitchers, then go to break again. After the lineups segment miraculously went off without a hitch, I removed my headphone, peeked at Ernie, and heard a "tick-tick-tick." Later, I learned that Mr. Scully had stood behind us, heard our segment, then started for his booth. To get my attention, he began a rhythmic tapping with his World Series ring on a Plexiglas partition dividing our booth from the Dodgers'. As I looked up, he said, smiling, "Welcome to the club!" Twenty years have passed since then. The Braves became a powerhouse, winning fourteen straight division titles and a Series in 1995. At Wrigley Field, my dad, grandfather, and I became the first three-generation family to broadcast a

game. I've gone from a rookie to a forty-six-year-old husband and father, still love baseball, and owe Vin Scully a debt I can't repay. I hope a heartfelt "thank you" will suffice.
— *Chip Caray*

The only good thing about interleague play is seeing Scully. In 1997, I interviewed him for our A's-Dodgers pre-game show. "What's broadcasting's essence?" I asked. Instantly: "That you are believable. If you always say everything is great for your team it won't mean anything when something great happens." In 2009, A's pitching coach Curt Young returned to LA for the first time since relieving for Oakland in the 1988 Series. Just before the game, Vin ran to our booth asking if Young had pitched then at Dodger Stadium. As partner Vince Cotroneo accessed the Internet, I ribbed Vin gently: "You're really hustling." He got serious: "This is what we do. We tie it all together. I'd feel terrible if Young went to the mound and I didn't know the last time he'd been on the mound here. Now, I can say that Young pitched in the sixth inning of Game 2 of the World Series and he is back twenty-one years later mentoring the A's pitchers." Believable? Here is Scully, then eighty-one, kicking everybody's butt at preparation when he could easily mail it in.
— *Ken Korach*

In the winter of 2004–2005, hurricanes battered Vero [Beach, longtime Dodgers' training site]. It was my first spring training with the Dodgers. I begin the opener hemmin' and hawin' about the devastation at Holman Stadium, how the new scoreboard had been erected and plugged in just in the nick of time, how the palm trees were a mess, blah, blah, blah. I'm nervous as hell: my first broadcast for the team for whom I wanted to announce since I was a boy. Then, in this wonderfully surrealistic moment, I introduce for the first time the guy I wanted to grow up to be. How cool is this? I'm going to watch and listen to the Maestro. Suddenly Vin goes into this rhapsody about palm trees. Palm trees! The trees that were damaged by the hurricanes. The old trees that didn't make it. The trees that managed to survive. The newly planted trees that just might make it. With a brilliant pause, he says, "Isn't that what spring training is all about?" My jaw dropped. I got up, left the booth for a moment, and took a deep breath. That's why Vin is Vin.

    — *Charley Steiner*

In 1950s and early '60s Connecticut, Mel Allen was all around you. I even announced fungoes in the backyard like Mel. At Christmas, I asked for a Ballantine beer glass to rehearse pouring the Three-Ring Circle. Mel had a great vocabulary, would weave stories, never caught short on a two-strike tale, and had a voice *Variety* Magazine called among the twenty-five "most recognizable in the world." Once, in Omaha, he hailed a taxi at night, the cabbie not seeing who it was. Mel says two words: "Sheraton, please." Pivoting his head, the cabbie almost drives off the road.

    — *Joe Castiglione*

Of all broadcasters in history, Mel may have had the most famous style: that mellifluous Southern voice, charming manner, and good fortune to air the Yankees. Back then the Series featured Voices of the participating teams. Since the Yanks almost always made it [at one point, fourteen pennants in sixteen years], Mel did, too. A hundred years from now, if people want to know what our baseball sounded like, they'll use a CD, DVD, or whatever they have then to hear him. Once a bartender insisted that Mel sign a $5 bill: "Write 'Good luck, George,' and add my name." Allen obliged, noting, "This is illegal." The keep didn't care: "For this, I die."

    — *Bob Wolff*

My dad, the Yankee fan, said that turning the TV or radio on he could tell by Mel's voice if they were ahead or not. In my family Allen was particularly popular, Dad's sister, my aunt, fantasizing aloud about becoming Mel's missus. That sounded great, because his demeanor suggested the perfect uncle: friendly, with a drawl fun to imitate, and passion for ball. We had a Polaroid camera. My mother took the empty black spool, attached it to some string, and tied it around my neck to replicate a microphone, which let me walk around all day and night saying, "Hello there, everybody!" or "How about that!" to no one in particular. In 1961, my father and I were on Yankee Stadium's mezzanine level near the booth. Between innings, Mel went to the bathroom. Seeing this, Dad told me to wait for Mel to come out and ask for his autograph. Clueless, I said, "OK, but what do I *do*?" I give a scorecard and pen to Mel, who couldn't have been nicer, but disappointed by not handing me a photo or drawing a picture. Somehow I didn't grasp the concept of an autograph, so dejectedly I hand Dad the scorecard, saying, "All he did was sign his name!" I thought I'd let him down. Instead, dad formed a how-about-that smile.

—*Howie Rose*

[In 2007, *The Voice* revealed why the Yankees fired Allen, fifty-one, in 1964 after a quarter-century of likely selling more Americans on baseball than any announcer who ever lived.] For years, people speculated, which heightened the mystery. In the early '70s I saw Mel at Yankee Stadium for the first time since he broadcast for the 1965 Milwaukee Braves. I ran into some people from Wisconsin, so I decide to do my pre-game show on them— their first impression of The Stadium. At that moment Allen passes me on the field, saying "Hi, Tom." People gasp. In their minds, I'm now a big-leaguer. Not because of me. Because I knew Mel Allen.

—*Tom Collins*

I did the Yankees in 1987–1988. Nothing like a couple years at The Stadium to validate your career. But I hated it when people introduced me as "Voice of the Yankees." There was only one "Voice of the Yankees," and it wasn't me.

—*Hank Greenwald*

This Red Sox fan found Aaron Boone's October 16, 2003, homer pretty unforgivable. Disliking him as a player, I was ready to dislike Aaron as an announcer until he wanted to meet each team's broadcasters and study the profession before joining it [at ESPN]. As a kid, Aaron idolized Harry Kalas and Richie Ashburn, his road connection to Phils catcher Bob Boone—dad. In 2008, I'm in the clubhouse when Boonie shouts, "Hey, Shul." I didn't know who he was talking to. Again: "Hey, Shul." I said, "Why are you calling me Shul?" He said, knocking me over: "You sound a lot like [ESPN Radio/TV's] Dan Shulman when you broadcast." Scrutinizing games piped into the clubhouse, Aaron made a connection no one else would. At season's end we're in Philly. "You *got* to hear this," he grins. "I just had Harry do my cell phone voicemail." I phone and there's Harry: "Thanks for calling Aaron's phone. Like a 3–1 fastball to his father, Bob, Aaron is out of here." To my knowledge, that was the last time he and Kalas talked. When Harry died, I asked Aaron about the phone greeting. "I'm not going to change it," he said. If you want to hear Harry, give Aaron Boone a call.

    — *Dave Jageler*

Ironically, Harry Kalas reminds me of growing up in Dallas, playing baseball four or five nights a week after Little League games ended but the lights stayed on. Waiting, we heard the Rangers' Mark Holtz and Eric Nadel, so familiar we knew their inside jokes, WBAP's silly theme, its Texas twang pitching Panhandle Slim shirts. One 1991 Friday my freshman year at Southern Methodist University, two friends and I decide to see spring training. Saturday, we're in Winter Haven, Florida, just awake enough to recall Roger Clemens, with the bases full, striking out Rob Deer. At our next stop, the Rangers' Port Charlotte camp, we send a note to the booth on a napkin from the concession stand — all we had — asking Mark and Eric to say hi to Dallas. Incredibly, they do, mentioning our *names*, followed by a crack about mustard on the napkin. I remembered that napkin when Mark died [1997, of bone marrow disease] and Harry passed away. Harry will always be revered in Philadelphia: his work, especially with Richie Ashburn in 1971–1997, maybe its best-ever baseball. Not growing up there, I knew from Mark and Eric how they'd aired some clunkers, but kept you coming back. So many letters after Harry's death, from casual listeners to those who didn't miss a game, hoped that *their* kids, growing up, would discover a "friend" like him. People ask what Harry taught. Mostly how to personally connect, shaking every hand, posing for every picture, or recording a voicemail message ending, "It's Outta Here!" — his home run call — on some kid's phone. Nothing beats baseball for making simple, small connections with fans, day after day, many with mustard-stained napkins of their own.

    — *Scott Franzke*

Ashburn may have been, next to Ben Franklin, the all-time most beloved Philadelphian. Knowing this, he could do anything, and did. Even during innings, you'd hear him shake a popcorn bag, dumping a crunchy handful in his mouth. One night, his call began "ground ball to third," but then Whitey began sounding utterly unintelligible. I jumped in: "He gloves it . . . throws to first in plenty of time . . . two outs." Worried, I said: "Are you OK?" Whitey didn't flinch: "Yep, bit my tongue, and just wanted to have you work on your play-by-play." Whitey didn't believe in preparation, once saying after messing up, "Boys, my fans expect that." And they did, like listening over and over to your favorite comedian do the same routine. A few years back he felt undercompensated for doing pre-game interviews. "Boys, if I screw up enough, maybe they'll take that show away." Sometimes Whitey'd grab the first person he saw: usually, the other team's Voice. Every guest got a watch, Lanny Frattare on so often he threatened to appear wearing our watches on both arms up to each elbow. Another time Whitey held his stopwatch under Marty Brennaman's chin, mike in other hand, where the stopwatch should have been! Fortunately, Marty mentioned this, and they started over. Richie's absentmindedness added to his persona. Packing for one road trip, he got to the park before realizing he'd left his suitcase on the curb.

— *Chris Wheeler*

Pirates 1948–1975 Voice Bob Prince was an unbelievable character: still a bigger baseball presence in Pittsburgh than any person who played there. Bob was named The Gunner when the husband of a woman he was telling a joke to in a bar pulled a gun. He'd blare, "We had 'em allll the way!" and "How sweet it is!" and "You can kiss it [home run] good-bye!" Before satellite radio, you followed a club like my dad did in Connecticut over Pittsburgh's KDKA: at 7:00 o'clock, getting a six-pack when I was pitching, and cruise around town looking for good reception. Finding it, dad'd turn off the car, drink, and listen, each year sending Bob an invoice for three batteries and twenty cases of beer. Bob loved the story, but didn't pay. Later we worked together. My first game, Prince called the press room—alcohol's forbidden in the booth—to say, "Send up two screwdrivers." For a moment, I wondered if there was a bolt loose. Next night Bob strings a series of expletives that would curl your hair. I think, "Oh, my God, it's over, we'll never do another game," not realizing he'd pushed the mute button. No one had heard a word. He looks at me with that Cheshire grin. The Gunner might shoot wildly, but he never shot blanks.

— *Steve Blass*

Tim McCarver, a big-league catcher since 1959, joined the Phillies booth in 1980. Replays were becoming a big part of a telecast, an analyst needing to complement the picture. McCarver also wanted to do play-by-play, so I said he needed to keep score. "*What's that?*" he said. I couldn't believe it. Then it hit me that players didn't sit in the stands, like us. Not surprisingly, learning how wasn't a problem for this voracious reader with a love of English. Once, after he'd dropped some multisyllabic words on the air, I said, "Timmy, I went to journalism school and you ate dirt for a living for twenty years, so why don't you leave big words to me?" We still get a laugh out of the one time I silenced him. Tim was like a concierge, arranging everything — restaurant reservations, wines, after-dinner plans. Harry and I would join him, but most nights Ashburn stayed in his room, saying, "Boys, I'll be in my suite" — he always called his room a suite — "reading a good book and dining with the most interesting person I know — *me*."

— *Chris Wheeler*

Since 1983, I've worked with about 100 play-by-play guys. Ernie, Costas, Dick Enberg, Jim McKay. On ABC, I did *Monday Night Baseball* with Don Drysdale and Uke, its other team Howard Cosell, Al Michaels, Keith Jackson. Not to mention Harry Caray. Before televising the Cubs, Harry was a radio legend over KMOX St. Louis. In 1982, he joins the Cubs, WGN using satellite to become a SuperStation. I join him in time for '84's perfect storm: "Cubs Win!" the NL East. Soon Caray's satirized on *Saturday Night Live*, does "Cub Fan, Bud Man" ads, a regional Voice turned national cult hero. For fifteen years, I was his TV partner: not always a bed of roses, but riveting and usually fun.

Harry taught, "You have to know when the game can speak for itself, and when you have to speak for the game." Score 3–2, it's play-by-play. Eleven-two, third inning, Harry'd make fun of my cigars, anything to keep a viewer. Each day he rode home from the game in his Hyatt Limousine car. Once, seeing a sign, "Seedless Grapes available," he has his driver stop the car. Next day, a dull one-sided affair, Harry starts speaking for the game. "Steve, I got some clusters from this place. Seedless grapes, amazing. How do they do that?"

"A hybrid, I think," I said. "Genetic splicing."

"*What*?" says Harry. "I don't think that's right."

"Alright, you come up with something," I said. A while later a Mr. Thomas, from the Napa Valley, calls up executive producer Arne Harris, saying, "Steve is absolutely right." Arne repeats that view, prompting Harry to accuse Arne and me of setting him up.

This goes on, hilarious, till Harry asks, "Hey, Steve, what do you think of seedless watermelon?" I say, "Uh, Harry, they've had seedless watermelon for some time." By this time, I doubt one viewer thought this game was dull.

— *Steve Stone*

From the start, Tim was warned about Whitey's penchant for saying almost anything, but he loved a good story. One telecast he talks about pitcher Larry Christensen, who'd recently returned to his native Washington State after the eruption of Mount St. Helens. L. C. had brought back some volcanic ash and was showing it to anyone interested, including Timmy, who expressed surprise on air at how smooth the ash was, expecting it to be coarse. Ashburn sat, occasionally saying something, then taking a drag on his trademark pipe. How many times had I witnessed that — and wondered what eventually he'd say? Finally, Whitey said, "Timmy, that's a fascinating story you've just shared with our viewing audience. But to be honest with you, I always thought if you'd seen one piece of ash, you've seen them all." Tim later told me how many thoughts at that moment ran through his head. One was the premature conclusion of his broadcast career. Another was simple incredulity — how could *anyone* get away with saying that on the air? As I said, only Ashburn could, and did.

— *Chris Wheeler*

May 1996, my first year with the Cubs. Harry leaves TV one day to join Ron Santo and me on radio, his purpose to say how well I'd been received:

magnanimous because a giant's blessing helps. That day, Sammy Sosa hits a game-winning homer. On post-game I hear "How about those Cubbies!" in the background — Harry, eighty, still a ten-year-old and a senior citizen. Late in his career, he had trouble with his voice, drinking hot tea and eating lemons to strengthen it. One night, a minute before airtime, he has a tea bag in the cup. They're saying, "Harry, put the tea down! Put your headset on! We're going on the air!" He said, "OK, right there!" Then: "Harry, thirty seconds, come on!" He's trying to get rid of the tea bag, they're handing him the headset, and as Harry puts it on the cord and the tea bag string get tangled. He opens WGN's telecast with a tea bag dangling down from his left ear: "Hello, everybody!" You had to see it to believe it. Another night, trying to face the camera in WGN's booth, he sits on the "cough button" you press to mute a cough. Sound gone, Harry does his post-game show in front of millions of people, none of whom heard a word. You can imagine the screaming in the production truck: "Why can't we hear Harry?" Finally, someone said, "Oh, my gosh, he's sitting on the cough button!" A writer said, "A great man is someone who never reminds us of anyone else." By that criterion, Harry was truly great.

— *Pat Hughes*

In 1982, I join White Sox TV, replacing Harry, off to Wrigley. How do you think Doug DeCinces felt replacing Brooks Robinson? What irony. As a kid in Savannah, I could only *get* Harry on KMOX. I learned from him — and later, from every guy I've worked with. You take A and B from one, C and D another. I learned the most from [White Sox partner] Don Drysdale, debating on and off the air. Once I'm driving, arguing hot and heavy about baseball, when I stop the car, get out, and say, "Let's do it, man." Thank goodness I thought again: Remember how Big D drilled batters? He'd a' drilled *me*! One guy who called all the time was Cosell — "Coach" — wanting me to work with him at ABC. I said no. He asked why. I said, "Because you don't know what the hell you're talking about." Coach laughed and said, "Don't tell anybody." He and Curt Gowdy taught me not to try to please everybody. The only thing I've wanted to do is tick off Cubs fans. As somebody told me, "Hawk, mission accomplished."

— *Ken Harrelson*

I worked with Harry for fifteen years, and am still getting to know Hawk, but my approach is the same. Remember Gavin MacLeod — terrific as Murray — on the *Mary Tyler Moore Show*? His part changed from week to week. One week he's on ten minutes, next five: either way, it's Mary's show. Same now: it's my job to adjust to them, not them to me. Unlike Harry, Hawk played the game, was great analyzing hitting strokes, close to guys like Carl Yastrzemski and Ted Williams. Thirty seconds into a conversation about civil war in China, you know, and Hawk's quoting "Teddy." His challenge was to take that to play-by-play. Like Harry, Hawk has idiosyncrasies: the Southern dialect, catchphrases. Plus, I've loved each guy's passion for their team, crucial to being accepted locally. [Once, after a Red Sox loss, Bob Starr said of Joe Castiglione: "My partner is sitting here, looking like he's been harpooned."]

— *Steve Stone*

Like Harry, Ron Santo was a wonderful piece of work. We're in the lunchroom at Arizona's park. A yogurt machine sign says, "Do not turn on until game time," so I don't. Ron, however, figures, "I can't wait until the game because I'm working once it starts, and besides I'm Ron Santo." He turns the machine on, fills the cup with yogurt, and is pleased till finding he can't turn it off, yogurt spilling on the counter. Panicking, cursing liberally, Ron starts shaking the machine, everyone laughing at this absolute spectacle. Soon yogurt's spilling on the floor, so Ron did what any mature eighth-grader would do, knowing he'd done wrong. He ran away, and let someone else clean up the mess. One cold April night at Shea Stadium, we stand for the National Anthem. Right above our heads in the visiting booth is an electric heater. Ron, who went prematurely bald, gets too close to it and halfway through the song I smell something burning. Sure enough, Ron's hairpiece is on fire! Smoke is billowing out the top of his head! So I do what any good partner would do — splash water on his head to put the fire out! He said, "How does it look?" I lied: "Not that bad." Actually, there was a *divot* in the middle of his head, like Phil Mickelson had taken a pitching wedge and whacked his noggin. A final irony you won't believe: The Mets' starting pitcher was Al Leiter.

— *Pat Hughes*

At '80s KMOX, in one day you'd see Jack Buck, hockey's Dan Kelly, and Bob Costas, who did a talk show and pro basketball, helping it dominate radio's pre-all-sports age. Bob aired *The Sporting News Report* and *Sports Flashback* series. Randy Karraker, now St. Louis sports talk host, wrote them, and I produced. KMOX had an incredible library of old play-by-play, and amazingly Bob didn't want a script, just bullet points, improvising to augment the call. For guys starting out, it was incredible to watch. Bob'd ad-lib, then say, "No, I didn't like it, let's do it again." Randy and I were on the other side of the glass, saying, "How can he do that again and make it *better*?" Incredibly, Bob's next take *was* better, using photographic memory to weave fact and tale.

— *Charlie Slowes*

Last week, 1998 regular season: the Cubs, Mets, and Giants neck and neck for the wild card. Leftfielder Brant Brown drops a fly that leads to three unearned Milwaukee runs — and a devastating Cubs defeat. Ron's call is a legend. As I say, "Brown goes back and he drops the ball!," Ronnie bellows "Oh, no!" — a hideous scream — like a guy losing a family member. I look at Ron, his forehead practically glued to the table. For a minute, I thought he had expired, jabbing him with my finger to see if he was alive. He was. Afterward, Ron is still in manager Jim Riggleman's office as I finish the post-game show. He's had a beverage or two, still despondent, saying, "How could he drop the ball in that situation?!" I then see what perhaps has never occurred in American sports history. Riggleman puts his arm around Ronnie, saying, "Hang in there, we're going to Houston, we can beat the Astros and still make the playoffs." I had to look away, thinking, "I just saw a *manager* trying to cheer up a *broadcaster*. I don't think Tommy Lasorda ever tried to cheer up Vin Scully; Whitey Herzog, Jack Buck; or Mike Ditka, any broadcaster with the Bears."

— *Pat Hughes*

As an East Baltimorean, I hope people know of our great baseball Voices: Ernie Harwell, Bob Murphy, Herb Carneal, Bill O'Donnell, Joe Angel, Jon Miller — and Chuck Thompson. When I got the O's job, Chuck showed how he knew Baltimore. "You have a special privilege," he said. "People

take you to baptisms, confirmations, at the beach, on the Chesapeake Bay: you're part of them." As a kid, my Colts kicked off at 2:00 o'clock every Sunday. Not everyone had air conditioning. People opened their windows in September and October, and you'd hear Chuck *everywhere*: old-shoe, that beguiling tone, the phrases. One was "Go to War, Miss Agnes!" borrowed from a golfing neighbor who never swore and used it when he missed a putt. The other pleased his sponsors: when the Orioles won, "Ain't the beer cold!" Add what Ernie called "the greatest voice in sports broadcasting history." Jon says he never cared what Chuck said— as long as Chuck said it.
— *Fred Manfra*

When I joined the Royals, our Voice was legendary Buddy Blattner. Sometimes, about to start a game in front of a small crowd, playing on the West Coast with games starting in the Midwest at 9:35, or any other game with people disguised as empty seats, Buddy would cry before taking the air: "Hi, anybody!" Nobody answered.
— *Denny Matthews*

Bob Uecker remains unbelievably recognizable. People even more famous want to meet Uke and hang around. Late-1980s Yankee Stadium: George Steinbrenner had a private box behind home plate, inviting actors and luminaries and diplomats. One night we get a note from Richard Nixon, rather well known himself, requesting Mr. Uecker's presence. On the monitor, I soon see Bob, Nixon, and Steinbrenner all laughing at Uke's stories. Next night we get another note from Mr. Steinbrenner's box. Joe DiMaggio would like Mr. Uecker's presence. On the monitor, I soon see Bob talking and the Yankee Clipper laughing. Uke let me meet a lot of people I'd never have met otherwise. A final note on meeting Richard Nixon. Afterward, I said on air, "How'd it go?" Bob said, "You know what, Richie was a pretty good guy." *Richie*!? Richard Nixon was an incredibly controversial person who was called every name in the book: Mr. President; Richard, Richard Milhous, Dick; by some, Tricky Dick. But never *Richie*!
— *Pat Hughes*

In 2009, the Astros hosted Milwaukee in a game that featured the home team batting out of order. Houston's Michael Bourn's leadoff hit prompts

Brewers skipper Ken Macha to come out of the dugout. Macha's and the official lineup's cards have Kazuo Matsui, not Bourn, leading off, so the umpires rule Matsui out and make Bourn hit again. In the Astros Spanish radio booth, Alex Trevino says he'd *never* seen that before—except lo and behold, he had. It turns out the last Astro to bat out of order had been in 1989. The second batter got a hit, but batted in the incorrect spot, and therefore was put out. Guess who he was? Alex Trevino! Next day Trevino was asked about it, *still* not remembering. At Minute Maid Park, glass windows divide the road and home booth. Uke's always funny, even without material like this. Looking over, I still see him laughing. Bob may not have batted well, but never batted out of order.

—*Brett Dolan*

Bob *literally* stops traffic. After home games, the traffic cop, raising his hand, changes the stoplight from red to green so Uke makes the highway onramp. Right behind, I raise my hand, too, more to apologize for running the light that quickly changes back to red. In spring 2010, I anxiously told our TV audience that Bob would require major heart surgery. Uke was concerned, saying he didn't want to "take a dixie on the road!" We were concerned, too, not wanting him to take a "dixie" anywhere. Bob asked us to keep things light, and we did, yet felt his void in the days before surgery and months in recovery. [Uecker returned to the booth July 23, doctors who performed his operation throwing out the first pitch. "I hope they do better," he joked, "than they did on my incision." In October, Bob underwent further successful surgery to repair a tear from the previous valve replacement.]

—*Brian Anderson*

[Of thirty-five Ford C. Frick honorees, a team-high seven have aired the Giants.] Their broadcast tradition dates back to New York: Russ Hodges, Lon Simmons, Ernie, Hank Greenwald, Al Michaels, Jon Miller, Duane Kuiper, Mike Krukow— wow—setting an impossibly high standard, but making fans so devoted we have license to be creative. Jon and I go way back to when I grew up in Washington and he did the Orioles. Despite my bitterness that DC didn't have a team, I reluctantly rooted for his. Fast-forward eighteen years to the Giants. My first game with Jon I told myself this must be how Vin Scully felt when the Dodgers hired him at twenty-two to join Red Barber. Probably the most I'll ever have in common with Vin.

—*Dave Flemming*

I could say Krukow and Kuiper work Giants games, except that it doesn't seem like work: the ex-teammate clubhouse-prankster sensibilities at their best when the team played at Candlestick. Before any night game, Kruk and Kuip augmented standard broadcast prep with a ritual of paper shredding. Walking by their booth and seeing them simultaneously tear paper into quarters, you'd think they were discarding old notes—until they breathlessly continued another fifteen minutes. When the wind was right, Kruk and Kuip would toss the paper from their booth, knowing that it would blow exactly two booths to the right into the visitors': a tickertape parade. They made a mess, but had better aim than some Giants pitchers.

—*Matt Vasgersian*

I joined the A's in 1996, Bill King's sixteenth as their Voice: apt, having long admired his staccato rhythm, passion, railing at officials, and preparation. At one time, Bill aired all three Bay Area big-league teams. Even growing up in LA, I fell asleep to his hoops play-by-play. Before our first game, Bill, I, and analyst Ray Fosse had dinner, barely past the appetizer when Bill laid down the law, like an intimidating teacher whose class you dreaded because he'd call on you when you were unprepared. Good news: except for three things, I could do what I wanted. Bad: the three things. First, "Don't thank me when I throw it to you for one of your innings." To Bill, it sounded phony—anyway, fans would soon know who we were. Second, he forbade saying "early on," the "on" being superfluous. Finally, never was I to say "grand slam home run," the "home run" repetitive. Bill often entered the booth in the decade we worked together bent out of shape hearing a Voice misuse the term. We lost Bill in October 2005 to complications from hip surgery. A week later a memorial service was held in the Oakland Arena. Each of Bill's three pro teams was asked to eulogize him. The Warriors picked former player and coach Al Attles. Al Davis spoke on behalf

of the Raiders. The A's asked me. Ending my speech, I violated one of Bill's rules. I thanked him, pretty sure he wouldn't mind.
— *Ken Korach*

[The ordinary Voice says, "There's a ground ball to the shortstop, who fields it and throws to first." Never ordinary, the Reds' 1942–1965 Waite Hoyt announced in past tense: "The shortstop fielded it, threw to first, and the runner beat the throw."] Waite broadcast in an age before kids had TVs in their rooms, my friend a 1960s old-style, box-shaped, clock radio. Here I found Reds players like Pete Rose, Tony Perez, Lee May, and Vada Pinson— some lineup—and Crosley Field, Forbes Field, Dodger Stadium, and the Astrodome—some world. After Hoyt, Jim McIntyre and Joe Nuxhall connected me to uncles with transistors at family picnics and led me to pester my parents to turn on the car radio. In high school, I graduated to my own transistor on a *Cincinnati Post & Times-Star* paper route, accompanied by a very young Al Michaels. On opening day 1974, now a senior, I drove a 1966 Mercury Comet home from school as Hank Aaron tied the Babe's career home run mark. Joining me: Marty Brennaman, in his first big-league game. In 1988, I filled in with Marty and Joe, Marty still doing radio today with son Thom, who's also on TV. In 2010, I aired Reds Fox Sports Ohio TV play-by-play, but the kid in me is glad that radio still casts its spell.
— *Paul Keels*

[Brennaman and Nuxhall almost *were* the 1974–2004 Reds. In Marty-speak, "frog strangler" meant tense game; "Grand Tour," dinger; "hit of the two-base variety," double. The Reds turned into "Redlegs"; Mets, "Metropolitans"; Astros, "Astronomicals." Joe was born in nearby Hamilton, Ohio, became the bigs' youngest player at fifteen, and squabbled with Marty, a writer said, "like an old married couple" on WLW's seven-state network.] My first bigs year the Brewers didn't daily televise, so I had days off to sit in the press box or radio booth, where there's never a day off. In Cincinnati, this let me listen to Marty and Joe, whom I'd heard breaking in on the Reds' Huntington/Ashland/Ironton affiliate, radio meaning more to the Reds than it does to most teams. This night, it began raining, and Marty's rain delay theater spun yarns of Milwaukee being the coldest place he'd ever visited. Listening in the back of the booth, I couldn't help but notice that Nuxie was out cold, head resting comfortably, fast asleep. Just as Marty seemed to be approaching empty, a groggy Nuxhall leaned forward, said "Put another log on the fire," slumped back into his chair, closed his eyes, and again fell asleep, having rekindled Marty's anecdotal blaze.

— *Matt Vasgersian*

This marks my twenty-second year at Turner Sports, where I've aired the Olympics to virtually every major sport, including, of course, baseball — and worked with a memorable assortment of athletes, from Charles Barkley — calling me "a nerd with a huge forehead" — to Cal Ripken Jr., David Wells, Dennis Eckersley, and, of course, my father. Dad likes to self-deprecatingly joke about his career, but Ernie Johnson was a pretty darn good relief pitcher with the '50s Boston and Milwaukee Braves. I was one year old when the Braves won the 1957 World Series, but Dad's line score is in the scrapbook my mom, Lois, put together: three games, seven innings, one run, two hits, one walk, eight Ks. Later, his second career gave me a broadcast education as I tagged with him to the park. Dad being Dad meant preparing, spending endless time around the cage, and talking with fans who waved from the seats, yelled his name, and for thirty-five years invited him into their homes, front porches, and cars — Braves viewers and listeners.

In the mid-'90s, Atlanta regional cable outlet SportSouth asked if I could work occasional games with a legend who happened to be my father. I can't describe the feeling, except that our few seasons at the mike are the highlight of my career. In 1999, Dad did his last game, our family behind us in the booth. I said, "I speak for all those Braves fans out there by saying thanks for all you've meant to so many people for so many years. When I grow up, I wanna' be just like you." Dad kept it light, as always focusing on the Braves, ending with his signature farewell: "This is Ernie Johnson, and on this winning night, so long everybody." Last year I did the Braves on Peachtree TV with Joe Simpson and John Smoltz and national Sunday TBS with John, Buck Martinez, David Wells, or Ron Darling. And with Dad: specifically, his 1954 Braves baseball card, next to my scorebook and game notes, which I bought one day at a card store for $7.50.

I know that in Cumming, Georgia, he and my mom are tuned in. When the Braves win a local telecast I use his signoff—"and on this winning night, so long everybody"—borrowed without Dad's permission, but with his blessing and my love.

—*Ernie Johnson Jr.*

Born in Massachusetts, Jack Buck tried to picture the Green Monster listening to the Red Sox' Fred Hoey as a kid. Later, he brought that power of description to the booth. We can recite Russ Hodges's call of Bobby Thomson; Milo Hamilton, Hank Aaron; Phil Rizzuto, Roger Maris. But if I had to pick a favorite home run call, give me Jack in 1985's NLCS Game 5. The Series was tied in games and score: 2-all, bottom of the ninth. Leading off for St. Louis, Ozzie Smith had never homered in 2,967 major league lefthand at-bats. "Smith corks one into right!" Jack said. "Down the line! It may go! . . . Go crazy, folks! Go crazy! It's a home run and the Cardinals have won the game by the score of 3 to 2 on a home run by The Wizard! Go crazy!" Dramatic, accurate, a wonderful rise to his voice, then dramatic pause before *Go crazy!* I still do, listening.

—*Pat Hughes*

I grew up with this game as a constant background and soundtrack for my life. I was born in spring training in 1969 in St. Petersburg, Florida. That is my birthplace because that is where the St. Louis Cardinals trained. If they had trained in Norman, Oklahoma, that is where I would have come out crying. My father was the Cardinals' play-by-play Voice, and from the day I was able to consciously keep my voice volume low, without constantly having to be reminded, I was with him in the booth. I followed him down to the field. I followed him into the clubhouse. I followed him into the parking lot after games, and held his beer while he signed autographs for fans he delighted from spring to fall, year after year. I've been asked what baseball means to me. Baseball is that which bound me to the man I most admired.

—*Joe Buck*

My dad Joe is a Red Sox announcer. Joe Buck's father, Jack, aired baseball for forty-eight years. One day I said, "Joe, were you ever doing something in high school or college that you shouldn't be doing when you hear your father's voice on radio and tell yourself, 'Whoops, I shouldn't be doing this?'" I wasn't graphic, but Joe laughed mischievously: something only the kid of an announcer would grasp. At the beach or a grocery or convenience store, I'd hear dad following me, on one radio after another! People talk about an inner voice. Mine was outer. There was no escaping him, not that I'd want to, of course.

— *Duke Castiglione*

[In 2010, Dick Enberg, calling baseball "magical," began Padres play-by-play after a quarter-century of other sports. Airing the '70s Angels, he welcomed a guest to the booth.] At the time I was doing the Angels' Triple-A Salt Lake team. After the game, I came back, got a guard to reopen the booth, and just sat in Dick's chair. I didn't stay long—just long enough. I said to myself, "I can do this," looking around the empty ballpark, and thankfully I did.

— *Jerry Howarth*

Tony Kubek was a great analyst, honest, smart, fearless, deservedly in the Hall of Fame. Having done *Game of the Week* with him from 1983–1989, however, I learned two things. First, as people know, Tony's playing career was shortened by Bill Virdon's famous bad-hop 1960 World Series ground ball that hit him in the throat. Once, referencing Virdon's smash, I felt Tony put his hand on my thigh to stop me. I relented so that circulation would resume. Second, Tony called Curt Gowdy his favorite [1969–1975] NBC partner. I've tried not to take offense.

— *Bob Costas*

White House, 1986. Several friends of Ken Coleman's and mine in the Secret Service help arrange lunch in the Roosevelt Room, accompanied by a Red Sox party. We're told no photos, above all, no recordings. Someone forgot to tell Ken. Then–Vice President Bush comes in, reminiscing about playing ball at Yale. Next, President Reagan enters at his theatrical best, talking about movies, especially 1952's *The Winning Team* about Grover Cleveland Alexander. Reagan had played Alex; Doris Day, his wife. Ken, knowing the script by heart, has a recorder, determined to tape the Gipper. Questions start, and Ken's is a doozie. In the film, Alex in relief strikes out Tony Lazzeri to save Game 7. How, Ken asks, did Doris Day take a cab all the way from mid-Manhattan to Yankee Stadium while Alex trudges from the pen? "Well, ah," Reagan says, a couple more questions, and lunch adjourns. The Secret Service must have seen the recorder, but didn't say anything. That night the taped president guested on Ken's pre-game show. With security, it could never happen now. Like most Sox fans, Ken and Ned Martin liked things the way they were. Ken's musical knowledge ended around 1953. Ned would listen on the plane, headphone on, channeling Sinatra, singing. Ned made the Sox from Duke via Iwo Jima. One moment he'd call Ted Williams "Big Guy," then quote Shakespeare: "Good night, sweet prince." Dick Williams introduced them to California's Crescent—renamed "Hard Bellies"—Beach, seals everywhere, great surf. In Anaheim, we'd go each day: Ken snorkeling, Ned diving and taking pictures. A clubhouse guy said, "There they go—two sixty-year-olds and a forty-year-old, playing in the sand." Like *The Winning Team*, in Boston a time warp works fine.

— *Joe Castiglione*

Ken was patrician, but exceedingly giving. In 1980, I join the Red Sox, who air almost every exhibition game. Driving around Florida, I tell him my repertoire of tales about Scully, Yankees PA Voice Bob Sheppard, like people around a water cooler. On opening day, there's a rain delay at Fenway, everyone listening to the *Sawx*. "In Florida," Ken says out of the blue, "you did this great Vin Scully impression. Do that!" Surprised? I freak out! I'd never done it on the air! On the spot, I recall the eighty-eight stations on our network and conclude I probably can't refuse. For an hour I talk till the game resumes. Back at my hotel, I find a pile of telegrams. Channel 4 puts me on the main newscast, the sportscaster saying, "I'm sitting on the Southeast Expressway, at 4:30 a parking lot, and I hear your Scully bit and even though I'm not moving I almost drove off the road. Do Scully," he says. I say, "Thank you very much." That week *The Boston Globe* critic Jack Craig writes: "Boston Welcomes New Voice[s]." I'd just been goofing around and I'm now invited to banquets and luncheons because of Ken. "I think you have something not many people have," he said, like a brother, "and you should do it on the air."

— *Jon Miller*

In New Hampshire, of our four TV stations, only one aired the Red Sox, so I spent boyhood nights in the kitchen, Ken everywhere: '67's Impossible Dream, Roger Clemens' twenty-strikeout single game, and Dave Henderson's 1986 playoff blast: "a beautiful horn," said Boston Bruins announcer Bob Wilson, "and, oh, he played it well." My parents said to reach for the stars. At twelve, I did, saying I wanted to air the Sox. Soonafter we moved to LA., hearing the Angels' Bob Starr, before I came back to Northeastern, taking a class from Joe Castiglione, who made me booth statistician in 1989—Ken's final year. Under *surreal*: Ken ends it by thanking me on air, succeeded by the burly baritone—Bob Starr! Graduating, I make the minors, getting a 2001 three-game Fenway callup: No matter what happened, I'd reached my parents' stars. Three months later NESN made me the Sox TV regular, its horn beautiful, too.

— *Don Orsillo*

I like the old style of broadcasting: humor, fact, some opinion, and wearability, drawing you in, not blabbing wall-to-wall. One such practitioner was the Blue Jays' Tom Cheek, Canada's longtime baseball Voice who tragically died in 2005. On July 23, 2004, Tom and I did a pre-game radio interview: his first game on the air after major brain surgery the day before his sixty-fifth birthday. We were in Toronto, but since he and his wife, Shirley, lived in the Tampa Bay area, they knew well wishers were likely listening. Tom spoke freely about his condition, optimistically about chemotherapy, and gratefully about the many who sent get well cards, letters, and e-mails. As a broadcaster, he gave the listener a chance to absorb and consider information. Tom showed how the old style works, less really *being* more.

— *Paul Olden*

By twelve, knowing I'd never wear a big-league uniform unless I bought one, I began to absorb every utterance of broadcasting's 1962–1978 Mets trio, later trying to incorporate each in my work, like Mets blue and orange derived from the Brooklyn Dodgers and New York Giants, respectively. Lindsey Nelson was magnificent at relating drama, his ninth inning different from the fifth, which differed from the first: more animated, quicker rhythm. If Mel Allen's voice told you which team was winning, Lindsey's told you the game's stage. Ralph Kiner was infamous for malapropisms — Howard Johnson became Walter Johnson; Marv Throneberry, Marv Strawberry; Gary Carter, Gary Cooper — but should be famous for storytelling, having a notebook with handwritten tales about seemingly every player: like the Marines, prepared. Bob Murphy *was* a Marine, rarely speaking of World War II but receiving the U.S. flag that flew on his birthday over the Iwo Jima Memorial. All you need to know was his phone number's last four digits — 6-3-8-7 spelled Mets — or how a dead tired Murph once signed into a hotel, "Robert E. Mets." At seventy-nine, Bob couldn't outlast death, but did outlast 112 Mets third basemen.

—*Howie Rose*

Raised in Oklahoma and Missouri, Murph brought to New York a grace, gentleness, and certain folksiness rooted in another time and place. A pop-up near the plate prompted, "It could have been hit in a silo." A fielder dropping a ball evoked, "That's why they put erasers on pencils." What happened in 1990 was so unlike the Murph we knew that it made a splash in a way no one imagined. The Mets led in the ninth, 10–3, before the Phillies rallied on a series of seeing-eye grounders on Veteran Stadium's Astroturf. John Franco relieved Wally Whitehurst with the score 10–9 and bases loaded. Tommy Herr then smoked the inning's first hard-hit ball to shortstop Mario Diaz, who caught it to end the game. What came out of Murph's mouth after this accumulation of events was "The Mets win! *They win the damn game by a score of 10 to 9!*" If you listen to the tape, I'm cackling in the background due to irony — after rinky-dink hits, the only drive's an out — and incongruity, *damn* the last word you'd expect from this most sweet and gallant Voice. In a sense, what's still known as "The Damn Game" defined the latter stages of Bob's career, bringing publicity that he'd not heretofore received.

—*Gary Cohen*

Ralph Kiner has been called many things, but never dull. Overweight, Terry Forster lost fifteen pounds because "his wife slept in front of the refrigerator. *She* gained fifteen pounds." Ralph said that another pitcher, Rick Sutcliffe, "does interior designing on the side." Partner Fran Healy was puzzled, so Ralph explained that, breaking chairs, "Rick redesigned Tommy Lasorda's office." Some lines were planned: "Statistics are like bikinis. They show a lot but not everything." Some clearly weren't. "The Mets didn't do well in the month of Atlanta." Tim McCarver calls "Mr. Kiner's ways wondrous." They are.

—*Howie Rose*

We're at Wrigley Field: Mets-Cubs. Spotting a nearby rooftop wedding, I turn to Ralph, who once dated actresses Elizabeth Taylor and Janet Leigh, for advice. "If the game gets rained out, does the wedding count?" I asked. Ralph didn't hesitate. "Only if it goes five innings."

—*Tim McCarver*

New York knows Ralph primarily as a Mets broadcaster since 1962. Before that, he was not only one of the great home run hitters of all time but an all-time great with the ladies. As Tim McCarver noted, among Ralph's one-time paramours was Janet Leigh, whose daughter is also a successful actress, Jamie Lee Curtis. Some years ago the Mets were in Philadelphia, and after the game Ralph was in the press lounge with his wife. Eventually, Ms. Curtis walked in, and Ralph remarked to Mrs. Kiner that he used to date Jamie's mom. DiAnn Kiner encouraged her husband to approach Jamie and introduce himself, so he did, saying, "Jamie, my name is Ralph Kiner and I dated your mom back in the 1950s." Immediately, with no prior warning of this introduction, Jamie Lee Curtis threw her arms around a stunned Ralph and yelled, "Daddy!" It was one of the few times Ralph was badly fooled and caught looking.

—*Howie Rose*

I did my first major-league game in 1953, have worked in a record fifty-nine big-league parks, been with the Astros since 1985. I coined *Ryno* for Ryne Sandberg. My mother somehow found twenty-five cents a week for a singing lesson. I'm not sure it got me to the Hall of Fame, but it didn't hurt. In January 1992, I'm home on a Friday afternoon when the phone rings. The voice on the other end didn't give his name, but I recognized it, because we talk so often: Bill Guilfoile, once head of Pirates', now Coopers-town's, PR. Due to our closeness, the Hall asked him if he'd like to make the call. Bill doesn't say hello, just "I'd like to speak to the newest member of the Baseball Hall of Fame." I'm alone, my wife's out playing bridge, and it came out of the blue. He said: "We're not announcing this till Monday." I said, "Well, can I tell my wife when she gets home, then my son?" Bill says, "Oh, yes." I call my son in Atlanta, playing the same trick on him that Guil-foile did on me. "Mark, do you know any airplanes that fly from Atlanta to Cooperstown?" I was so high by then, I didn't need a plane.

　—*Milo Hamilton*

Jerry Coleman is a living legend in San Diego, and in baseball gener-ally. His nickname is "The Colonel" because Jerry was an Air Force Lieu-tenant Colonel in World War II and Korea, flying 120 bombing missions. He's 1949 Associated Press Rookie of the Year, plays 1949–1957 with the Yankees, makes the World Series every year but one, and is 1950 Classic MVP. He enters broadcasting: CBS, the Yankees, Angels, and Padres, calls more batting titles than any National League announcer—nine, eight Tony Gwynn's—and even invents a language. ["Here's the 2–1 delivery. Strike 3, he's out!"] In 1981, Jerry called a Tokyo-Taiyo game during the baseball strike for U.S. syndication. Partner Lindsey Nelson was impressed, saying, "Colemanisms even work in Japanese!"

　—*Mark Neely*

Chapter Eleven

Our House

In 1956, Robert Creamer called baseball "bound by certain hard unities: nine innings, three outs, one pennant. Within these unities baseball presents a variety as endless as the waves of the ocean, as intricate as a fugue by Bach." Its ballpark fugue binds three unities, or acts: the urban plant, Stepford mausolea, and coming back to a future of look, sound, and feel.

For a half-century after 1908, in ten big-league cities, on fifteen fields, the Golden Age of Parks knocked boredom down. Fenway Park had the Wall; Crosley Field, a berm; Yankee Stadium, Death Valley. Each was heavy with individuality. "Across America entire cities revolved around them," said Larry King, growing up near Brooklyn's Ebbets Field.

Through Ike, ballparks prized quirk and angle — "anything can happen here!" more dead-on than cliché. Then, Suburban-Ho: Baseball threw a 1960s through '80s curve, trading creativity for sterility. Out: being able to almost touch the field. In: antiseptic clones, with faux grass, vast foul turf, bad sight lines, and seats in another county.

"When I'm at bat, I can't tell where I am," Richie Hebner said as football stadia snatched baseball's soul: Three Rivers, Kingdome, and Olympic Stadium's Big O, as in zero. In 1992, act three began at Baltimore's Oriole Park at Camden Yards, built on the site of Ruth's Cafe, owned by George Herman Ruth Sr. "When this park is complete," the late commissioner Bart Giamatti had said, "every team is going to want one."

An arch facade mimes Comiskey Park; triple-tiered leftfield, The Bronx; right-field wall, Flatbush USA. Beyond right, a restored B&O Railroad Warehouse *looms, the Yards' frame of reference, like houses near Wrigley Field. Since 1992, twenty-one new parks have tried to match it. Coming closest: Houston, San Francisco, Seattle, and Pittsburgh, the Allegheny River flowing slowly to the sea.*

Each is scene and actor, like the deceased Shibe Park, Griffith Stadium, and Polo Grounds' Sahara of a centerfield. When Frank Sinatra sang, "There used to be a ballpark," he bespoke shrines—it may off-put; no other word will do—in which it mattered where you played. "We shape our buildings," Churchill said. "Thereafter, they shape us."

Kids today can't grasp not daily seeing their favorite team on TV. They won't believe it, but a world once existed where radio was all we needed because the listener participated. Living in New York I grew up a Giants fan, which meant Russ Hodges and Ernie Harwell, who evoked awe and wonder. To me, that was especially true when the Giants hit the road. Each game I opened my copy of their yearbook to a page showing an aerial view of the park. When the Giants played in Cincinnati, I'd eye Crosley Field as Russ noted the "laundry" behind the leftfield wall or rightfield "sun" or "moon deck." In Boston, I stared transfixed at Braves Field's tiny bleachers called "The Jury Box," as in twelve-person size. Russ made Forbes Field mean Schenley Park; Wrigley Field, ivy; Ebbets Field, the high wall in right; Sportsman's Park, a large centerfield. Each photo left me mesmerized. If radio was *my* friend, imagination was *radio's*.

—*Dick Stockton*

At Griffith Stadium, a select audience including the White House, navy, army, and other federal officials watched and listened. One time an army colonel called: "Bob, last night, third inning, foul behind the first-base dugout." I knew what was coming: "I made that catch," he said, wanting me to name him. "Tell you what," I said. "Keep me posted on your future baseball exploits." Griffith's *biggest* day was *opening* day. With everyone watching, I couldn't afford a muff. Before the game, players stood near the presidential box, hustling for the first-ball lob. I'd say, "Which player will get it?" I felt pressure like the president's to throw a strike. A rare win and I'd say, "Amazing. *Washington leads the league!*" Next day, we're at .500. By the second week we were already so bad I never said who was ahead, just gave the score: 5–3, 10–5, 4–2. You knew who was winning, and it wasn't the Senators.

— *Bob Wolff*

In Texas we do things big. Our first year [1962], the Colt .45s trained near Arizona's Superstition Mountain, where Indian spirits and a Dutchman's ghost were said to guard lost gold. Geronimo's warriors roamed there. Our first uniforms were as wild, owner Roy M. Hofheinz making the team wear western outfits with black cowboy hats and boots, an orange tie, and white shirts with red and blue baseball stitching. Players hated them, but fit right in. Doug Rader later used the clubhouse as a driving range. Turk Farrell put snakes in players' lockers. In 1965, the first domed all-purpose stadium — the Astrodome — opened with a roof, air conditioning, and skyboxes. Glare from the ceiling made it hard to catch fly balls, so Hofheinz applied a blue translucent acrylic to the roof. On one hand, this cured not seeing flies. On the other, daylight was cut, killing grass bred for indoor use. That led to artificial grass, displeasing Richie Allen, who said. "I don't want to play on no place my horse can't eat off of." Big.

— *Gene Elston*

Shea Stadium was christened with Holy Water from Brooklyn's Gowanus Canal and the Harlem River at the point it passed the Polo Grounds. It may not be the prettiest ballpark ever, but it might have been the grandest of its time. In 1964, Shea and the next-door World's Fair opened in Flushing Meadows. To this six-year-old growing up in Queens, the park's incredible size and scope, like the Ford and General Motors pavilions, meant the possibility of tomorrow. Driving by, you saw Shea's speckles, as I called them. Inside, an expanse of field stretched as far as the eye could see. Later, most new parks had bleacher seats encircling them. By contrast, at Shea you could *gaze* forever, then turn around and see stands seem to go *up* forever. In 1969, I watched the Mets sweep the LCS from Section 48 in left field, five rows from the top. Was Shea great art? No. But for grandeur it was tough to beat.

— *Gary Cohen*

Most new parks put the press box somewhere between the clouds and the foul poles. I liked it better in places like Shea before it yielded in 2009 to Citi Field: the press box low and between home and first base, prime foul ball ground. In the minors, I used a giant fishing net to catch fouls. At Shea, I needed it out of sheer self-preservation, knowing if you didn't catch the ball it would likely hit the wall and club you in the head. Sure enough, Mark Loretta spanked a liner in my direction, giving me a split second to grab the net and attempt a play. Instead, the ball hit the net's rim and deflected into my lip and mouth. New York fans cheered, then groaned. I groaned, too, seeing blood leaking from my mouth. Dave Raymond took over play-by-play while medics put gauze in my mouth, complicating play-by-play. A bubble inside my lip from the beaning is my lasting souvenir from dear demolished Shea.

— *Brett Dolan*

I was a man—really, boy—in red before I broadcast the Big Red at Busch Stadium—ushers, like announcers, baseball's face to the fan. I'd get asked about seat location, concession stands, meeting people from Arkansas, Tennessee, Oklahoma. Even in the 1970s, you had to be at least sixteen to apply. Our ushers spent game time on the field: three innings behind a wall door in right and leftfield, at the end of the dugout on a folding seat, and on a bullpen chair farther beyond it.

Once Ron Fairly hit a foul at me. I dive and fall on my face, the ball hitting where my face had been. Fans booed me for bailing out, but wouldn't if they knew about Jerry Reuss. One game the Expos' Bill Stoneham hit Richie Allen, who walked to the mound, benches emptying. I look into the Cardinals dugout, see the only player *not* on the field, and tell a photographer, "Look at that!" He snaps the picture. Next morning's *Globe-Democrat* page 1 showed two photos—the brawl, and Reuss! Fast-forward twenty years. Working with Jerry on ESPN, I tell the story and he's flabbergasted. "*You're* the guy who caused that picture. I've been waiting to *deck* you." Next time we worked together he brought in his scrapbook and there they were—The Brawl and Mr. Reuss—ushering now full circle, full life.

— *Bob Carpenter*

In 1976–1980, the Royals won the AL West every year but one. Royals Stadium was electric. One night they're behind by four or five runs before rallying. Suddenly, my partner Fred White and I see a gangly fellah standing on the third-base dugout, dancing, waving, fired up possibly with a few adult beverages. Two policemen motion for him to come over, like a parent to a child. We looked at the field, then back at our friend, escorted by the officers toward the back of the lower level, likely headed for the slammer, arms hanging around the officers' shoulders like they're long, lost buddies. Suddenly, amused, the policemen stop to ask a question, our guy pointing eight rows up to an empty seat. Next to it sits a woman who's clearly embarrassed, got her head in her hands, obviously his wife or lady friend. The officers say something to her and she shakes her head: "Yes, that's my guy." He sits down and the gal keeps shaking. I doubt that at that moment she thought that opposites attract.

—*Denny Matthews*

I've been with the Red Sox for almost thirty years, and every day it's still a thrill to go to Fenway. It would be a great place to play hide-and-seek. Most fans never see the passageways and shortcuts: a little door that leads behind the scoreboard, up the back staircase for player interviews, or into the batting cages or even bullpen. And what this grand old park brings to the game! First, the Wall. I always have to wait longer before I call a home run or not. No one can control Fenway, meaning unpredictability. Want the ball to travel well? Hope the wind blows out. Want to see a fielder stretched to his limit? Try a ball hit to the Triangle. Want a grounder over first to go for an inside-the-park homer? You've come to the right place. I call Fenway my office. I never tire of seeing fans who arrive hours before a game. I love knowing the ushers and groundskeepers. I always look for that one peanut vendor who's been there forever and the sausage guy across the street. They're all part of the feeling of a city neighborhood, which continues inside the park. My favorite image always thrills me. When I come back from a road trip, I often don't get back to Fenway until two or three in the morning. The place is mystical, even magical. To walk alone up a gangway, view the field lit only by the clock, see the lights on Ted Williams Way, and watch Fenway just before dawn — well, it's breathtaking. I'll always be grateful to have had Fenway be a part of my life.

— *Joe Castiglione*

Fans in Fenway, like Philly or New York, are said to be hard. It ain't necessarily so. I'm in centerfield, it's 1982, and a bleacherite yells "Okie Joe!" I'm from Oklahoma. This guy had done his homework. Soon: "Ok-ie Joe! Ok-ie Joe!" A little later the fan starts singing the title song of the musical *Oklahoma!* I turn around and start conducting: He's singing, pals join in, and we converse. Next night I'm back in center. The same fellah brings Xerox copies of the words, passes 'em around, and soon the *bleachers* are in song! A year later I'm traded to Kansas City, not even playing, and from the stands I hear "Where the wind comes sweepin' down the plain." Amazing. The musical ends, "Oklahoma! OK!" — a good word for these fans.

— *Joe Simpson*

Minnesota's Metrodome featured weird hops, lost fly balls, two World Series, an All-Star game, and crowd noise that was, depending on the time, deathly silent or ear-splittingly loud. I recall fan reaction most. In 1987, the Twins took the AL West, upset Deroit in the LCS, and came home for a supposedly modest pep rally that packed the Dome. Just before the team bus arrived, Kent Hrbek's mother Tina came to me in tears, having lost husband Ed to Lou Gehrig's disease five years earlier and desperately wanting to be the first to greet Kent as he walked off the bus. Not knowing who she was, security refused, so I took her to a Twins executive. The bus arrived a minute later, Tina giving Kent a hug. On closing day 2006, the Twins, having clinched the wild card, could win the AL Central — homefield edge — if they beat Chicago and the Royals beat the Tigers. A rain delay in Detroit meant the Twins started first. Winning, we then saw the Tigers game on our scoreboard with 40,000 fans. When KC won, Twins players, still in uniform, celebrated with a victory lap around the field. Even the maligned Metrodome showed that whatever a stadium's shape, turf, or roof, being home beats being not.

— *Dick Bremer*

The tunnel that led from the visitors' dugout to the Metrodome clubhouse was long and steep: eleven steps, then a landing that's six feet deep, eleven steps, a landing, eleven steps, a landing, and eleven more steps. Cal Ripken would finish his pre-game infield and sprint up the stairs. The idea, which only he would invent, was to get to the top in the fewest strides. Ripken could do it in six strides, which was positively Bob Beamonesque. Before one game, teammate Rene Gonzales made it in six. That was unacceptable to Ripken. He couldn't stand to not be the best, not even for one night, so he went back to the bottom, did it again, and made it in five.
— *Tim Kurkjian*

Modern parks are great for fan and broadcast comfort, yet can't match, as Ernie Harwell described, the "grand lady at the corner of Michigan and Trumbull." Radio/TV boxes hung below the upper deck barely higher than the top of the screen behind the plate. Fouls rocketed back, booth walls inundated with dents: Usually I wore my baseball mitt, ready for any shot. In June 1992, the Indians are two years away from becoming a rest-of-the decade powerhouse. Detroit puts up a six spot in the first. This starts Mike Hegan and me telling stories, trying to keep our Cleveland audience. In the sixth, Lou Whitaker, the great second baseman, fouls a pitch above the screen. Inexplicably, I hadn't brought my glove, so I lean to my left, Mike his right, the ball screaming by. Normally Joe, our audio engineer, was outside in the production truck. Tonight each club shared TV's broadcast feed, meaning Joe sat next to me. When Lou's foul hit our back wall, it ricochets, hits Joe in the head, and knocks him unconscious. With his fingers on the slider bars for various sound inputs, Joe, falling forward, pushes every button to full capacity, the feedback incredible. A TV truck and announcer can talk to each other without a viewer hearing it. Panicked, producer/director Pat Murray asks me about our sound gone kablooey. "Where's Joe?" I say, "Joe is out," leaving Pat flabbergasted. "Where'd he go?" I tell him Joe hasn't left, just been knocked out cold. Another audio engineer relieved him, but the audience in Cleveland must have wondered what happened the night Lou Whitaker made the sound go crazy in Detroit.
— *Jack Corrigan*

Tiger Stadium, 1984, Tigers-Angels, NBC's *Game of the Week*. Tony Kubek and I are in the TV booth: as noted, almost on top of the plate. Between innings, you could be heard like a bell yelling to a person in the first row. In his previous at-bat, Reggie Jackson had cleared the roof above the rightfield grandstand — maybe not as crushed as his 1971 All-Star blast off the light transformer — but a moonshot nonetheless. Reggie's next at-bat leads off an inning. During break I hear this piercing whistle from the on-deck circle, first-base side. It's Reggie, about to show his broadcast savvy and healthy ego: the two, I guess, related. He makes eye contact, then pantomimes tying his shoe. I look quizzically. Reggie draw his hands apart — TV's sign for stretch — before pantomiming again. Right there, it clicks what Reggie's trying to say. I nod, give the thumbs up, know what he's going to do. He's going to dig in, hold up his hands, and ask for time. Next, he'll back out of the batter's box, tie his shoe, and then slowly get back in. What will this achieve? Give us time to play the mammoth homer yet again, marvel at it, comment on it, give it a full measure of appreciation. We do, Kubek comparing the moonshot to some by Williams and Mantle at Tiger Stadium. Reggie's next at-bat then unfolds. He singles to centerfield, gets to first base, looks up at me, and tips his cap. Quintessentially, Reggie Jackson.

— *Bob Costas*

Tiger Stadium was the only place I've worked where I could *see* the spin of the ball on its way to home plate. In 1987, Rangers catcher Geno Petralli had an awful time trying to catch Charlie Hough's knuckleball, tying a major-league record with six passed balls in one game. Each time Geno chased another knuckler to the screen, almost directly beneath our booth, his frustration became more audible. Seeing the amazingly late break of the knuckleball, I felt for Geno each time he arrived. To me, Tiger Stadium was its era's classic double-deck site, twin-tiered around the entire park, the smell of grilled hot dogs permeating from when you walked in the gate. Tiger dogs were never the same after the team moved to Comerica Park. Neither was our view.

— *Eric Nadel*

In the early '90s, this New Yorker, living in Baltimore, saw a changing of baseball's guard. On October 6, 1991, the Orioles' Memorial Stadium closed. A limousine then took home plate to their new park, Oriole Park at Camden Yards. ["The field was cleared," Chuck Thompson recalled. "First, the background music began from *Field of Dreams* over the PA. Then Brooks [Robinson] emerged from the dugout to take his position at third base— followed by Frank [Robby] in the outfield, followed by Jim Palmer," then Boog Powell: former players returning to say good-bye. "The crowd hadn't expected this. When it happened, they were stunned." More than seventy-five players ran to their position, each wearing the age's uniform: no introductions, just the song and tears.] Next April 6, I saw Oriole Park open near the Inner Harbor: a *ballpark* of nooks and crannies after a cookie-cutter age. At its '93 All-Star Game, John Kruk comically flailed at Randy Johnson and the crowd booed AL manager Cito Gaston for not using Mike Mussina after the Orioles pitcher warmed up. Opening, Camden Yards wanted to be Fenway or Ebbets Field. Since then, new parks want to be Camden Yards.
— *Kenny Albert*

For a long time Baltimore was thought a football town: the Colts, Johnny Unitas, "The Greatest Game Ever Played." That changed in 1979. A new radio flagship marketed the O's, the song "Orioles Magic" everywhere. The gas crisis kept people at home, with baseball inexpensive. Most of all, the Birds had a new hero every night. Inevitably, Memorial Stadium got old, a new park necessary. Beside free agency and Jackie Robinson, George Will calls Camden Yards baseball's biggest post-war story. In a pre-opening day tour, I understood for the first time the inferiority of circular stadia like Cincinnati and Pittsburgh: seats here up-close, painted green, the Warehouse [1,016-feet-long and 51-feet-wide] seemingly as near as the first-base bag. Between it and the field Eutaw Street became a carnival, where I do my pre-game TV show, Boog Powell joining me, "Boog's Barbecue" nearby. Pull hitters take dead aim at the Warehouse. Customers take dead aim at the beef.
— *Tom Davis*

The Astrodome hosted many events, but baseball had its best home-field edge. Away teams had trouble seeing for the first one or two games of

a series. Since the Dome seemed darker than outside, visiting players could lose the ball while running. Finally, they got frustrated, a long home run elsewhere a warning track out here. In 1992, the Astros took baseball's most famous journey: a 26-game, 28-day, 8-city, 9,231-mile road trip because the Dome was hosting the Republican National Convention. We began July 27 in Atlanta, logistics planned by traveling secretary Barry Waters, who gave players, coaches, and staff $59 per day meal money. They got a one-time laundry allowance, returning August 17 for "Laundry Day," like cowboys on the Chisholm Trail. In Chicago, each player got a single room, first class airfare for a guest, and team T-shirt reading "What It Takes—It's all You've Got." Our prior road record suggested a 9-17 trip: a lot to take, not much to get. As the GOP moved toward renominating President Bush, a shutout by the Cubs' Greg Maddux ended seventeen games in as many days. After "Laundry Day," we rallied to sweep our first series of the year. Almost as good was the trip's 12-14 record, our team outscored by just twenty runs. We had traveled to each NL city except Montreal, New York, and Pittsburgh, glad to be back in Houston, even if Houston had locked us out.
—Bill Brown

[In 2000, Sports Illustrated wrote: "(Houston) has built a ballpark . . . of idiosyncrasies and intrigue"—then–Enron Field's centerfield berm, in-play flagpole, retractable roof, and 1860s life-size coal locomotive and steel tender on a track atop the leftfield wall. Rain delays were improbable, but hurricanes were not.] On Thursday, September 11, 2008, only a few were on hand of the announced 31,000 to see Roy Oswalt blank the Pirates, 6-0. With Hurricane Ike moving toward Houston, most were boarding up houses, stocking up on food, and getting out of Dodge. Wind and flooding made the Astros postpone Friday's and Saturday's games of a three-game series against Chicago. I got a call Saturday at 6:00 p.m. to be at our park next morning to fly to a rescheduled "home" series in Milwaukee with the Cubs! Players staggered in, some with families. Water blocked roads. The only people at the airport were a few TSA agents to help us. It was empty, quiet, weird. Our plane barely reached Miller Park in time for Carlos Zambrano's no-hitter—the Cubs' first in thirty-six years and first at a "neutral site." I'm not sure how rested Carlos was. I do know Astros starter Randy

Wolf started his day at 8:00 a.m., carrying a suitcase and computer bag down ten flights of stairs in his high-rise apartment: no power, elevator, or reason to ask why he wasn't sharp. Almost all the crowd wore enemy apparel, making Lance Berkman say, "I can't believe our fans cheered so lustily for the Cubs."

—*Brett Dolan*

Some neutral series: ninety miles from Wrigley Field. Ours was the only aircraft to leave Houston on Sunday, and some of us almost missed it. I heard the news at 10:00 p.m. Saturday on an emergency crank radio we had in our house, but didn't know how to get to the airport, when to drive, or how the team was leaving. I couldn't get a signal to make a call, so I went to [Astros TV analyst] Jim Deshaies' home in my neighborhood, left my headlights on to see, found the doorbell didn't work, and yelled through an open window. We reached the airport *just* as the plane is leaving. That day I call the no-no: rare enough. Rarer was that with Houston's power out, Zambrano's tree fell in the forest. I'm calling history, and almost no one can hear a word.

—*Dave Raymond*

The old Yankee Stadium was special. Ever since his 1985 firing as manager, Yogi Berra had stayed away. When Joe DiMaggio died in 1999, George Steinbrenner made peace by apologizing to Yogi. That July 18, the Yankees reunited. First, manager Joe Torre gave Yogi a 1998 World Series ring, many former teammates there to celebrate. Next, Yogi crouched for Don Larsen's pre-game toss. "Mr. Larsen," said starter David Cone, referencing 1956's perfect game, "are you going to jump into Yogi's arms?" Larsen laughed. "You got it backward. *He* jumped into *mine*." Yogi caught the pitch, then gave his glove to Yankees catcher Joe Girardi, who used it to call *Cone's* perfect game against Montreal! Amazing. Girardi said: "I don't want to be superstitious but so many great things happen here, you wonder." In 2009, moving across the street, the Yankees traded one Yankee Stadium for another. They also won their twenty-seventh World Series, leaving Girardi, now manager, still wondering.

—*Bob Wolff*

Dodger Stadium and the old Yankee Stadium reflect two teams, and coasts. In the Bronx, you'd look out, spot elevated trains, and see and smell the city. The Stadium *was* the city: noisy, harsh, elbows flying, people screaming about a parking space. One guy: "Hey, that's mine!" Another: "Fuhgetaboutit!" The ever-present 4 train rickets by. In LA, you see the palm trees and San Gabriel Mountains beyond right- and right-centerfield. Not a day goes by that I don't talk about the weather, temperature, and radiance of distant peaks. Is there a haze? A bright Dodger Blue sky? You marvel at the beauty. Dodger Stadium opened in 1962, when a lot of parks were old and big. I marvel at this, too: Ours is now baseball's third-oldest stadium, with a big-league-largest 56,000-seat capacity. I hope I age as gracefully as Dodger Stadium.

    —*Charley Steiner*

Coors Field opened in 1995, to hitters' delight and pitchers' horror. Start with baseball's smallest foul ground. Then add light air helping the horsehide carry, making outfielders play deep, and letting flares fall in front. Next, consider distant alleys making gappers triples. All that helped Andres Galarraga, fourth to homer in three straight innings; he, Vinny Castilla, and Ellis Burks, the second team of three guys of forty or more homers; and MVP and batting champion Larry Walker, winning the percentage Triple Crown of average, on-base, and slugging. Later, for several reasons, hitting declined a bit, still the best playground to end a slump. Actor Jack Webb, as TV's Sergeant Joe Friday, said, "Just the facts, ma'am." Fact: A dinosaur bone was found during Coors' shafting. Must have been a pitcher's.

    —*Wayne Hagin*

My favorite stadium is Wrigley Field, by a mile, the atmosphere inside and out fantastic. The Cubs have made the most of its charm and history, almost creating the feeling of a pilgrimage to a holy shrine. I thought Fenway was equally charming until they started messing with it. The Cubs have resisted that: It's all pure ball. You can hear batting practice from outside the park. No loud music, just vendors, an organ, guys throwing the ball around, a Dixieland band near the ticket windows: *baseball sounds*. A

lot of organizations have lost track, trying to "entertain," which is incredible. How can a business be oblivious to the product it's selling?
— *Denny Matthews*

I grew up in Phoenix a Dodgers fan, Vin Scully making Dodger Stadium a wonderland. In 2003, I saw a July 4 game. In 2004, there to *broadcast*, I gaze at an open centerfield gate, spot two buses, and say, "Those look like ours." Producer Leo Gilmartin says, "They are. That's where we connect after the game." On the field I phone my Dodger-loving brother. "Guess where I am?" I said. "Centerfield at Dodger Stadium." He says, "Pull up some grass." Next year's even better: my first game, a Sunday, at Wrigley Field. Leo suggests I fly there a day early. I ask why, not airing Saturday's game. He says, "It'll take you a day to get over the *wow*." *What*? I say. He says, "You'll see." I fly in, take a taxi, inhale the North Side neighborhood, and see the park straight ahead. Inside, I climb the ramps — one per level — glimpsing the packed crowd, ivy, flags in the breeze. Leo was right. Sunday I call my best friend — great Cubs fan; in the '80s, we argued Vin *v.* Harry Caray — asking, "Guess where I am?" Don says, "Wrigley Field." How did he know? "I saw your schedule." Neither of us could speak for ninety seconds. A little different than my first game at Riverfront Stadium.
— *Jeff Munn*

[John Rooney joined the White Sox in 1988, working there through 2005.] I'd grown up in Missouri, often going to Comiskey Park as a kid. It was strange now seeing it broken, chipped asphalt everywhere. One night the Sox go to Detroit, where Steve Lyons reaches first base. Next thing I see, he's pulling down his pants, forgetting that he's in a baseball park before thousands of people. "It may be an overcast night," I said, "but the moon's shining brightly inside Tiger Stadium."
— *John Rooney*

May 8–9, 1984: Brewers at old Comiskey. We played a game each night — the *same* game, taking eight hours and six minutes. The first night we stop, tied after seventeen innings, due to local law barring an inning from starting after 1:00 a.m. Next night we resume before the regularly scheduled game. Scoreless inning by inning passes till Ben Oglivie hits a three-run homer: 6–3, Brewers. Tom Paciorek's single soon reties the score at 6, going 5 for 9. One irony: Tom hadn't started, replacing Ron Kittle in the fourth. Another: "This is the first five-hit game I've had," he told me. "Little League, high school, or American Legion!" In the twenty-fifth, Harold Baines's homer gives the Sox a 7–6 victory. Twenty minutes later the nightcap begins: Tom Seaver scheduled to start, his problem the opener, where, Chicago out of pitchers, he'd thrown the twenty-fifth and winning inning. Despite that, Tom pitches and wins again: two victories in a day. The moon must have been full over the South Side that night.

   — *Pat Hughes*

   I loved [1910–1990] old Comiskey, but it needed a facelift: paint, make-up, and perfume. A lot of fans hated that it had to go, especially when new Comiskey opened in 1991: boring, the upper deck in Indiana. Later, U.S. Cellular Company, buying naming rights, made the new park sing: intimate, had a roof, eight rows cut from the upper deck, every seat now green, more bleachers, ivy on the hitter's backdrop. They dressed up the young lady, and now each game's a date.

   — *Ken Harrelson*

   I've broadcast twenty years for the Cubs, and the last three the White Sox: great fans, but from different planets. As Hawk notes, the Sox beautifully restored U.S. Cell, improved the neighborhood, made ballpark food sensational, yet must win to draw. Cubs fans come out regardless. Some think such fanaticism hurts the Cubs: Wrigley's packed anyway, so why improve your record? *Ridiculous.* Since 2003, the Cubs have spent or obligated more than $1 billion in salary. Meanwhile, teams spending a lot less made the Series: Colorado, Tampa Bay, Florida, the *White Sox!* It's not money, it's the judgment, stupid. Until that improves, neither will the Cubs.

   — *Steve Stone*

   In 1968, Montreal deemed its 25,000-seat football stadium, the Autostade, not suitable for the expansion Expos, saying it would cost a "fortune" to house baseball: actually, $12 million for a roof and 12,000 seats.

Later, the City and Province of Quebec paid a hundred "fortunes" to build a 1976 Summer Olympics Stadium better fit for bocce ball than baseball. Till then, city and club officials needed a temporary site. The '68 search led to 3,000-seat Jarry Park, near a subway, expressway, and commuter railroad, just north of downtown and Mount Royal. The NL OKs it, if *Parc Jarry* — Park Jar-*ee* — is converted to 28,000 seats, which it was, baseball played there through 1976. Olympic Stadium then became their park — really, prison — hurting the Expos as much as the labor stoppage that killed the 1994 Series and, though we didn't know it, baseball in Montreal. That August 12, the 'Spos' .649 percentage led the bigs, the strike costing them nearly $16 million. Next season we finished last. Everyone knew the team needed a new park, and each year it went nowhere. Upset, new owner Jeffrey Loria yanked baseball off 1999 TV and English radio, sending me to Cyberspace. The Expos moved to Washington in 2005, by which time I'd moved to Miami, whose Marlins will soon open a new park. Expand the Autostade or Jarry, and *L'Expos* are still in Montreal.
    — *Dave Van Horne*

The 1977–1999 Mariners somehow survived what *Newsday* called "the worst baseball arena *ever*." The roof leaked. Balls struck speakers, hit roof support wires. In 2000, even the M's wanted to sell detonating plungers for the Kingdome's razing. For a long time we'd been unable to get State funds for a new park, crucial to stay in town. Then, in 1995's best-of-five Division Series against the Yankees, Grandma got out the rye bread because Edgar Martinez made it grand salami time, winning Game 4, 11–8. Next day, we're down, 5–4, two on, bottom of the eleventh, everything at stake. I remember saying, "Right now the Mariners are looking for the tie." [Then: "Swung on (by Martinez), lined down the leftfield line for a base hit! Here comes Joey (Cora), and Junior to third base, and they're going to wave him in! The throw to the plate will be . . . late! The Mariners are going to play for the American League championship! I don't believe it! It just continues! My, oh, my!"] The M's lost the LCS, but won something else: an intimate, gorgeous park — best of all, outdoors! That year the Legislature OK'd Safeco Field.
    — *Dave Niehaus*

Rogers Centre, then SkyDome, mid-1990s: Detroit's Lou Whitaker gets a personal milestone hit. To make sure I knew, our statistician, Scott Carson, pivoted on his chair, reached to point at a chart, and inadvertently knocked my glass of water out of the booth. For those who haven't been to Toronto, it's a long way down to the seats and that plastic cup seemed to hang in the air forever before apparently soaking a woman. Not thinking, I lean out to see what's happened, letting the woman in question see where the cup came from — *me*. Moments later, security enters the booth and tries to drag me out. Usually announcers have to talk fast to describe, say, a triple. Here I had to fast talk my way just to stay on the air.
    — *Dan Shulman*

[In 1995, LA Raiders owner Al Davis, plotting a return to Oakland, got it to add *five outfield* tiers to the Oakland-Alameda County Coliseum, blocking the Athletics' old view of the East Bay Hills and ruining its baseball suitability.] Since then, the A's have tried to leave. Hey, why wouldn't they? For a long time, nearby Fremont was felt to have the inside track, the team dedicating a page in their 2009 media guide to Cisco Field: "Future Home of the Athletics." That media guide will be a great collectors' item since, after a few hundred people demonstrated against it, A's owner Lew Wolff dropped the plan. I've lived in Fremont for more than thirty years: fourth most-populated city in the nine-county Bay Area, yet like a place with a few gas stations and no movie theater. That year Toyota in effect closed Fremont's largest employer. The city awoke too late, trying to use the land for a stadium. Lack of leadership is why people opposing the team's move from Oakland don't have to worry. Only a new park in the Bay Area will save the A's. Thank you, Mr. Davis.
    — *Amaury Pi-Gonzalez*

On September 28, 2000, Milwaukee County Stadium, forty-seven, closed after housing the 1953–1965 Braves, 1970– Brewers, and Vince Lombardi's Packers: for many Wisconsinites, the only venue they'd known. Maybe that's why they forgave it having one functioning elevator; taking the blame for the Brewers' two-decade financial plight; or getting showered with ice-cold water when frozen plumbing burst. Maybe that's why tonight people cried you a river. County Stadium was the crazy aunt you rarely visited, yet mourned after a long, fulfilling life: a bucket of bolts, but *ours*. After the game, ex-Brewers, Braves and Packers walked one-by-one from the bullpen to home plate: crowd roaring; many players for years not having seen one another. Once-Brave Bob Buhl wanted so badly to pitch that he took ten wonderful minutes to reach the mound, letting fly one more time. Next year he passed away at seventy-two, Milwaukee not wanting to give him up, or County. The Apollo may have had Aretha Franklin and Grand Ole Opry Hank Williams, but County Stadium had Aaron and Spahn, hard-hitting and -living Gorman Thomas, second baseman Jim Gantner, and huge applause for Robin Yount. Not born yet, I felt I'd been alive for the Boston move, '50s dynasty, and four straight years of unheard-of two million attendance. The move south lingers, but so does baseball's, then Aaron's, return, a 1982 pennant, and Yount riding a Harley on his Day across the field. My partner, Bill Schroeder, and I studded the night's TV pictures with story, while then-broadcast head Tim Van Wagoner produced a Bob Fosse-like good-bye. I'd only aired the Brewers since 1997, but tonight forged a oneness that's never gone away. September 28 is also my birthday, fueling introspection. I left the park thinking of the line from *Wayne's World*. "Milwaukee, or *Mil-ee-wah-kay*. It's Algonquin for *the good land*." Part of me still calls it home.

—*Matt Vasgersian*

I grew up in New England, living and breathing baseball 365 days a year. After baseball left Washington in '71, a generation followed the Yankees or Orioles or Red Sox, if they followed the game at all. When baseball returned, we played at RFK Stadium: quirky, charming, great vantage. Less charming: the stale scent of beer; long run to the restroom, meeting lots of odors; and visiting third-base booth literally shaking when fans jumped up and down. Nationals Park's booth is much higher than RFK's. Compensating is the view looking to your left on a clear night and seeing the Capitol Dome, so close you feel you could give it a hug.

—*Dave Jageler*

I broadcast from Forbes Field, Ebbets Field, the Polo Grounds. In Pittsburgh, a guy'd hit a ball down that rightfield line, the outfielder'd vanish from view chasing it in the corner, and it was Clemente! The batter thought, "Hey, I got a double easy," and looks up and there's the ball and he's thrown out by eight feet. Center was so far [457 feet] they'd wheel the batting cage there before the game, in play. At Ebbets, the press box was an afterthought, hung under the upper deck, and if it was quiet, you'd hear the third-base coach 'cause you were right above him. Thank God you could turn the mike off because, well, you know how third-base coaches talk. Carl Furillo playing balls off the wall. Junk homers and a centerfield canyon in the Polo Grounds. I love Camden, Minute Maid, the Pirates' new park, a jewel, so much like baseball's past. Compare 'em to Three Rivers Stadium in Pittsburgh. The best thing about it was when they blew it up.

—*Milo Hamilton*

Chapter Twelve

We Shall Overcome

"The grass was green, dirt was brown, and players were white," Roger Kahn wrote of baseball before 1947. Later Jackie Robinson, Larry Doby, Juan Marichal, and Roberto Clemente, among others, fueled color-blindness on the field. Above it, vision lagged.

In 1965, Robinson became the bigs' first minority TV analyst: "a high, stabbing voice, great presence, and sharp mind," said ABC producer Chuck Howard. Bill White was then a Cardinals All-Star first baseman. In 1971, he became baseball's first black play-by-play man. "My first year I was terrible. The next year I was a little less terrible. The Yankees could easily have fired me."

Blanche DuBois relied on the kindness of strangers. Improving, White relied on work. Commuting two hours from Bucks County, outside Philadelphia, he critiqued his taped segment of every game on radio, auguring such black analysts and play-by-play men as Darrin Jackson, Gary Matthews, Joe Morgan, Paul Olden, Harold Reynolds, Billy Sample, and Dave Sims.

White made the big leagues in 1956. A decade earlier Rafael (Felo) Ramirez cracked Cuba's amateur and later professional baseball, adding play-by-play in Puerto Rico and Venezuela and co-anchoring Gillette Cavalcade of Sports with Buck Canel. "If you have cardiac problems," Felo told the listener, "back away from your radio now." Forewarned, few did.

Ramirez began as media U.S. Latinos were often laughed at or condescended to. Carmen Miranda's come-on was a befruited head. The Cisco Kid soon made English elementary. Pancho: "Oh, Cisco." Cisco: "Oh, Pancho." Unbowed, Felo aired Don Larsen, Hank Aaron's number 715, and the World Series, All-Star

Game, and Little League World Series: said fellow Cuban Amaury Pi-Gonzalez, "like a god to the people."

In 1993, joining the expansion Los Marlins de la Florida, Ramirez christened "Estaaaaan ganando los Maaaarlins!" – the Marlins are winning. Florida is now among eleven bigs teams with a Spanish-speaking network, Voices like Juan Avila, Jaime Jarrin, Eduardo Ortega, and Pi-Gonzalez reaching America's fastest-growing minority. "Tomorrow lies as much with them," wrote Peter Gammons, "as Ozzie and Harriet suburbs."

The Spanish "mi casa es su casa" means "my house is your house." Increasingly, many are leaving baseball's back porch for an open front door.

In 1946, I was a fourteen-year-old kid living in western Canada. My Dad coached the Montreal Canadiens, who that spring won the Stanley Cup, one of twenty-four. Hockey was, and is, a religion in Montreal. Then, the season ended each April: hockey stopping as baseball starts. In 1946, Jackie Robinson played his only year with the International League Montreal Royals — as big a hero as any Canadien. Branch Rickey had signed him the previous October, knowing that a black player would be accepted far more easily in Montreal than in the States, where segregation existed. This way Robinson could prepare for the majors, which he entered in 1947 and where he became a star. The first time I saw Robinson play was that year at Wrigley Field. By then I felt I'd seen him — because of what I'd heard in 1946. He won the league batting title, and the Royals the Little World Series. Nobody batted an eye in Montreal about his being black. Once fans rushed him for autographs after a home game at Delorimier Field, a writer saying, "It was the only time where white fans were chasing a black guy, and everybody was happy." The rest of the league didn't show Montreal's tolerance. It was tough, but so was he — we can't imagine what he felt. The last time I saw him was in 1972, the year he died at fifty-three. I was emceeing a dinner in Montreal that Jackie attended. I was shocked at his condition, diabetes: Robinson could barely see. He got up and talked for three minutes, totally spontaneous, about his year in Montreal, his friends there, the street he lived on. You could hear a pin drop. The gods in Montreal are named Morenz, Richard, Beliveau, Lafleur. But for one year a deity played baseball, too.

— *Dick Irvin*

In 1987, Dodgers veep Al Campanis said on *Nightline* that he didn't think blacks had the "necessities" to be a manager or in the front office. That got me into broadcasting, because baseball started to look for blacks to be more representative of America. It wouldn't have happened without Robinson making the bigs seven years before the U.S. Supreme Court case *Brown v. Topeka Board of Education* outlawed segregation. I didn't face — nobody could — what he and [the first AL black, Cleveland's] Larry Doby did: death threats, pickets, *teammate* petitions to go back to the minors. This so, I'm asked about the low percentage of black players now: maybe 10 percent. I don't know that it's ever been much higher. That's true too of *watching* the game. In 1987, the *New York Times* reported black *attendance* about 5 percent of baseball's total versus 12 percent of the overall population. A lot is kids lacking people to reinforce them: dads and moms busy, or a one-parent family. You can shoot hoops, play a video game, or worse, get into trouble by yourself. That's not what Jackie wanted. As a writer said, "Without Robinson, there's probably no Rosa Parks."
  — *Billy Sample*

Like many young black kids growing up in 1960s LA, I wanted to play big-league baseball. Alas, I wasn't good, so I decided to do play-by-play, unconcerned about not having black role models. I could still hear Vin Scully and Dick Enberg, even writing asking how to get started. Dick suggested getting a tape recorder — then, a small reel-to-reel model — and doing youth league games or those off TV. I sold programs at Dodger Stadium, getting out my recorder after cashing out. Later, wondering why no one could explain the lack of African American play-by-play men, I decide to be the first black non–ex-athlete to call ball. Meanwhile, Bill Wilkerson earns a journalism degree from Southern Illinois University–Carbondale and is recruited by KMOX St. Louis's legendary head Bob Hyland, broadcasting heretofore not crossing his mind. Wilkerson goes to St. Louis after getting a salary large enough to give up his weekend job selling suits at J.C. Penney's: hired as a newsman, happy till out of the blue he's given football Cardinals color.
  "Maybe I should tell Hyland I've never done sportscasting," he said, soon rethinking saying no to the guy who hired him. Before long Bill's

doing ESPN play-by-play of sports he'd known nothing about—Greco-Roman wrestling, swimming, diving—and the pre-season Cardinals. Jack Buck then resumed his regular-season role till having an "emergency" one quarter. Bill took over, knowing that Hyland was listening. Next week the same thing occurred, Bill now knowing something was afoot.

"Did the boss [Hyland] call while I was away?" Buck asked.

"No," said Wilkerson.

"Well, brother," Buck chirped, "play-by-play is yours because I'm going to [KMOX parent] CBS!" becoming *Monday Night Football*'s marquee. Bill added Missouri football, St. Louis Spirits color, and Cardinals *baseball*: the pastime's first African American balls and strikes *non–ex-pro player*. "It just happened," he said, as it *didn't* for other blacks, blooming in studio and network but not local TV color or play-by-play. Dave Sims and Darrin Jackson do Mariners and White Sox TV, respectively, David Kelly University of Arizona radio and Internet, Robert Ford Royals radio. The late Mike Lockhart aired Class-A baseball and Notre Dame hockey, destined for great things before his 2009 death. Why not more?

In the late '80s and early '90s, ex-NFLer and then-Orioles official Calvin Hill began a minority broadcast internship. Jon Miller, at Baltimore, and I, at Tampa Bay, tried to help. We need to try again to get minorities when they're young. Bill Wilkerson would agree, now a businessman involved in the Boys and Girls club with "Reach Out St Louis!"—an initiative to curb the public school black dropout rate. Bill works with former coach Tony Dungy and ex-player Troy Vincent and hopes the program spreads. How do we honor him? Get more blacks playing and calling baseball: another chapter in a groundbreaking life.

— *Paul Olden*

Being called up scares you: black, white, or brown. In late '78 I joined the Rangers in Milwaukee, went to the clubhouse, and saw I'm leading off and playing second base. It surprised me that I played right away—and at a position I hadn't played in more than a year. I ask someone, "Does Mr. Hunter [manager Billy] know this?" He said: "The Brewers are starting [lefty] Jerry Augustine, and [switch-hitter second baseman] Bump Wills has been having trouble from the right side. So they want to give him one less at bat." I lead off, line the first pitch to right-center, and get a hit when Sixto Lezcano dives, ball bouncing off his glove. I'm at first base, a big grin on my face, when, sure enough, here comes Wills to run for me! Some debut, huh? It was downhill from there! My day is over as soon as it begins.

— *Billy Sample*

We need guys who play baseball as a kid, are mentored, and love its history. I was lucky that way — and to play nineteen professional years. In late 1999, retiring, I became a Sox announcer, different than I expected. I thought you went to the booth, watched, and talked to the guy next to you. Boy, was I misinformed! I found that you study, try to be accurate, and what's more that after playing all my life, I'm an outsider: not a player, but *former* player involved with — *gasp* — the media! As a player, *I'd* had bad things said about me that I used for motivation. I learn now that not every player thinks that way, upset with what I "said." Some players heard things I *hadn't* said or someone misinterpreted, a wife or girlfriend relaying third-hand stuff. I'd say, "I didn't say that." Some wouldn't listen. Others did, saying, "OK, well, I see." Reliever Bobby Howry was a 1999 teammate. Next year the team gets its butt kicked three straight by Kansas City. In the booth Hawk [Ken Harrelson] and I give accolades to KC. When the series ends, I go in the locker room and Howry says, "What's going on?" I ask what gives. "You and Hawk are kissing the Royals' a—." I asked what he meant. "You act as if we suck and they're the best ever," Bobby steams. "Well," I said, "they *did* score ten runs each game. Do you want us to say you're a bunch of bums?" Overnight I'd gone from fighting *for* and *with* these guys all the time to *fighting* them half the time. Whatever your color, you hang in there, like facing a dancing knuckler or drop-dead curve.

— *Darrin Jackson*

In one sense, we absolutely need to work on race relations. In another, they've come a long way. I grew up in northern Philadelphia, able to look south and see the lights of Connie Mack Stadium. It seemed an odyssey to get there — actually, a ten to fifteen minute walk partly through the Italian neighborhood around 20th Street. I remember mid-'60s racial riots around the country — and the great tension in my town. In 1991, I'm with CNBC

TV, just off the ground, and interview basketball '76ers owner Pat Croce, a physical therapist and entrepreneur. Pat asked, "Where'd you grow up?" I said: "Northern Philadelphia. What about you?" Pat said, "20th and Somerset." I laughed: "Going to the ballpark, I wanted to race through, get out of there. Just to survive we felt we'd have to fight." Pat said, "Oh, *you* were that guy!" Again I laughed, something we didn't do much of forty-five years ago.

— *Dave Sims*

Once Hawk and I did a TV breakdown of Frank Thomas's and Miguel Olivo's 3–0 swing. Right-handed Thomas fouled the ball over the first-base side: unacceptable, since ahead in the count his barrel should be going. By contrast, Olivo pulled. Next day I approach the batting cage, see Frank, and start talking: former mates and long-time friends who like to rag the other.

"D. J.!" he booms. "What are you *doing* comparing me to Miguel? You can't do that."

"What you are talking about?" I say. "And, yes, I can."

Frank: "We're different kinds of hitters."

Me: "That's not the point. We're comparing you in the same situation."

He's not buying. "That's a bunch of bull."

Frank is making a point, which Frank likes to do. I have my view, which usually is right. We go jawing into the locker room when suddenly from the other side of the room reliever and relative Sox newcomer Billy Koch yells, "I'd kick his" — *my* — "a —." Where did *this* come from? I go over to Billy and say that Frank and I are friends, we do this all the time. Issue over, right?

Frank and I resume our needling, when Koch again screams, "I'd kick his a —." This routine's getting old, making me think I've done something to offend. I know Koch gets to the park early, so next day at 2:00 p.m. I confront him: "Is there a problem between us that I don't realize?" — maybe, as I noted, an on-air comment that gets misconstrued.

"No, no, no, I was just trying to get Frank going," Koch says. When you travel with guys each day for seven months — especially different backgrounds, attitudes, in close proximity — a flareup can become a crisis if you don't nip it right away.

— *Darrin Jackson*

[Improving, Bill White famously partnered with 1971–1988's Phil Rizzuto.] Scooter had this unique way of scoring: "WW" — wasn't watching. I loved to listen to him. He made me laugh. Phil starts reading a long list of birthdays, and eventually I interrupt: "Hey, don't you have a name in there that doesn't end in a vowel?" [Phil began another telecast: "Hi, everybody, this is New York Yankees baseball. I'm Bill White. Wait a minute! I swear to God I didn't."] One day the camera spotted a teenage girl. Phil said: "She reminds me of that old song, 'A Pretty Girl is like a Memory.'" I said, "Scooter, I think that's Melody." Phil: "Really. How do you know her name is Melody?" It clicked, even though he always called me "White." How'd you like to work eighteen years with a guy who never learned your first name?
— *Bill White*

I was a decent player growing up, big for my age, attending a 1969 Phillies tryout camp at sixteen in [Philadelphia's] Fairmount Park. There were a lot of coaches, and a black gentleman was working with infielders. The gentleman came up and said, "Young man, you did all right." He tells my dad, "He's too young, but has a chance." My father's smile lit the field. The gentleman was the Negro League star, Judy Johnson, who made Cooperstown in 1975. Fast-forward to a 1994 ESPN game in Kansas City, where I introduce myself to the great Buck O'Neil, who's off and speaking: twenty minutes of incredible tales. Three years later I'm with WCBS New York covering a Long Island University symposium on the fiftieth anniversary of Jackie Robinson breaking the color line. One of the guests is — Buck O'Neil! I reintroduce myself, Buck saying, like we're old pals, "Man, give me some love." Judy to Buck, one story spawns another, baseball our link. For proof, check the Negro Leagues.
— *Dave Sims*

I'd take a 1930s train from Long Island to New York to see Negro League teams like the Homestead Grays, a big part of the game coming *before* it: players smiling, laughing, and wooing the crowd. Pepper games don't exist now. Then, you marveled at gifted athletes' ability to keep a ball in play. A favorite routine was "invisible ball." In infield drill, the batter

pantomimed hitting to the third baseman, who threw to the "first sacker," scooping up—or maybe the shortstop, who flung to the second baseman, pivoting and dropping the "invisible ball," teammates all over him! Later something *visible* preceded me to DC. The 1937–1948 Grays played many games at Griffith Stadium, Josh Gibson thrice clearing a wall behind the distant leftfield seats. In 2010, the *New York Times* bemoaned the dearth of similar prominent black players, naming Gary Matthews Jr. the Mets' only African American. This has little to do with prejudice. Fewer blacks now play high school baseball because football and basketball draw crowds and have more full college scholarships. Playing baseball means finding money elsewhere. Another factor is time likely spent in the minors *v.* a quick ticket to the NBA. It makes sense—dollars and cents—to seek financial opportunity. Why so few blacks in baseball? The color that counts is green.
   —*Bob Wolff*

   The rise of Hispanics is a great story of the last fifteen to twenty years. In 1996, Texas's Juan Gonzalez and Seattle's Alex Rodriguez finished first and second for American League Most Valuable Player: the first Hispanics to place 1-2. Since then, the trend has grown: Rafael Palmeiro, Pedro Martinez, Manny Ramirez, David Ortiz. Yet what about *before* the rise? In 1871, Cuban-born Esteban Bellan became the majors' first Hispanic. Progress was erratic: The 1911 Reds had to file affidavits to prove two Cuban players were European. Adolfo Luque began a twenty-year career in 1914, twice leading in National League ERA. In 1938, Miguel (Mike) Angel Gonzalez managed the Cardinals. Two years later scout Joe Cambria told a young prospect to forget the bigs. Fidel Castro did, pitching at the Universidad de La Habana. The 1940s ended with Cuba's Orestes (Minnie) Minoso: baseball's first dark-skinned Hispanic. The '50s began with Venezuelan shortstop Chico Carrasquel: first All-Star Hispanic. In 1954, Mexico's Bobby (Beto) Avila hit .341: first to win a batting title. Before long, Venezuela's Luis Aparicio and Puerto Rico's Orlando Cepeda were voted league Rookie of the Year. Hispanics were changing beisbol, even as some were slow to see.
   In 1959–1970, Hispanics helped the NL hold a 13-2-1 All-Star Game edge. 1960: the Dominican Republic's Juan Marichal, twenty-two, throws a

one-hit debut, six times winning twenty games. 1961: Puerto Rico's Roberto Clemente wins his first of four batting titles. Tony Perez drove the Big Red Machine. Felipe and Matty Alou doubled an outfield's pleasure. Cuba's Zoilo (Zorro) Versalles became AL MVP on the same 1965 Twins team as Camilo Pascual and Tony Oliva. Dagoberto Blanco (Campy) Campaneris and Cesar Tovar were first to play all nine positions in a game. 1969: Pedro (Preston) Gomez managed the Padres all season. 1971: Clemente became Series MVP, dying a year later in a New Year's Eve plane crash trying to help victims of a Nicaraguan earthquake. The Pirates retired *Arriba*'s — The Great One's — legendary number 21.

At fifty-three, Minoso became oldest to get a hit. Venezuela's Tony Armas won a home run title. Mexico's Fernando Valenzuela and Puerto Rico's Guillermo Hernandez won a Cy Young award. Jose Canseco founded the 40/40 club: home runs and steals. The firsts go on. I often cook on special occasions like *Nochebuena* (Christmas Eve) a traditional Cuban meal for friends and family: Cuban Lechon Asada (roasted pork) with black beans and white rice. Add plantains, a good Merlot wine, and Cuban and Spanish dessert like *Turron* (nougat). Next day, Christmas, we have Cuban sandwiches. We need to remember when for Hispanics baseball was not a holiday.

— *Amaury Pi-Gonzalez*

[In the 1860s, U.S. sailors porting in Cuba and Cubans once schooled in America brought baseball to the isle.] I was born in Bayamo, in the province of Oriente. I always liked baseball, but knew I didn't have ability to play. My family wanted me to [be a lawyer], make more money, but I knew where my heart was. [As a teen] one day me and four of my friends went to Havana and met the people at Radio Salas, a pioneer in Cuba. Later the owner of COCO Radio and El Crisol News asked how much Salas is paying me. I told him. He said he would pay nearly four times that amount. I took the offer. I remember there was an association called ACRI [association of radio and newspaper reporters]. I was in the sports department, but they had all kinds of people — singers, musicians. When you think about it, that's what we try to do — bring music to the game.

— *Felo Ramirez*

Clark Griffith had little scouting money, so he turned to a former laundry owner from Baltimore, Joe Cambria, who turned to 1930s Cuba, signing Bobby Estalella and Venezuela's Alex Carrasquel, pitching in Cuba when Cambria spotted him. By wartime 1944, *twelve* Cubans dotted the Senators spring roster. In 1954, Cambria signed Carlos Paula, who next year tied for third with *six* home runs, showing the team's power shortage. Carlos was released a year later, not stopping Mr. Griffith from signing Jose Valdivielso, Julio Becquer, Sandy Consuegra, Julio Moreno, Mike Fornieles, 1950s pitching ace Pedro Ramos, so fast he beat Mickey Mantle in a match race, and Havana's Camilo Pascual, blooming later, like his curve. What an influx — and indicator. Mr. Griffith didn't care what color a player was, only if he could do the job. Someday, reopening, Cuba will surely produce more big-league players and announcers. When that happens, remember him and Joe Cambria, who showed how it should be.

— *Bob Wolff*

God has given me a long life. I can say that no one has presented more games than I have, announcing continuously since 1945: first amateur, then professional. The Cuban League's four teams were the Almendares Scorpions, Cienfuegos Elephants, Havana Lions, and Marianao Tigers. I did each [also, Puerto Rican and Venezuelan clubs like Caguas, Santurce, and San Juan; 1993– NL Marlins; and thirty-two of 1951–1983's World Series, missing only 1961's when Fidel Castro banned professional baseball and refused to let Cubans leave]. That year I permanently left the country but remember teams playing in the same Havana stadium each night, especially a Sunday doubleheader. One reason U.S. players liked our Winter League was they didn't have to move from one place to the other. They could live on the beach! Ah, the Havana beach, which was a sweet thing, and they enjoyed it. So did fans, who could always see our sport. Everything helped me transmit as much as I did.

— *Felo Ramirez*

Baseball began with my Spanish-born father leaving as a young man for Cuba and introducing me to a game that at age sixty-five, I love more than ever. We went each Sunday to the doubleheader at Estadio de El Cerro. The first game was Cienfuegos and Marianao. The second matched Havana *v.* Almendares, a historic rivalry like Dodgers-Giants. By the '50s, Felo meant Cuban baseball. As my mother said: "Amaury would go in the patio of our house, grab a broom, turn it upside down to look like a microphone, and imitate Felo's play-by-play!" Imagine getting a call in 1988 from the Caracol Radio Network to work the NLCS over stations in the U.S. and Latin America with him! — like a child hearing Vin Scully, then joining him in the booth. That year I also teamed with Jaime Jarrin on the network: with Felo, the sole Spanish-speaking Voice still living to win the Frick Award. Only in America — even when your dreams start somewhere else.

— *Amaury Pi-Gonzalez*

In 1949 I met Buck Canel, whom I'd heard in Bayamo at the first Caribbean Winter League Series in Havana. He spoke Spanish and English perfectly. During World War II Buck had a series, NBC's *El Juego de Hoy* [Today's Show], a slice of a game, on its twenty-four-hour Latin American Division. He'd re-create games played in the day and at 6:00 o'clock, when the short wave came perfectly into Cuba. One day a program boss heard me on the air and invited me to broadcast with Buck, beginning our [more than thirty-year] partnership. We did NBC Radio's *Cabalgeta Deportiva Gillette* aka *Gillette Cavalcade of Sports* on more than 200 U.S. and Latin America stations, then TV when it came to Cuba. I'm proud of being the only person Buck would invite to work with. I have my own style and fortunately I leave behind some quotes that the public has chosen to enshrine. For that I take satisfaction. My life has been full of Cuban, Caribbean Winter League, and big-league baseball. And I once worried that I wouldn't get invited by anyone!

— *Felo Ramirez*

With many thousands of refugees, I arrived in Miami in 1961 after Castro declared Cuba a Marxist-Leninist government, seizing my family's property. Soon I played in high school and, when I didn't have a game, in baseball lots near the Orange Bowl. Many fine players fled the island after Castro eliminated professional sports, including Cuban-born Roberto Ortiz, a [1941–1944 and 1949–1950] Washington Senator who drove a beer

truck, delivering the popular Cerveza Hatuey, as he had in Cuba after retiring. At lunch, Roberto joined the mostly Cuban kids in the lots, showing how he faced big-league pitching. Ortiz died in Miami, in 1971. In 2012, the Florida Marlins will open a new stadium on that site. Guess who I'll remember on my first visit to the park?
    —Amuary Pi-Gonzalez

In 1951, I aired my first World Series, at Yankee Stadium. A foul ball went rolling down the net, and I did what anyone would do—I reached out to try to snatch it, and I ended up with it. Little did I know an immortal from the movies was next to me: Humphrey Bogart. He just laughed. Even then, getting a baseball back was a real big thing.
    —Felo Ramirez

Fernando Valenzuela is the most significant all-time baseball figure in Mexico: El Toro—the Bull—still hailed for his magic Rookie of the Year 1981 and beyond. He transcended athletically and socially, his 173–153 record not beginning to tell how this kid from the town of Etchohuaquila in the northern state of Sonora took Mexico and the baseball world. In a nation of 105 million people, half in poverty, Fernando, from a humble family, encouraged many, like me, who loved baseball but felt goals were for richer people. In Mexico, Fernandomania was everywhere: streets, soccer fields, or baseball diamonds, kids imitating his trademark windup, eyes almost rolling over his head, parents taking kids to practice. Futbol—soccer—is our favorite sport, but Fernando passed it—still the only baseball player. As Vin Scully said after Valenzuela's 1990 no-hitter: "If you've got a sombrero, throw it to the sky!" We'll never see such a phenom again.
    —Juan Angel Avila

[In 1997, Jaime Jarrin called Edgar Renteria's World Series–winning single on the Latina Broadcasting System, 35 million matching Scully's audience on CBS Radio. Next year Jarrin became the Frick Award's third Hispanic, joining Canel and later Ramirez.] As I'm taking the call of my selection, my wife began to cry. Emotion hit me Induction Week. Only if you're there can you feel how the impact registers. I think it shows how you must devote yourself to your profession, rising above bigotry to be regarded as an equal. I hope people see someone in me who came to this country without knowing the language, but through hard work and responsibility was able to go places. The cliché is true: Only in America could my story happen.

—*Jaime Jarrín*

Recently, a foul ball in San Francisco arced toward our booth at a high rate of speed. I closed my eyes, ducked out of the way to avoid getting hit, and was fine, but scared. As I quickly bent down, I heard a sound: the screen on my laptop, breaking. As any fan knows, ruining a suit or dress trying to make a catch, a foul ball can be expensive, the difference being that dry cleaning can't restore a screen.

—*Eduardo Ortega*

I was born in a beautiful town called Mazatlán, on the Pacific Ocean, where we breathe our winter league team, the Venados. Whitey Ford played there, like Kent Tekulve, Rick Sutcliffe, Jeffrey Leonard, and Lyman Bostock, among others. They made the majors, and so did I. As a kid, I heard the Mazatlán native and longtime Venados Voice, Eduardo Valdez-Vizcarra. My summer friend was Padres' Spanish broadcaster Mario Thomas, who lived more than fifty years in Tijuana, the border town near San Diego. Cable TV reached Mazatlán in 1987, yet radio was my bigs listening and talking "ticket." At this time Eduardo joined Thomas. In 1998, I joined *them*, making *two* Mazatlán Padres Voices—until Thomas told me that his real place of birth was not Tijuana, as I thought, but believe it or not, *Mazatlán*! That makes three, or would have had not Gilberto Delgado done the Padres in 1970: he, *too*, from our home. Four people, from one town, Mazatlán, with one team, the Pads! The American Dream is Mexico's, too.

—*Juan Angel Avila*

My 1980s A's partner was Nicaraguan-born Evelio Areas Mendoza. Not traveling, we did road games live from a regular-size nineteen-inch television monitor at radio station KNTA. Jose Canseco was el hombre because he hit, ran, hit for power, even caught the ball. In a TV game, Jose

hit a typically kilometric home run, Evelio calling it as I returned from the bathroom. A pitching change and TV break then followed at the very time Evelio also needed to "go." Taking over, I see a long drive on the screen. Not knowing it's a replay, I call the homer like it's live. Learning differently, I add, "Sorry, folks, that might be the first time a player hits two home runs with one swing." Canseco, in his prime: two for the price of one.
— *Amaury Pi-Gonzalez*

Raised in Tijuana, I idolized Dave Winfield, who reached the big leagues from college. My older brothers worked to help cover household costs and my sister's education and mine. Without me knowing it, Dave made my first Padres game possible: the first athlete to create a community foundation, helping low-income people watch baseball in San Diego Stadium's rightfield section — "The Winfield Pavilion." At ten, I rode in a van having special access through the border. The "Big Red Machine" played the Padres, but I mainly recall sitting behind the wall near Dave, who soon became an AL free agent. I made the Pads and did postseason, including '95's Atlanta-Cleveland World Series: Dave not on the Indians roster, but still in uniform. I thought, "Wow, my first Series and Dave's last year," deciding to introduce myself, nervous at meeting someone who inspired my career. "I'm the Spanish Voice of the Padres," I said in break, "working the World Series for CBS Americas Radio Network, and one of those kids from Tijuana you invited to the Winfield Pavilion. I just want to tell you, on behalf of my family, *thank you very much*. You motivated me to pursue a life in baseball." With a heartfelt smile, he said, "Congratulations! The drive to reach your goal was all your own." I again felt ten years old.
— *Eduardo Ortega*

If being a rookie 1998 Voice was the second-most important thing to happen to me, the first was working that year's Series. The 1998 Padres were solid as a rock, with Tony Gwynn [.321] our superstar, and pitchers like Trevor Hoffman [bigs high fifty-three saves] and Kevin Brown [18–7], a legitimate Number One. Greg Vaughn hit fifty homers. Ken Caminiti was in his last Padres year, a warrior and great third baseman, sadly dying young [forty-one, of a drug overdose]. That fall Yankee Stadium was seventy-five years old. Imagine the odds of someone from the Pacific Coast of Mexico, so far from The House that Ruth Built, working in this cathedral. It overwhelmed me, like the Yankees did the Pads. Despite our loss, '98 led to Petco Park, opening in 2004: seating sections separate; people sitting on grass beyond the fence; a next-door building the leftfield pole. For a Padres fan, that was even more important than my most important thing!

    — *Juan Angel Avila*

Hispanic broadcasters call baseball in a lively way. In the Padres' first years at their Peoria, Arizona, spring training home, the Brewers, in nearby Chandler, played at Compadre Stadium: a unique venue, to say the least, the field funneled toward home plate, booths behind the last row of fans. One day there was no radio transmission to Milwaukee: just the Padres' English broadcast team on one side of the press box and Hispanic, other. It must have been a weekday: fans stayed away in droves, letting you hear players talking on the field. When the umpire called "ball" or "strike," we'd describe the pitch with our "festive Latin" style. At first, the few fans there turned around and stared, as in "Who the heck are you and what are you doing here?" Most, I suspect, were Chandler retirees. By game's end, no one was sitting directly in front of us, moving to different sections to get away. I haven't taken it personally.

    — *Eduardo Ortega*

In 1953, the Braves left Boston, leaving the Jimmy Fund in the lurch. Thankfully, the Red Sox made it their official charity, fighting childhood cancer. Owner Tom Yawkey spent untold dollars. Ted Williams visited untold patients, insisting no one be told. Like Curt Gowdy and Ken Coleman, I've made the trip from Fenway to the clinic with Sox players to visit patients. In 1994, I met twelve-year-old Uri Berenguer, the nephew of Juan Berenguer, "Señor Smoke," a pitcher with most notably Detroit. Uri had come here because he had bone cancer and doctors in Panama were going to remove his leg. After surgery, he didn't know till waking if the leg would survive. By sixteen, pronounced cured, Uri was interested in broadcasting, so we invite him to keep out-of-town scores, do odd jobs, between treatment and playing high school ball. A few years back the Red Sox start

a Spanish network. Uri ran the board, went on the air, and became our Spanish Voice, then NESN TV host: still close to the Jimmy Fund, runs in its yearly Marathon. P.S. A woman named Rosie Lonborg — to Uri — "my play lady" — volunteered weekly at the clinic. One day he sees a 1967 video of Jim Lonborg pitching. "Look," Uri says, "there's Rosie's husband!"
    — *Joe Castiglione*

I have had a lot of bad news in my life, and have thankfully been able to overcome it. This helped me deal with the death of a friend. [On May 29, 2005] I did a Sunday night game in Yankee Stadium with my partner, Juan Pedro Villaman, getting back to Fenway about 2:00 a.m. J. P. was talking about how ESPN games take forever with all their commercials. We were laughing about how we should be home by now. I was the last person to say good-bye. We gave each other a hug, and I said, "See you tomorrow, Papa." We never did. [Villaman, forty-six, shortly died in a car accident north of Boston. Berenguer, then twenty-three, somehow aired that night's game.] I did a lot of crying that day and composed myself. As soon as I entered the gate, I started crying again. J. P. was like a brother, every "hello" a hug, every "good-bye" a hug. It's Latino culture, and that's who he was: the most passionate broadcaster I've ever known.
    — *Uri Berenguer*

Once at Coors Field, Mario Thomas was sitting during break when Steve Finley hit a foul that he barely had time to duck. "Oh, the ball has landed in our booth and look out!" I said on air. "It hits my friend [Thomas, striking a table, then his head]. He is getting up and I think he's going to have to visit Padres trainer Todd Hutchinson," which he did. Mario returns with a red lump on his head and at break starts talking: "I just spoke to my wife on the phone. Your play-by-play scared her to death! I had to convince her that everything's alright. She wanted to jump on the first flight to Denver!" Mario called the rest of the game with an icepack on his head. Next day, someone yelled in the clubhouse, "Hey, we have something for you, don't leave." They gave him a closed box. Inside was a batting helmet. In 1993, we held a special banquet, which I coordinated, at a Tijuana hotel to celebrate Mario's twenty-fifth Padres year, inviting team executives, colleagues, and long-time friends. At the podium, Jerry Coleman prepared to present a plaque: "Mario, I congratulate you on your twenty-five years with San Diego but I'm very mad with you. I've known you so long and you never told me your real name." The room fell silent. "I didn't know your first name was Donald." Jerry then gave the award, everyone laughing because the plaque read: "In recognition of DON MARIO THOMAS," who died in 2009. In Spanish, the term *Don* is a sign of respect for someone who is older and considered wiser, like Don Pedro, Don Luis, and Don Corleone. By that criterion, Jerry's real name is Don, too.

— *Eduardo Ortega*

Airing baseball thirty-five years, I know that things are cyclical, but let's go back to when interleague play began: 1997 Giants-Rangers at The Ballpark in Arlington. I was there and had no idea how the format would develop. Many opposed it, because baseball was the only major sport where one league never played the other outside of pre- and postseason. Currently the American League has a 1,808–1,652 game regular-season edge, winning every year since 2004. The All-Star Game is more lopsided: 12–1, with one famous or infamous tie in the 2002 Mid-Summer classic. The World Series is 8–6, including the Giants over the Rangers in 2010: the very clubs that kicked interleague off! Teams that draw are in the same area: Yankees-Mets, Cubs-White Sox, Giants-A's, Dodgers-Angels. Forget Florida and Tampa Bay. These are geographical rivalries. The rest are a stretch: even good baseball cities like Seattle *v.* San Diego. Baseball faces a challenge keeping interleague play from becoming dull. That's one cycle it *doesn't* need.

— *Amaury Pi-Gonzalez*

A few years back, I was doing a game at Veterans Stadium on a muggy ninety-five-degree day when a ball was fouled in our direction above our booth. A fan reached for the ball, lost track of his beer, and dropped his suds on me—I think, a Bud. The rest of the game was a stinky affair, uncomfortable until I finally got back to the hotel. An old beer ad went, "Tastes great, or less filling?" This beer went 0 for 2.

— *Eduardo Ortega*

I worked on CBS's *The Jackie Gleason Show*, was involved with Lorimar Productions' *The Midnight Caller*, and broke in re-creating A's away games in-studio. Recently colleague Ken Korach described distinct parts of parks where'd he'd announced. My most memorable was in 1986: Jose Canseco, a rookie; Jose Rijo, in his third year; Joaquin Andujar, the A's highest earner — $1.3 million. Times change. The Oakland Coliseum, if not ideal for baseball, at least had no Mt. Davis with that cement monstrosity behind the outfield. KNTA now broadcasts in Chinese. Then, it did A's games in Spanish. One day GM Gene Hogan had a brainstorm: erect a *canopy* behind home plate in a space behind the backstop. Fans talk about feeling like you're on the field. We *were*, the canopy keeping fouls from hitting us on the head. At that time, advertising wasn't sold behind the plate, so the canopy's station ID letters, seen on TV from centerfield, gave us a promotional monopoly. Players like Rijo, charting pitches, sat with us, our view not good, liners over first and third getting lost in the corner. In the end, management, fans, or players didn't kill the canopy. Rival *scouts* thought we were stealing signs. We weren't — couldn't *see* well enough! On the other hand, our equipment never got wet.

— *Amaury Pi-Gonzalez*

You can't repay parents for what they do: in my case, helping me reach what I call baseball's "second-best job after the players themselves." We share a goal: the "big show," falling, getting up, acquiring priceless experience. Behind every player and announcer, a story lingers. Mine is my mother's. I was seventeen on December 11, 1980, my first day in radio, returning home to hear these words: "Your brothers tell me there was a beautiful voice on the radio. I congratulate you for following your dreams and I love you very much. Remember, while you may not be before me, I will always listen with my heart." Baseball means connecting with the audience: Exciting and engaging, you succeed. For me, this involves two emotions: becoming the eyes of people, who, like me, love baseball; and filling my mother, who loves me, with pride. My mother has clipped articles, photos, periodicals, or game programs: anything that notes my work. One day, I reflected on twenty-five years of Padres baseball, fifteen World Series, ten

All-Star Games, and ten Caribbean World Series, and working for ESPN Deportes Radio, CBS Americas, and other networks. The one person, above all, who I wish could have heard me, is my mother. The irony! She is deaf. Each game she watches, thrilled to see the Padres, but at the same time nostalgia creeping in. She wonders how her son's voice must sound. My voice! A voice she hears not with her ears, but heart.

    — *Eduardo Ortega*

Chapter Thirteen

Make 'em Laugh

A half-century ago Joe Garagiola wrote Baseball Is a Funny Game. *It still is. Game 2 of 1990's Reds-A's World Series was tied at 4 in the ninth inning. Cincy's staff spent, Marty Brennaman was asked to make a plea: "We understand that Tom Browning's wife Debbie has gone into labor," he said on WLW. "He has left the ballpark, and a call apparently has just come up from the Reds clubhouse to make an appeal over our airwaves for Tom Browning to come back to the ballpark in the event that they have to use him to pitch tonight." He did. They didn't.*

A year earlier Bob Uecker stole film's Major League *from Tom Berenger, Wesley Snipes, and Charlie Sheen. "Diehard Day coming up at The Stadium," Uke intoned as boozy Voice Harry Doyle. "Free admission to anyone who was actually alive the last time the Indians won the pennant." A batter "crushed the ball toward South America. [You'd] need a visa to catch that one." The peepul's choice: "just outside" as a wild pitch hit the screen.*

For twenty-seven years, Harry Kalas and Richie Ashburn kibitzed on the air like two sides of the Phillies' coin — "friends immediately," said Kalas, "and best friends, eventually." The 1992 Phils placed next-to-last. Harry: "What are they going to name their highlight film?" Ashburn: "How about, 'The game's not so easy?'"

One day the former centerfielder said: "Harry, you know I did something Babe Ruth never did?"

Kalas: "What's that, Whitey?"

"Hit a home run in Dodger Stadium."

Harry paused. "Yeah, Whitey, I guess that Babe Ruth wasn't the player he was cracked up to be." Once the Phillie Phanatic mascot crashed the booth, scaled a ledge, and worked his way around Veterans Stadium. "What does it say," Richie asked Kalas, "that you're one of our biggest stars — and the Phanatic is the other?"

The Giants and A's Lon Simmons liked to turn gotcha on himself. A listener admitted a crush since childhood. "You must have been terribly deprived," mused the Bay Area funnyman. Of pitcher Robb Nen, Lon said, "It looks like he's trying to overthrow it. Which is fine, if you're pitching against a government." One night the bases were loaded. "And I wish we were, too." Another game entered the bottom of the fifth. "Boy, I wish I was at the bottom of a fifth."

At eighty, Simmons moved to Maui, feeding peanuts to a cardinal he named Stan Musial. California was sad to see him go. "I wish you could broadcast baseball," a woman rued. Lon said, "That's what they used to tell me in the broadcast booth, too."

In 1941, I homered twice in my first exhibition game with the Pirates. I got a little fat-headed, which didn't please our manager, Frank Frisch. "Kiner, why aren't you running laps?" he said. I said, "Mr. Frisch, I have only one pair of baseball shoes, and if I wear them out running, I won't have any for the games." He reddened. "Well, that's fine. You can take those shoes to Barnwell [South Carolina, Bucs minor-league camp], because that's where you'll be playing your next game."
— *Ralph Kiner*

In World War II, I served in Okinawa with the Marines. In 1945, returning to Brattleboro, Vermont, I was twenty-one and asked a former cheerleader at my old high school for a date.

"What do you do?" Lois Denhard asked me.

"I play baseball," at that time in the Eastern League.

"I know, but what do you do for a *living*?"

We got married in 1947.
— *Ernie Johnson*

Things happen. In 1951, Detroit's Pat Mullin's late-inning home run tied the Yankees. Broadcaster Bud Blattner was beat, and Mullin was due to hit again in the tenth. Except for him, Bud would have been driving home, so Blattner wrote "The bastard" beside his name. His partner read:

"Now to the bastard, I mean batter." A few years later Sarasota, Florida's, mayor is about to throw out the first pitch at a Red Sox spring game when the press steward asks Curt Gowdy about a drink. Too far away for Curt to answer, the steward passed a note with "milkshake" as a suggestion. Gowdy misread its meaning, saying, "To throw out the ball, here's the Mayor, *Mike Shane*." Then, there's a story attributed to many about spotting a couple in the bleachers. "That's interesting," the announcer says. "He's kissing her on the strikes, and she's kissing him on the balls."

— *Ron Menchine*

On July 31, 1954, Joe Adcock hit four homers, had eighteen total bases, and helped Milwaukee rout Brooklyn, 15–7. That week a man from North Carolina sent a letter, saying I'd made him drive off the road. Don Newcombe had been bombed early in the game. "Aaron is coming up, Newk is still out there," I said, "and in the bullpen Clem Labine is throwing up." I could have said "heating up" or "warming up," but somehow my malapropism fit better. To the guy, pulling over, laughing so hard he couldn't drive, a Dodger vomiting was the perfect image.

— *Nat Allbright*

In 1960, Ronnie Held, like me, was eleven. I was a Yankees fan, since the Dodgers had moved and the Mets hadn't yet arrived, and I bet Ronnie on the Series. He hated the Yankees. We bet a dollar — four weeks of allowance — big money. Game 7 was a Thursday afternoon, the time each week when Miss Segreta picked me up at elementary school, drove me to my home, and gave my piano lesson. I pleaded, "Can't I have today off? It's the seventh game of the World Series! I got a *dollar* riding on it." I might as well have talked Sanskrit. She said: "No, no, we have a lesson!" It starts, I'm fuming, and I begin playing "On Top of Old Smokey," take twenty-two, when Ronnie runs up, hits the doorbell, and says, "You owe me a dollar! The Pirates won the Series! Mazeroski homered!" I'm mortified because a) I didn't get to see it; b) I'm playing "On Top of Old Smokey"; c) I'm out a buck; d) the Yankees lost. I probably knew two curse words at age eleven, and I unleashed my entire vulgar vocabulary on (to this day I believe the entirely deserving) Miss Segreta. It was the last time I played piano. The first time I met Mazeroski, I told him the story. Whenever I've seen Bill since, he asks about my piano playing.

— *Charley Steiner*

Good friends Mickey Mantle and John Blanchard had next-door lockers. John was a fortunate guy, not catching much, Yogi Berra and Elston Howard starting, but cashing all those World Series checks. In 1965, Mick comes into The Stadium, goes to his locker, and sees tears running down Blanchard's face. "My God, what's wrong?" he says. John: "Mick, today I got traded to Kansas City." Mantle says, "That's great, you'll finally get a chance to play." Blanchard: "That's why I'm crying. You know I can't play."

— *Steve Blass*

Phil Rizzuto and I are doing the Yankees, we're in a rain delay, and somebody calls us: Name the all-time Yankee team. We can't choose between Bill Dickey and Yogi Berra at catcher. First base, Lou Gehrig, best guy there in baseball history. Second, Joe Gordon: Till he made Cooperstown in 2009, I'd bitch to the Hall each year. Shortstop, the Scooter. Third base, Red Rolfe. Outfield: We put Mantle in left, Joe D. in center, and Roger Maris in right. Great team. We're feeling good till the phones light up. "Hey, fellahs, did you forget somebody? Where the hell is Babe Ruth?" Oops. A time like that, you want to curl up in a fetal position and find yourself a closet.

— *Jerry Coleman*

By 1968, reliever Elroy Face had already set a then–National League career record for games. Friday, we find he's being traded to the other league — Detroit. Next afternoon, I start against Atlanta, face two batters, and move to leftfield. Elroy comes in to get a batter to build his total. I retake the mound, finish the game, the Braves not scoring, but because Face pitched I don't get a complete game or shutout, ending with seven shutouts, one short of the Pirates record. Elroy lived in a Pittsburgh suburb, near a country club, where one day I play golf, have too much beer, and decide I shouldn't drive. Remembering Elroy's house, at 3:00 a.m. I park in his driveway, not wanting to wake anyone, so I get out of the car, lie down on the lawn, and fall asleep. At 6:30 Elroy gets a call: "Mr. Face, I live next door and think there's a dead person on your lawn." That's how it was: You helped your teammates awake, asleep, live, or dead.

—*Steve Blass*

Many listeners ask if I ever made a blooper on the air. Yes, and it was a doozy, describing a sharp grounder to third as "a harply s— ground ball." It always brings a laugh when I tell the story. Depending on the audience, I may add, "I feel very fortunate I never broadcast ice hockey. I hate the thought of having to describe a flying puck."

—*Ron Menchine*

Former pitcher Pete Harnisch helped work his way through Fordham University by appearing in police lineups. "Twenty-five bucks for a regular case," he said. "Fifty bucks for a murder case." Former major league infielder Casey Candaele was equally pragmatic. His mother played in the Women's Professional Baseball League, which was glorified in the movie, *A League Of Their Own*. "She had a better swing than mine," Candaele admitted with a smile. "She was the only mother ever to be banned from playing in father-son baseball games at school because she was too good."

—*Tim Kurkjian*

On the road you like bars with a good mix of people and atmosphere. Fred White, I, and other Royals were at a Steak & Ale. Outfielder Jim Wohlford came up to where we're talking. He'd been slumping, wasn't playing much. When things got quiet, he said to Fred and me, "Guys, will you pray with me?" Understandably, the request threw most of us off base. Prayer is good, but we were in a bar with loud music and a lot of commotion. Fred said, "Wolfy, I'm not sure this is the time or place." Wolfy replied, "I really, *really* have to get rid of this slump. Won't you please pray with me?" Fred paused for a second before saying, "How about if I just buy you a beer?"

—*Denny Matthews*

We used to call Russ Hodges "The Fabulous Fat Man," and he was more fabulous than fat. "Here's what we'll do," he told me. "If we win the game we'll drink because we're happy. If we lose we'll drink because we're sad. The only way we won't drink is if we tie." One night an extra-inning error tied the game. Curfew extended it. Said Russ: "We're just gonna' break a rule."

— *Lon Simmons*

Hungry, Richie Ashburn wondered on the air if the people from Celebre's Pizza were listening. Fifteen minutes later pizza arrived in the booth. Soon management called him in. "Richie, you've got to stop these plugs. Celebre's not a sponsor." Whitey asked if he could still salute birthdays. Sure, they said. That week Richie said he'd like to send "very special birthday wishes to the Celebre's twins — Plain and Pepperoni."

In 1971, his first year in Philly, Harry Kalas was told to solicit Richie's analysis as a future Hall of Fame outfielder. One night a player broke his bat. Harry said, "Whitey, a game bat must have been very important to you."

"Hey, it really is," Richie said. "When I was going well with a particular bat, I wouldn't trust leaving it around the clubhouse. On a road trip, I'd take my bat back to the hotel and go to bed with it."

"Is that right?" Harry said.

"Sure," said Richie. "I've been to bed with a lot of old bats in my day."

— *Chris Wheeler*

TV is sport's main stage, but as long as people listen on the porch or go places in a car, there'll be a place for radio. My wife Marlene and I were talking in a hotel elevator in Baltimore. A couple elderly ladies heard us, and started looking at each other. When the door opened, one asked, "Excuse me, are you Fred Manfra?" I said yes, and Marlene and I began laughing as the woman said, "I go to bed with you every night."

— *Fred Manfra*

I invented the batting glove, necessity the mother of invention. Once the Yankees' Jim Coates was supposed to pitch: like me, a righty. No way I'm in the lineup. I play thirty-six holes of golf, get to the park, see lefty Whitey Ford's starting, so guess who's playing? In batting practice, I have a big blister, which is trouble, except I remember a golf glove in my locker pants. I put on the glove, Whitey throws a curve, I homer, and later go deep again. Next day, the Yankees all have red golf gloves on. Mantle'd had their clubhouse guy go out and get a couple dozen. That's how you start a trend. The same thing later happened with the one-handed catch, which I didn't invent, but popularized. Our manager, Dick Williams, steamed when I practiced it: "Don't drop one. Don't drop one." I didn't, because you never like to let your skipper down.

— *Ken Harrelson*

'Seventy-eight's last game, Dodgers at Padres, a big crowd for Fan Appreciation Day. Gaylord Perry's Padres are in fourth place, twelve games behind us, so why he is pitching? Perry wants his 3,000th career strikeout before everybody goes home. By the fifth inning, I'm in the outfield, giving a Dodgers regular the rest of the day off. In the tenth, Gaylord's still pitching. I bat with two out and Perry at 2,999, getting two strikes before fouling off four super wet spitballs. Finally, I take a pitch a foot off the plate. Big Lee Weyer yells, "Strike three!"—me cussing him in vain. The stadium goes berserk. Gaylord gets his milestone, the Padres carrying him off the field. At least I've made history—victim 3,000! Two weeks later, I see in *The Sporting News* that baseball had miscounted. *Another* strikeout had been number 3,000 two innings earlier. Know who it was? Me! I already *held* the record when in the tenth I *set* the record.

— *Joe Simpson*

Hal McRae was our long-time clubhouse enforcer, including a short-lived Royal. George Scott joined them in 1979 after thirteen years with Boston and Milwaukee, having nothing left. Whitey Herzog mainly used him as a pinch hitter or fill-in at first. George's nickname, "Boomer," had nothing to do with his high-pitched voice: Mike Tyson before Mike Tyson. Arriving, Scott wanted his Boston number 5. The problem was that we already had a star named George wearing number 5. Still, for the life of Boomer, he couldn't figure why he couldn't have it, complaining constantly: bus, cage, probably in his sleep. "I'm George Scott," he'd say in that voice. "I deserve number 5. Boomer gets no respect. I'm number 5." As a part-timer, Boomer routinely hit into an easy double play in his only at-bat, then went into the clubhouse and began yada yada: "I'm number 5. I get no respect." (Fittingly, he wore number 0.) Three weeks later, hitting less than his 215 pounds, Boomer went 0 for 4 in a game, afterward again whining. Finally, our enforcer, his locker near Scott's, had heard enough. "Boomer, shut up!" McRae shouted. "I'm sick and tired of listening to you talk about number 5. We have another number we're going to give you . . . 6-4-3." The room was silent. We didn't hear another word from George before the Royals released him, which wasn't long. The Yankees signed him, and he played the final month of his career there. They wouldn't give him number 5 either. It belonged to another guy, retired.

    — *Denny Matthews*

In baseball, you need a thick skin. In the mid-'80s, I'm doing a Padres game in Montreal. Goose Gossage has just come in from the bullpen. His third baseman is Graig Nettles, good friends from playing together in New York. Goose walked his first two guys on eight straight pitches. Nettles came to the mound, said something, and Goose put his glove by his mouth, in the days before players worried about people reading lips. It was a long way from the booth to the mound, but I could see Goose doubled over, laughing. After the game I asked, "What'd you say when you went to the mound?" Nettles smiled. "Ah, nothing, I just asked if they had any home plates in the bullpen."

    — *Dave Campbell*

The 1985 Giants lost a hundred games for the first time in their century-old history, compiling their worst team batting average, a mark that still stands. One night during batting practice, the Giants' Jeffrey Leonard and Dan Gladden got into a dispute. I was in our booth and couldn't tell what had precipitated it. Suddenly, they began swinging at each other and then rolling on the dirt beside the cage. Teammates poured out of the dugout trying to break it up. It occurred to me it was the only baseball fight I'd seen where only one dugout cleared. The next day the *San Jose Mercury* ran a headline that read: "GIANTS START HITTING — each other."

    — *Hank Greenwald*

In the '80s, the White Sox' Shawn Hillegas was one out from a complete game when our director showed a shot of his wife standing and clapping

with the team's other wives. Seeing her, I blurted, "There's Shawn's wife, looking forward to watching her husband go all the way for the first time this year." My partner, Steve Busby, burst out laughing. When he lost it, so did I: There was lots of dead air before the final out. Later, someone praised me for not overtalking at a highlight moment. If they'd only known.
   —*Bob Carpenter*

September 25, 1986. A year earlier the Astros had told Mike Scott to get another pitch or his career's over. All of a sudden, he came up with the spitter—and now in one game he no-hits the Giants and helps clinch the NL West. What makes it amazing is that the day before Nolan Ryan had pitched a two-hitter. It reminded me of Dizzy Dean who in 1934 scattered three hits in the first game of a doubleheader. Brother Paul threw a no-hitter in the nightcap. "If I knowed Paul was gonna' pitch a no-hitter," Diz says, "I'd a' thrown one, too."
   —*Milo Hamilton*

In 1987, Toronto pitcher Mike Flanagan was driving to Exhibition Stadium with former teammate Mike Boddicker in a Blue Jays rental car. New players to the team drove these rentals until their cars arrived. Flanagan saw me as I was walking to the ballpark, lugging my computer and oversized bag of books, and gave me a ride. "This was Phil Niekro's car," Flanagan said of the ancient pitcher who had just been released. "How do you know it was his car?" I asked. He said: "I found his *teeth* in the glove compartment."
   —*Tim Kurkjian*

My first year broadcasting, pitcher Osvaldo Fernandez, a Cuban émigré, is on third base, and the Giants try a squeeze play. The ball gets past the catcher. Osvaldo seems a cinch to score until he very gentlemanly stops near the catcher, not wanting to hurt him, and the catcher, having retrieved the ball, tags him out. I can't believe it. I turn to Jon Miller, who's great at Spanish, and say, "Jon, how do you say *pussy* in Cuban?" Jon mumbles a few syllables, getting back to English as fast as he can.
   —*Mike Krukow*

It's easier to play tired than to broadcast tired. As a player, it can actually help, too tired to lunge at the slider. On the air, every word is measured, as my late-'80s Braves showed. I have a dull monotone voice that needs a high energy level to pierce crowd noise. Ronnie Gant is at the plate when, sure enough, I go for energy. "There's a drive—deep leftfield—[Herm] Winningham's back at the wall—he leaps—home run, Ronnie Gant!" Man, was I over the top. My partner, Skip Caray, points to the monitor: Uh-oh, Winningham has brought the ball *back*. We go to break, and I say, unclassily, "I sound like Phil Rizzuto." So I have to write to Phil and apologize. He writes back, very kind: "Billy, it's OK. I don't care if you use *huckleberry*." By then, I was more tired than after a road trip to Nepal.

—*Billy Sample*

Memorial Stadium 1991: I did a half-hour 7:00 o'clock Home Team Sports show before each Orioles game: the first part live, second pre-recorded. You're not too nervous, except with royalty. The Queen of England, Her Majesty, the most famous woman in the world, is coming to the game, and I don't know how to *act*. All that security, no players to interview, and I don't know what to *say*. Brit Hume, then of ABC, spots me and yells, "Hey, Tom, how you doing?" I go over, tell him I don't know anything about the Queen, and ask, "Would you mind joining me at 7:00?" "Sure," Brit said, getting me through the show. Today I think of the great movie *The Naked Gun*, a lady falling from the upper deck foiling Reggie Jackson's attempt to assassinate Queen Elizabeth. *Then*, all I thought of was how to stop perspiring. I look up at the owner's box and the real Queen hasn't broken a sweat.

—*Tom Davis*

In 1992, the front office told me Miss Illinois was at our game and would I interview her on radio? What twenty-seven-year-old male would say no? I'm still learning play-by-play, let alone how to interview, but give it my best: at that time, not good. As the inning went on and on, Miss Illinois' answers got shorter and shorter. Finally, I said, "Are those real?" She replied, "Yes, I just got them done." I said, truthfully, "I noticed them when you walked in the booth. They're beautiful." Thankfully, the inning

ends, I say good-bye, and a few moments later a woman from our front office races in asking what I'd been _talking_ about. Phone lines are jammed. I
said, gee, I'd asked Miss Illinois about her well-manicured fingernails. I've
tried to be clearer since.

    — _Dave Wills_

I can't remember who the '90s Giants batter was but he fouled off a
pitch which struck Cubs catcher Todd Pratt in the one place you don't want
to get hit with a foul ball. The poor guy is rolling around on the ground
and my partner Duane Kuiper and I are relying on such euphemisms as
"He'll be singing soprano in the church choir this Sunday" and "We hope
he wasn't planning on having any more kids," since you can only be so
graphic describing such an injury. The trainers from both teams attend to
Pratt. Finally after several minutes they got him to his feet and he's stagger-
ing around when Kuiper, in the height of innocence, declared: "He's just
gonna' have to shake it off."

    — _Hank Greenwald_

In 2001, Jack Buck stopped by the Wrigley booth. He had Parkinson's
disease, a pacemaker, arthritis, but was still smart and funny. I said, "We've
been talking about your appearance at the Chicago Museum of Broadcast
Communications, 5:30 to 7:30. Admission is free. It should be a good time."
Jack didn't miss a beat: "Well, that shows you how important I am when
the admission is free." Of his many lines, my favorite was how Jack had
been in the Ninth Infantry Division, got shot crossing the Remagen Bridge
into Germany, and spent V-E Day in a Paris hospital. He'd tell people: "I've
always had a fondness for French women. In fact, during World War II a
French woman hid me in her basement for three months. Of course, this
was in Cleveland."

    — _Pat Hughes_

In 2001, I did a seventeen-inning Blue Jays game against New York at
SkyDome that lasted until 1:00 a.m. My youngest son, Ben, was six months
old, and as babies do from time to time got up in the middle of the night.
My wife, Sarah, got up to take care of him, noticed I wasn't home, and went

into panic mode. She called the police, who told her if someone is only a couple of hours late he's not considered missing. She persists, telling them how punctual I am and how something must be wrong. Finally, they agree to take information. When's the last time you saw him? Where was he going? When the officer realized who it was, he told his colleagues, and my wife could hear laughing through the phone. "Check the TV, ma'am!" they tell her. "The game's still on!"

    —*Dan Shulman*

To his credit, the A's Bill King thought interleague play a "sideshow," even putting a clause into his contract that the only away games against the National League he had to broadcast were those in San Francisco—no "sideshow" on the road. Bill's wife, Nancy, died in 2004 after a beautiful marriage that lasted decades, her wrenching death coinciding with the start of a Coliseum homestand featuring the Pirates and Reds. Naturally, Bill, grieving, missed the games. It was slightly awkward when he returned to the booth. How do you find the right words for a wonderful friend who has lost a spouse? Typically, Bill broke the ice: "At least Nancy had the good sense to die during interleague play."

    —*Ken Korach*

Everybody remembers 1962's World Series Game 7. The dentist let me listen on radio, hoping it'd distract me. Today, I walk in the Giants' clubhouse. One day, there's Willie Mays; another, Willie McCovey; another, Orlando Cepeda. I still ask about the game. The tying run, Matty Alou, bunts safely to start the ninth. Mays doubles into the rightfield corner and Alou's held at third because on a wet field Roger Maris made a great pickup and throw to cutoff man Bobby Richardson. Mays put it nicely: "I'm not saying Matty *should* have scored. I'm saying if it had been me, I *would* have scored." Being Mays, he probably would have. Yankees manager Ralph Houk, bullpen ready, stuck with [starter Ralph] Terry, who strangely wanted to pitch to lefty McCovey, not Cepeda, a righty like himself. Orlando explained that he'd had a double earlier against Terry and in that game hit a foul home run. Ralph had an aversion to him, like me to dentists since.

    —*Jon Miller*

In 2006, we're supposed to go to Texas and Tampa Bay, with Monday off in between, until a rainout forces a Monday afternoon makeup game in Pittsburgh. On Sunday night we endure a convention at our hotel—not your normal clientele—of people dressed up like cats. Some getups were downright scary, like people meowing in the elevator. Next day Pirates Voice Lanny Frattare asked me on his pre-game show, presenting a cigar as a gift: huge, pungent, and expensive. That night, it's warm, humid, and miserable in Tampa as Greg Schulte and I go outside to the pool. Seeking relief, I open the cigar, take three puffs, absolutely puke, and return to my room, where I drink water, lie down, and puke some more. Still, nobody knows, right? This is between me and the bed sheets. A day later Schulte tells the world that I "nearly vomited on Lanny Frattare's cigar."

—*Jeff Munn*

Since 2009, I've been Yankees PA Voice, following the great Bob Sheppard. In the mid-1990s, I televised fifty games a year with Bobby Murcer and Phil Rizzuto. Return with me to Sunday, August 6, 1995, sixth inning: the day Phil and I confronted a bee while trying to telecast from Detroit. I'm on play-by-play. Phil's rummaging through a fans' plastic bag filled with anniversary and birthday cards to read on the air, a homey touch seldom heard today. I've never been stung, have no cause to believe the worst, yet panic when this fat bloodthirsty bee invades our booth. Soon I'm waving frantically, further annoying him, as Phil tells director John Moore what's going on, using his last name like he did with everyone when not using "Huckleberry." Moore tells his centerfield cameraman to shoot my—actually, *our*—distress, since the bee, an equal opportunity annoyance, is now lashing Phil. Picture us as our audience did: two grown men in suits calling the action while fighting this intruder. Recall the plastic bag? Phil grabs it and in one fell swat—the bee is going, going, gone! Dead! On camera! Our next TV game is Wednesday, where Phil and I recount our escapade, Scooter saying he'd got letters from bee-lovers accusing him of cruelty. Friday a *This Week In Baseball* TV crew made a—sorry—beeline for a "special report," Phil and I interviewed separately. I tell the story straight. Phil being Phil plays it for all it's worth, saying, "I think the reason that bee liked Olden is because of all the cologne he wears . . . the bee was attracted to him. I've told Olden in the future not to wear so much." Scooter, of course, was joking. I hate cologne, wouldn't wear any under punishment of being stung. Still, his quick mind added more comedy to the story. I don't miss the bee, but I do miss Phil.

— *Paul Olden*

Fenway Park's press box was once close to the plate, putting you in peril. "Here's a swing," Olden said, "and a foul ball coming back toward . . . *me!*" The chair with four wheels spun out from under him and down he went, ball hitting the rear wall. "Paul, are you *OK*?" I said. He laughed, "I wanted no part of *that* one!" Next day we saw a body outline masked with tape on the floor and wall where Paul fell, like a police murder scene. Credit Rays TV's Joe Magrane, a zealot about Olden. Glass divided Fenway's TV and radio booth, each monitor having the same remote control, which Joe used during Paul's play-by-play to change the channel to snow with the volume up. In response, Paul taped the TV electronic eye to void the remote; another time papering the glass so Joe couldn't see. Undeterred, Magrane had the press box page Paul, who went to answer as Joe removed the paper: a true prankster, though I doubt Paul sees the humor.

— *Charlie Slowes*

In baseball, you may do 200 games a year and each day see something different, as 2007 proved. Because the Astros didn't take a radio producer or engineer on the road, we used a freelance radio professional. In DC, that gentleman also trained seeing-eye dogs, whom he brought to the booth. In a late inning he says he's leaving, to be back shortly, and leaves the dog with us, not to worry. As the Astros rally, I lean forward, hands on knees, staring at the field, before experiencing one of the creepiest feelings you can: wet flesh you didn't know was there, the seeing-eye dog putting his nose on my hand. I nearly jump out of my seat, scaring myself more than him, adding to baseball's sound of bat against ball a man's scream, dog's bark, and tail vaguely thumping against a chair.

— *Dave Raymond*

In 2010, Willie Harris was hit by a pitch by the Mets' Francisco Rodriguez. Turns out, Harris didn't say anything to him, just shouted out in pain. Misinterpreting, Rodriguez ran toward him as dugouts and bullpens emptied. That night I asked reliever Tyler Clippard, "Have a good sprint from the bullpen?" He replied, "I was in the bullpen bathroom. When I came out, no one was there. I knew the game wasn't over, and didn't know what had been going on." Players returning from the infield told Clippard what he'd missed: nothing, since like most baseball fights, punches are illegal.

　—*Charlie Slowes*

I was born on Mom and Dad's oleomargarine run to Chicago because we couldn't get colored margarine in Milwaukee. My mother was with child, and suddenly pains started. So Dad pulled off the road into an exit area, sort of a Nativity-type setting, the light shining down and three truck drivers present. One guy was carrying butter. One had frankfurters. The third was a good baseball scout. I remember the coldness of the asphalt on my back. Immediately I was wrapped in swaddling clothes, and put in the back seat of a '33 Chevy, without a heater. That was the start of my Cinderella story. In eighth grade, I made a team. Trying to help, Mom made me a supporter out of a flour sack. The guy guarding me in basketball knew where I was always going because little flecks of flour kept dropping out. Right on the front, it said "Pillsbury's Best." In 1953, the Braves came from Boston. In a tryout, I was asked to toss a fastball. I told them I was. I became a catcher, got a tiny bonus, and signed in a swanky restaurant. Dad was thrilled, but so nervous he rolled down the window and the hamburgers fell off a tray. I began at Class-C Eau Claire, where, talk about your vision, an early manager suggested I announce. I did, making Cooperstown in 2003. I was honored, but still think I should have gone in as a player. After all, anyone with ability can make the majors. To trick people year in and year out is, I think, a much greater feat. I only wish the forty-four Hall of Famers there that day agreed. A lot of them were my teammates, but won't admit it.

　—*Bob Uecker*

Baseball can be wonderful, but a little parochial. Early in 2009, a Mariners backup catcher read that there was a big deal being made about an important person due to visit Seattle. The catcher said to no one in particular, "Hey, who's this Dalai Lama chick?"

　—*Dave Sims*

Chapter Fourteen

That Vision Thing

Passing radio, free TV became baseball's post-war prism. Late 1940s: WPIX and WOR New York put base runner and close-up cameras near each dugout and above first and third base. 1951: WGN coins the centerfield camera. 1956: CBS's IFB — Intercepted Feed Back — earplug ties the Voice, director, and producer, easing on-air flow. July 17, 1959: Jim McAnany's ninth-inning single ends Ralph Terry's no-hitter. On a whim, Mel Allen asks if the Yankees can reshow the hit, the first replay aired five to ten minutes later.

The first Telstar satellite hookup telecast a 1962 game from Wrigley Field to Europe. Pay cable seemed around the corner, except that systems tied few U.S. burgs. In 1976, Ted Turner bought the Braves, renamed Atlanta's WTCG Super-Station WTBS, and used satellite to "sell us a world from Georgia." Soon other SuperStations included WOR, WPIX, and WGN, flinging Harry Caray into every corner of the country. Basic subscription cable now wires nine in ten homes.

In 1990, the Entertainment and Sports Programming Network (ESPN) launched baseball: Baseball Tonight, Sunday Night Baseball, *and postseason using the K Zone, bat track, first official's replay call, and BaseCam. In 1996, Fox bought network exclusivity, miking managers, players, walls, and bases, the "Fox Box" listing score, inning, out, ball, strike, and men on base. A decade later, renamed TBS ditched the Braves for the Division Series, LCS, and* Sunday MLB.

Today the Internet shreds walls between print and electronic coverage. Every team has an official website, linked to programs like baselllibrary.com, ESPN. com, and Fastball.com. "Entertainment options" include Direct TV, Extra Innings, *Sirius XM Satellite Radio, MLB.com's* Gameday Audio, *iPod, DVD, CD, and text messaging. In 2009, baseball's MLB TV Network began 24/7 coverage in 50 million homes — sports' largest-ever cable start-up.*

MLB mixes highlight, play-by-play, talking head, and archive from 1940s Series to 2011 spring training. Quick Pitch *segues from one game to another. Matt Vasgersian hosts* MLB Tonight Live. *Back from the Olympics,* Dateline, *and* Later with Bob Costas, *Mr. C. interviews and does balls and strikes. Among others, he has a fine sense of what coverage should and should not be.*

[By the 1930s and '50s, respectively, sponsors helped radio and TV outlets do baseball. Philadelphia's Byrum Saam hailed Phillies cigars. Later, Bob Prince hyped Iron City beer; Harry Caray, Busch-Bavarian; Curt Gowdy, "Hi, neighbor, have a [Narra]gansett." Mel Allen called a home run "Ballantine Blast!" or "White Owl Wallop!"] Announcers help the bottom line, the most interesting Vin Scully, selling, among other things, Farmer John's sausage. Can't you just hear it? It's 3:00 or 4:00 a.m. The lights are off. Vinny wakes up, he's hungry, puts his bathrobe on, and wanders toward the refrigerator. Does he always talk this way? "Good evening, wherever I am. Can't wait for some Farmer John's. Freshly drenched, Eastern-fed, pure pork sausage. Um-um." Just wondering.

— *Jon Miller*

[In 1953, Saturday's *Game of the Week*, network TV's first sports series, debuted on ABC. In 1955, it moved to swanker CBS, *four of five sets* in use hearing Dizzy Dean sing "The Wabash Cannonball," call a viewer *pod-nuh*, and assault English like no one had, or will. Runners retook "their respectable bases." A hitter "stands confidentially at the plate." Mayberry loved Ol' Diz's 300 pounds, string tie, and Stetson — the whole rustic goods. In 1957, CBS added a Sunday *Game*. By 1960, three-network coverage augured today's Fox, ESPN, and TBS. Pro: Saturday heirs included Curt Gowdy, Joe Garagiola, Vin Scully, and Joe and Jack Buck. Con: Network baseball spurned Sunday from 1966 till 2008.] Today's MLB and the *Extra Innings* package give baseball access anywhere. But, as a child in Georgetown, Texas, it meant static-filled AM radio, making me an Astros and a Rangers fan, and NBC's *Game*, its different teams making me more crucially a *baseball* fan. Vin and Joe were preceded by Johnny Bench's *The Baseball Bunch* and

Mel Allen's *This Week In Baseball*, a fantasy world existing in my imagination and fortunately on TV. In 2009, I began TBS' *Sunday MLB*, really started by Diz: an old-turned-new window on the land. I'm asked who my audience is. Me! Or, at least the fourteen-year-old me, sitting in my living room soaking up the game. If you live in a big-league city, you're lucky. Millions don't, especially small-town and rural America. Sunday is for them.

—*Brian Anderson*

From 1962–1964, Dean and I telecast baseball each Saturday and Sunday on CBS and NBC, respectively. We both valued language. I tried to facilitate it. Diz tried to incinerate it. I certainly wasn't going to be Diz, and he wasn't going to talk like me. My style was to be as accurate as possible and the best announcer I could. Dean's style was to be Dizzy Dean: kid around, butcher names, didn't know players — didn't know the score. People didn't care, since he was such a monumental personality. Lesson? There's no one way to broadcast, just a warning that whatever your style, be good.

—*Bob Wolff*

As kids, we liked radio, a more refined art (I think). We wanted to call its games. Today most young Voices want TV, because that's what they've grown up on. When I was young, there were no highlight shows. No *SportsCenter*s. No home run calls heard over and over again. Now each highlight's a *SportsCenter* wannabe moment, a home run or catch, as if that's all baseball broadcasting is. Maybe you have one, two moments a game. The rest — baseball's core — is conversation used properly with a batter up. I'll hear a frantic play, a "You've got to be kidding me!" and I'll think, "Do I care if you've been kidded or not?" *Sshhh!* I'm not blaming ESPN. It's the culture: scream, have a shtick. The beauty of calling a baseball game is its totality from first pitch to last. Maybe you find a diamond: a grand-slam call or circus catch. Don't go looking for it. Mostly you're in the mine, trying to make it as colorful, entertaining, informative, and as interesting as you can.

—*Charley Steiner*

Football is an analyst's sport. Run a play; see instant replay, a guy describing a pass or off-tackle run. Baseball's different, most pitches not worth review. It's the best sport for an announcer because of the history and context and time for storytelling and exchange of opinion. Baseball means play-by-play.

—*Bob Costas*

Baseball's a radio game, due to imagination. Before I went to Houston in 1985, the Yankees wanted to sign me. I met Clyde King, an old friend who'd worked for Steinbrenner since Methuselah was a pup, at Gallagher's Steakhouse in New York. "George wants you to announce the Yankees," he said. "I'm going to write on this napkin what I think you want to do. You do the same." We unfolded our napkins, and each had written *radio*. I decided to stay, but later told the Astros, "I don't want TV anymore. People like Jack Buck and me, our strong suit is stories, and we can't tell 'em if the director's saying, 'We're showing this, talk about it.'" I took a pay cut to get off the tube. Incidentally, a word on style. Scully is the greatest announcer of all time, so you can't argue with him being the only guy to do the game solo. He and I differ. Especially on radio, I enjoy having the former player to play off of. They have the authenticity because they *did* it. I like having the ex-athlete interpret.

—*Milo Hamilton*

I grew up on radio disc jockeys who were personalities—entertainers—playing a record but also theater of the mind. I talk about Willie Mays, and you conjure sliding, a great catch, going yard. I mention him on TV, and you see some other guy spitting tobacco juice. TV's a film, to be seen; radio's a novel, translating prose into images. Maybe we read the same novel, and see it differently. Maybe your hero's better looking than mine. Same thing in a game. If the announcer describes it well, your radio moments are more vivid. At the park, seeing Willie McCovey's pop-up as a ten-year-old was breathtaking: "Oh, my God! Will it ever come down?" On TV you never see the ball!—only bat hitting it, outfielder waiting, then the catch. In Minnesota, Dave Kingman's pop went through the *roof*! On TV, you don't even *see* it. In person or on radio, you *remember* it.

—*Jon Miller*

I do WGN TV, but cut my teeth on Brewers radio. Before then, my only TV gig was as sideline reporter for a Michael Bolton charity softball event in Appleton, Wisconsin. The players were Green Bay Packers, and if you happen to see that game and my performance—my condolences. Radio and TV are like singles and doubles tennis: similar, technically; in fact, different. Radio accents nostalgia and memory. On TV, you're a traffic cop hearing the analyst, ballpark sounds, press box PA, producer, director, and associate producer—all while trying to sound coherent. Good luck! I try to give fact, have fun, and use technology to gloss the screen: camera angle, slo-mo replay, continuous score graphic, strike and ball box. As the French would say, "Viva la différence!"

—*Len Kasper*

Raised on radio, I fight the urge to talk too much on TV. On radio, you're a town crier, Paul Revere's midnight run: empowering but challenging, announcing that the British are coming, and how they're doing it. Local *v.* network TV is different, too. Locally, you're allowed—*expected*—to be homespun, have yucks. Network games reach a more neutral audience. When people say "baseball broadcasting," I'm tempted to say, "Which one?"

—*Josh Lewin*

I've done local *and* national TV: Fox individual-team and network coverage. July 30, 1998: Steve Lyons and I air Fox Sports Net Mariners-Indians. Rico Rossy bats three times with the bases full in extra innings and doesn't reach the outfield. April 17, 2010: Tim McCarver and I expect just another day on *Game of the Week*'s Mets-Cardinals. Instead, it's an *amazing* day: scoreless for eighteen innings. Next inning each team scores, New York winning in the twentieth after six hours, fifty-three minutes, despite *no* extra-base hits. Forty-six of fifty players in uniform took part in the Mets' inning-wise longest victory. Most important to Fox, the game stretched into prime time, winning its ratings slot. [Fox Sports exec Ed Goren says that, while ratings often drop in spring and summer, "What seems to still resonate is original programming." *This* game was original.]

—*Kenny Albert*

TV or radio, good coverage needs perspective. Retiring in 1996, Ozzie Smith was my next-season partner. In his first game, best friend Willie Mc-Gee hit a walkoff homer against the Expos. After we took off the headsets, I said, "OK, future Hall of Famer, what do you think of this broadcasting stuff?" He said something I'll never forget: "Partner, the game sure looks easy from up here." To me, it *had* looked easy for Ozzie all those years at shortstop. Down there it's different.
— *Bob Carpenter*

[Good coverage means paying, not compromising to pay, bills.] Bob Wolff wrote a book entitled *It's Not Who Won or Lost the Game . . . It's How You Sold the Beer*, describing a 1930s through 1990s broadcaster, when sponsors owned rights. The team now usually does, so you work for it or its TV or radio outlet, which doesn't mean guys don't shill. A Mets TV partner was ex-big-league catcher Fran Healy, who knew where his bread was buttered. When it came to sponsors, Fran could plug three of them while calling a ground ball. Former Mets owner Nelson Doubleday loved Krispy Kreme donuts, one night sending a boxful to our TV booth. I started to thank him on the air: "Hey, look what Nelson Doubleday just sent in . . . a delicious, great big box of . . . " At this point Healy took his hand, literally covered my mouth, and pointed frantically to Shea Stadium's leftfield signage, screaming "Dunkin' Donuts!" It was fattening, but seamless. Or to paraphrase Chuck Thompson, "Ain't the donuts sweet!"
— *Howie Rose*

Coverage has got to be personal, being yourself a cliché, but true. In 1974, I'm twenty-two when the A's Monte Moore hires me. I'm in spring training, nervous, not wanting to screw up. "Not exciting enough, nothing's happening," I kept muttering of my play-by-play. One day Monte broadcast an exhibition game. I'm sitting nearby trying to practice: "Ground ball, *right at the shortstop! Unbelievable! Oh-boy! He could have hit the ball anywhere! But right to him!*" Monte looks at me like I'm in a loony bin before turning off the mike: "What the hell are you doing?" Between innings I confess my fear. He says, "That's ridiculous. We hired you because you're the best guy for the job. You sound great. Just do it." I then exhaled.
— *Jon Miller*

Being yourself makes sense. To fill dead time, I used the road to act and write. My first book was *The Official Fan's Guide to the Fugitive* [ABC 1962–1967 series], with which I identified. He was a loner, and so was I. It was fun to learn about David Janssen, a social animal who loved wooing gorgeous women, which is, when you think of it, a key demographic for radio/TV baseball.

— *Mel Proctor*

Coverage must be professional. My baseball career began a year *before* I joined 1975 Red Sox TV. I got a call from Sox assistant GM Gene Kirby, whose career dated back to Dizzy Dean. As Ol' Diz's producer, Gene had some hilarious stories. Dean was awful at pronouncing surnames. [Once, bases full of runners of Italian and Polish lineage, a batter hit to left-center-field. "There's a line drive," Diz said, "and here's Gene Kirby to tell you all about it."] Gene now wanted a baseball tape for the Sox likely new UHF flagship station. I didn't have one, so he suggested I go to Shea Stadium, the Yankees' home while their park was being renovated, record a game, and send it for his critique. Obediently, I did, thinking that Gene might recommend me, or say I wasn't what they were looking for. Instead, he called — "Do you have a legal pad handy?" — picking apart everything I'd taped, from starting lineup to final out. I filled seven pages, front and back: pretty shattering. Return to Shea, he said, and try again. Six times I did, Gene insisting that I phrase correctly — baseball's "patter," he called it — and properly inject things and describe plays. Finally, progress glacial, Gene called after *another* tape, now able — Eureka! — to recommend me to the Red Sox. I teamed with analyst Ken Harrelson of 1967's "Impossible Dream" in a 1975 just as great. Boston won the AL East, swept the world champion A's in the LCS, and opened a wonderful door when NBC TV named me to the Reds–Red Sox Series. Amazingly, I was behind the mike when Carlton Fisk hit his twelfth-inning home run to win Game 6. ["There it goes! A long drive! If it stays fair . . . *home run!*"] Who could have predicted when I was enduring the grueling exercise of taping and being harshly but honestly critiqued that one year later I would call such a play? I wouldn't have, without Gene.

— *Dick Stockton*

Good coverage respects, not fears. Over 162 games, travel, time away from family, reaching a city at 5:00 or 6:00 a.m., maybe team futility, all test one's sanity. Players have to laugh, clubhouse humor cutting and personal, but usually good-natured. I learned long ago the line between laughing when one player rips another (OK for an announcer) and you ripping them (not OK). You need to be polite, not intimidated. One then-Met didn't understand *another* line between derision and praise, as I found emceeing the club's annual Welcome Home Dinner. My job was to say chicken will be at people's tables in five minutes, introduce players, and please don't bother them for autographs while they eat. Todd Pratt, Mike Piazza's fine backup catcher, was the first bench player I introduced, calling him an example of how a good team can't win without depth. Even the Three Stooges had Shemp, I said—not "A" material, I admit, but it got a chuckle. I glowingly praised Todd, then introduced his teammates. Time for the chicken—except that Pratt, forgetting about not bothering people on the dais, approached me to say, "We're through, dude."

"Huh?" I said, eloquently, not knowing what he meant, just that my mashed potatoes were going to get cold.

"I know how it works," Todd said. "You say great things about our stars, but when you introduce me, you call me Shemp. You think I'm a bleeping stooge. I've been a scrub my whole career, so I know how it goes—but you and me, we're through."

I think he's kidding. Learning better, I try to calm Pratt down as my green beans spoil. For ten minutes, not getting anywhere, I say I'm not belittling him before Todd inexplicably walks away. Next day, Pratt didn't apologize or say he misunderstood the comment but amazingly from then on was terrific. Maybe teammates explained. Maybe he reflected. Maybe he preferred Joe Besser to Shemp (although I can't imagine how). At any rate, he struck up conversation, did everything but buy me flowers.

For me, it was a lesson more reinforced than learned. Player frustration or insecurity can distort even well intentioned comment. Next season, players approach me before the Welcome Home Dinner and wonder if I'll call Todd Shemp? No chance. I introduced him like he was a Hall of Famer, complete with wink and smile. This time, Todd Pratt understood.

— *Howie Rose*

[Coverage should use statistics wisely.] Some people kidded me for overusing numbers. On August 23, 1989, Vin Scully had waived the Dodgers' trip to Montreal. Our other announcer, Don Drysdale, was away expecting his wife's baby. As inning by inning unfolded, I was talking to my audience and myself. Finally, Rick Dempsey homered to give the Dodgers a 1–0 victory in twenty-two innings. The game time was six hours and fourteen minutes. Often, statistics fill pretty well.

— *Ross Porter*

[Coverage can use luck.] On opening day 1990, Kansas City has a runner at first with one out and George Brett up. The natural thing would be to discuss Brett, an all-time great. Instead, for some reason I noted that Baltimore's Cal and Billy Ripken led the league in 1989 double plays. Next pitch Brett one-hops to Cal, who tossed to Billy, who threw to first for a double play. "Nice call, Mr. Carpenter," said analyst Norm Hitzges. At break, I thanked him for the compliment, returning it when lefty slugger Sam Horn homers after Norm says Royals manager John Wathan lacks a left-handed reliever ready to face him. Norm and I are now a trivia answer. Question: Who called this game — ESPN's first-ever regular-season telecast?

— *Bob Carpenter*

Coverage should use the analyst. In 1989, Joe Tait left the Indians. My new partner was Cleveland native, twelve-year big leaguer, and Brewers analyst Mike Hegan, his dad Jim a longtime Tribe catcher and fan favorite. Since Mike and I had attended the same high school, I joked about watching him play football and basketball as a child. In April Mike got revenge on our first TV game, from New York. Two lefties met: Greg Swindell, twenty-four, yielding one run in seven innings; and Yankees' Al Leiter, twenty-three, not always controlling his fastball and great slider. In the fifth, Andy Allanson doubled, Mike saying in replay that he saw Leiter struggling with his middle finger grip. I was caught off-guard because Yankee Stadium's booths were so distant from the field. How could he *see*? At half-inning's end, we shucked our headsets. I asked how Mike could tell the position of Leiter's middle finger from such a length. He eyed me disdainfully: "You mean you *can't*?" Knowing most hitters' keen vision and how ex-players-turned-announcers could be difficult if they felt the "broadcaster" didn't possess their knowledge, I imagined a long and awkward year. Then I felt a playful punch and saw Mike's Irish grin: he was giving me a dig. Mike said the replay showed a flatter trajectory for the pitch—and how it likely stemmed from the position and/or tension of Leiter's middle finger. Incredible. We worked thirteen years together, the "broadcaster" amazed by Mike's knowledge.

— *Jack Corrigan*

[Coverage should use technology.] I join the Angels' Dick Enberg in 1969. In 1973, Don Drysdale does, too. On one hand, we followed Vin Scully's example of don't cheerlead or make excuses. On the other, we differed from Vin's talking to the audience alone. Trying to compete, Dick got the Halos to install toggle mikes. Lets you hear a partner, push the button down, and respond. Pioneering then: Everybody does it now. Gotta' love those technological bells and whistles.

Still, broadcasting's about chemistry. I loved my two partners: nice and easy, conversation, lots of humor. One night Drysdale noted, "I'm going to have dinner tonight at singer's house."

"Bill Singer, the pitcher?" I said.

"No, Dave," said Don. "The singer is Frank Sinatra."

— *Dave Niehaus*

Good coverage uses mikemen you never see: PA announcers giving us starters, substitutions, and scoring decisions. In the '20s, Cleveland's Tom Manning yelled batteries with a megaphone. Later, using a mike, Brooklyn's Tex Rickard said, "A little boy has been found lost." In Baltimore, Rex Barney said of each foul catch, "Give that fan a contract!" By 1962, the Senators' Charlie Brotman was too busy for an eighty-one-game home schedule, his replacement Phil Hochberg, a twenties graduate student and later noted cable attorney. In new DC Stadium, only the Yankees really drew. One night Roger Maris came to bat, hitting sixty-one homers the year before. The big crowd pumped Phil up: "Batting third, the right fielder, number 9, Roger Maris," stretching and accenting "Maris," as many PAers do now. Hearing him, the *Washington Post* reporter Bob Addie marched over and said, "Roger Maris? Roger Maris?" — extending the syllables, imitating Phil—"You introduce him like you would anyone *else!*" In 1962, DC hosted the All-Star Game, introductions prepared by the Senators' front office, which left out a player. Phil welcomed the entire AL team, and Elston Howard's still in the dugout. Another time he missed a Yankees batter, saying, "Batting ninth, the pitcher, number 23, Ralph Terry." Below, lead-off man Bobby Richardson prepared to bat. In Phil's defense, the Senators later taught me how losing can affect your concentration.

—*Ron Menchine*

Speaking of coverage, players mostly get the kind they want. Fans cheer (most of) them. Owners pay handsome salaries. We generally say nice things. Sometimes, though, we don't. Praise a guy thirty straight days, but criticize him on the thirty-first and you hear about it. Many times a player has been ticked off by something I supposedly said, like Keith Miller, a Mets utility infielder asked to try centerfield. After a rough April game, a post-game caller gave Keith the business. I defended him by saying give it time. Somehow, Miller heard *I* was ripping him, to which I said I hadn't, even produced a tape. Listening, Keith was apologetic: a best-case scenario for how things work out. By contrast, Brett Butler, a 1995 Metsie, had what I termed on air the worst game I'd seen him play. In next day's papers, he essentially said the same thing, but was furious since his wife, hearing the game, thought I should be ashamed for being so disrespectful! I said my comments mirrored his, and would he like to hear them? Brett took the tape, but we haven't spoken since. To review: Many players think play-by-play should be an infomercial. Criticized by an announcer, the player rarely hears it first-hand. Fact is bent, spindled, and mutilated as to be unrecognizable. I tell a player upset over a critical comment that I don't mind as long as he thanks me when more often I say something nice. Gary Carter, Dave Magadan, and Mike Piazza are three of a small group of players who thanked me for all of the platitudes I delivered on their behalf. Classier people you'll never find.

—*Howie Rose*

Good coverage has context. In New England, 2004 was for dead relatives and friends who hadn't lived to see a title, many going to a cemetery to put bats and balls and Red Sox paraphernalia on a gravesite, including my brother-in-law on my late dad's. We had the rolling rally in Boston, signs saying, "You won one for my grandma" — a remembrance. 'Oh-seven was about being the best team in baseball. We went up in the Series, three games to zero, the final, as it happened, Sunday. That morning Mike Lowell, a close friend who'd been on fire, and our families were at Mass. I tell my wife Jan: "If he gets a double and a home run tonight, he'll be Series MVP." Maybe I should play Vegas: Mike got a home run and double and was named Series MVP. In the ninth, Jonathan Papelbon fans Seth Smith. I said, "The Boston Red Sox become the first team in the twenty-first century to win two world championships!" — a subtle reminder to Yankees fans that they hadn't done it, and the Red Sox had. Different coverage than 2004's, not worse. Winning never is.

— *Joe Castiglione*

Coverage demands thinking on your feet. In 1997, joining Padres TV, I wrote and rewrote material, then memorized it, knowing I couldn't use it all each game. I might use five percent of the stuff I compiled in each of five straight games. Then you use 75 percent in one clunker. Each inning you make decisions. Do I use story X? Do I save it till later? Can I mention fact Y before break? If it's 2–1, do I stray from balls and strikes at all? A close game focuses you on the field. Twenty to one, you rely on preparation. Late that first year Harry Caray told me: "When the game is at its worst, you have to be at your very best."

— *Rick Sutcliffe*

[As Rick Sutcliffe notes, coverage requires judgment. In 1955, Vin Scully went "back and forth" about mentioning Bob Purkey's at-work no-no. "I asked the audience to vote. The mail strongly indicated it was with me. That means we got two postcards in favor and one opposed." In 1956, he declined to note Don Larsen's in-progress perfect game. "Today I would have started in the seventh inning," Vin said in 2009. "Hey, call your friends. This guy's pitching a perfect game."] Debate still roils about mentioning a no-hitter. Vin was on NBC TV. On Mutual Radio, I succeeded Bob Neal after 4½ innings, Larsen having retired fifteen up and down. I told our producer, Joel Nixon, that I wasn't going to use the term "'perfect game.' I'll use every synonym in the book so that everyone knows what's happening. As long as they know, they'll listen." I also liked the tradition and novelty of not using it: "eighteen up and down"; "only the Yankees have reached base." At the end, I said, "It's a no-hitter! A perfect game for Don Larsen!" Mostly I felt a sore arm. My body had been so tense, concentrating on the broadcast, that I was pitching the last inning with Larsen. It's not in the scorecard, but it took me a week to recover.

— *Bob Wolff*

Knowing that Hank Aaron would break Babe Ruth's career home run record in 1974, I wanted the call to be made by the home run, not me. That's why my trademark "Holy Toledo!" for a great play or homer isn't on the call. My former partner, Larry Dierker, says I'm the only man he knows who can make "holy" into a five-syllable word. Here, it didn't matter. I had all winter to think about it. Where'll the ball be? What if I can't see it? What if it's an inside-the-parker? What's more, he and Ruth were the same age, forty-two. They both would do it in a Braves uniform — people forget Ruth hit his last homer at Forbes Field. For a while I thought of using the first fact when Henry went to first base, and the other at second. Well, thank goodness I decided to be as spontaneous as the call. Ruth himself expected someone to break his single-season record of 60 home runs, but thought 714 would stand forever. ["Swinging! There's a drive into left-centerfield! That ball is gonna' be! . . . Out of here! It's gone! It's 715! And there's a new home run champion of all time, and it's Henry Aaron!"] Running through my mind: It was Henry Aaron's moment, not mine.

— *Milo Hamilton*

A broadcaster can't edit mistakes: terrifying if history looms. How should I call it? What words, in what sequence, with what inflection? Unlike 1961, when Roger Maris's last-game homer broke Ruth's record, it was clear in 1998 that both Sammy Sosa and Mark McGwire would top sixty-one. But when, who'd be first, and who'd hit the most? Milo made a classic call of Aaron's 715th. "It's okay to plan a few words," he told me, "but you have to sound extemporaneous." The 1998 Cubs had already been magical — Kerry Wood struck out twenty in a game, Sosa hit a ridiculous twenty homers in June — so the two words I think of are "magic" and "historic." If the moment happens, I decide to use both. By coincidence, Mac broke the record against the Cubs September 8, drilling a low liner, not his typical launch. "McGwire drives one to deep left! — this could be! — it's a home run! Number 62 for Mark McGwire!" I said on WGN. "A slice of history and a magical moment in St. Louis!" Thankfully, words tumbled out, ESPN and many radio stations replaying them over and over. McGwire ran to the box seats to hug members of the Maris family: people crying, I had tears. Next Sosa ran in from right and jumped into Big Mac's arms. What respect and friendship the two briefly shared! Since then, we've seen The Steroids Era; St. Louis winning a Series; and Cubs, having not. At least 1998 shows how easy it is to fall in love with baseball again and again.

— *Pat Hughes*

Hank's 715, McGwire's 62: You go to the park, not knowing what'll happen. In 1969, Atlanta hosts the Cubs: Chicago up, two on, no out. "Kessinger third, Beckert second, first base empty. Santo is due next. Got a no-ball, two-strike count on Billy Williams, left-hand batter waiting. Off-speed, swung on, first base. Cepeda runs to the bag [one out]. Holding the runners, may have a runner cut down at second base. Garrido now will chase one of them! Now he will throw to the plate! There'll be a run back toward third! Now Boyer will turn the play on Kessinger! Now Jarvis has the ball! He is throwing back there . . . he's out at third! [Out two.] Now they may have the runner between second and third! Carty's there! [Third out.] Jarvis is out of the jam! What about that! Listen to this crowd!" A triple play. You never know.

— *Milo Hamilton*

As Milo says, the best thing about baseball is not knowing the script. In 2008, Milwaukee had missed postseason since 1982, but is tied for the wild card with New York with four games left. Bob Uecker justifiably did each ninth, so the only way I ever had a walkoff was if the game went extra innings. This night, in the tenth, Ryan Braun grand slams to beat the Pirates: easily, my top call. A contender was opening day 2010, Atlanta's Jason Heyward, twenty, debuting at home: baseball's "top prospect," not always what that's cracked up to be, except he might be a generation's. Carlos Zambrano throws two first-inning fastballs. Jason crushes the next ten miles to right on his first big-league swing, my call ending, "This stadium is upside down."

On May 20, the Reds, ahead, 9–3, turn inside out, gallantly not having a ninth-inning runner steal. In the booth, Mark Lemke and I say of the move, "Six runs aren't completely out of hand." Soon it's 9–6, two Braves on, one out, and Heyward up, having earlier that year hit a game-tying ninth-inning homer. "Anyone *not* expect Jason to hit a home run?" Braves skipper Bobby Cox said then. Tonight, chuckling "We've seen this script before," we expect him to. Surprisingly, Arthur Rhodes fans Heyward. Stunningly, Brooks Conrad's drive off Francisco Cordero then hits left-fielder Laynce Nix's glove, bounces on the fence, and goes over: 10–9! A grand-slam game-winning homer! The first time the Braves rallied to score seven ninth-inning runs in the history of the National League's longest continuously operating franchise!

My hands shook all during post-game. Without a script, you never know.

— *Jim Powell*

Chapter Fifteen

Baseball on My Mind

Billy Joel sang "A New York State of Mind." Baseball's state of mind can inveigle, too. Ernie Harwell's baseball life began at age five. Mine began a year or two year later. Hitting fungoes, citing averages, or trading two A's playing cards for a dog-eared Cal Koonce, friends and I thought of little else.

Winter ended with catch and pepper. Spring "boiled down to Little League," as pollster John Zogby says. Summer meant pickup games, for me in a field near a cemetery: rites grass stain, broken glass, and our Xanadu — a long belt, an automatic homer — clanging off a stone. One batter took me beyond the farthest grave. Playing, I was same old by ten.

"In our youth," Jon Miller referenced post-war America, "baseball fit the age" — unslambang and uncutting edge. Today, when in your face means a snarl, not pie, a sweetly unhip sport gropes unsurely with trash talk and toxic taunt. "Screeching PA and blaring boombox!" said a friend. "That's not what baseball is." What it was could be again: Voices spurning vanilla for meringue.

Joseph Alsop wrote, "If I feel that there were giants in the Roosevelt years, I claim the right to say so." There were, not long ago. Jack Buck and Brickhouse. Harry Caray and Kalas. Gowdy and The Gunner. Thompson, Nelson, Harwell. Today's stylists include Miller Time; Uke's catcher in the wry; and Ken Harrelson, putting interest on the board. The Marlins' Dave Van Horne still hooks a listener. Dave Niehaus will always mean the Mariners, despite his death in late 2010. "No one could draw you into the moment, the drama of a game, like he could," said twenty-eight-year M's producer/engineer Kevin Cremin. Baseball could use more.

"To express the game you have to follow it from childhood," said Mel Allen, using memory not to forget with but to recall time and place. Among his reverie: a

1942 game at Yankee Stadium — Tommy Henrich, later termed "Old Reliable" by Allen, about to go to war.

"Ladies and gentlemen," the PA announcer said, "this is the last time that you will see Tommy Henrich in a Yankee uniform for the duration."

The crowd burst a lung. Detroit pitcher Dizzy Trout left the rubber. Henrich stepped into the box, yelling, "Come on, Dizzy, throw the ball."

Trout cupped his hands: "Stand there and listen to it, you SOB. You'll remember it as long as you live."

Like your everyday Voice, he was expressing something on his baseball mind.

I got into baseball on 1945 Armed Forces Radio. How many people years later can't wait to get to work? Having done football and basketball, I can't imagine calling a game each day, yet counting exhibitions I've often done 200 baseball games a year. I love the camaraderie. I love baseball's unpredictability. I'll call a game, and something happens that'll make me say, "You ever see that before?" My partner laughs, "No." One game triggers another, which begets one story, then another. When I entered the Hall, my favorite player was there, Stan Musial, and manager, Al Lopez. So was Bob Feller, like me, from Iowa. We talked about the 1930s and the Depression, and I began thinking about my mom and dad. Ultimately, inductees and their families were taken by bus to a special room at the induction ceremony. That's when palms get moist. All of a sudden I see Brooks Robinson and Johnny Bench asking for autographs, like twelve-year-olds. I grew up with grown men playing a kids' game with short pants. Really, what's changed?

—*Milo Hamilton*

[In 1996, Orioles owner Peter Angelos, finding Jon Miller insufficiently bleeding "black and orange," invited him to join the Giants.] In 1997, a questioner at Washington's National Press Club asked if a play-by-play man should be a fan or reporter. "I think the announcer should be an advocate for the team," I said, having fun. "I think the announcer should bleed the colors of the team. I have seen the light. Hallelujah!" In San Francisco, we built a house on Moss Beach, near where I'd grown up. I can see my boyhood home across the bay. At the ballpark, I study ships in McCovey's

Cove, which, like my boyhood team, comes full circle. I once saw FDR's ship [the *Potomac*] there, and wish I could travel by boat everywhere. Instead, I fly about 100,000 miles a year. When the season's over, I take a cruise. I can't wait to take it, then can't wait for its end. What's next? *Baseball*! Man, now I'm juiced. Forget spring training. I'm ready for the new season by New Year's Day.

 — *Jon Miller*

Before broadcasting baseball, I endured a baseball tragedy. My first major job was KDKA Pittsburgh sports director, doing a five-minute report on its 6, 7, and 11:00 p.m. TV newscast. When Larry Shepard was fired as Pirates skipper in 1969, two members of the 1960 world champion Bucs vied to succeed him: Don Hoak, feisty and aggressive, named "The Tiger" by legendary Bob Prince; and Bill Virdon aka "The Quail" in centerfield. The night before October's Decision Day, I reiterated my view that Don's personality was needed after Shepard's quiet manner. Next day's 5:00 p.m. press conference would reveal the new manager on a boat from Gateway Center to nearly completed Three Rivers Stadium. Imagine my shock when GM Joe Brown introduced Danny Murtaugh, the 1960 skipper who'd retired in 1964. For a young team, in a new stadium, Murtaugh, fifty-two, seemed to symbolize the Pirates' past. I interviewed him and Brown, then checked my watch: 5:45. Back at the office, I took a call from Hoak: hurt, furious, wanting to come on and blast the Pirates. Dissuading him, I joined the 6:00 o'clock *Eyewitness News*, a first-of-its-kind idea, anchors and reporters speaking amid live news room activity. When film or commercial ran, our police radio was turned on full. At 6:20, it reported that Hoak had been found dead in suburban Shadyside. The news editor confirmed the report. Stunned, I told the audience: "We have just found out a shocking and incredibly sad development. Don Hoak, who had been a prime candidate to become new manager of the Pirates, has died of a heart attack. Details to come on the 7:00 p.m. newscast." After the half-hour *CBS Evening News with Walter Cronkite*, I led with how apparently someone had tried to steal the car of Don's brother-in-law. Hoak got into his own car and chased the other auto, never catching it, and was found slumped over the steering wheel at the bottom of a hill. To this day, Hoak's wife believes that

Don, who so badly wanted to manage the Pirates, died of a broken heart. (Footnote: I was wrong about Murtaugh, hardly too old to manage. In 1970, Pittsburgh won its division. The 1971 Bucs seized a classic seven-game Fall Classic. It took Murtaugh two seasons to recapture 1960's, which was the Tiger's, glory.)
    — *Dick Stockton*

[Once a student asked Bart Giamatti about basketball. "You want me to talk about *thumpety, thumpety, thumpety swish?*" huffed the boyhood Bobby Doerr buff: in his heart, a baseball "lifer." Player/coach Jimmie Reese bridged John McGraw and John McNamara. Cal Ripken Jr. was born into and breathes the game. Voices can be "lifers," too.] Dad grew up near Pittsburgh, married a local girl, became a top Washington coal lobbyist, moved to Harrisburg when he found DC no place to raise seven kids, and loved the Bucs — our thread. In 1970, one baseball "lifer" took a future one on a business trip to Pittsburgh, he and I seeing a game at new Three Rivers Stadium. Each year I'd go back, dad asking whose autographs I got and my thoughts on the game. Later I was a Pirates intern, front office staffer, and Buffalo Bisons, Bills football, college hockey and hoops Voice. Dad critiqued tapes: being a lifer, liking baseball's best. An ex-congressional speechwriter, he would have loved giving his 1992 take on Bill Clinton's victory over George Bush forty-one. Instead, that summer Dad took ill, our election-night talk brief. It was the last time we spoke, since next month he passed away. A year later I was hired to announce the — *Pirates* — wishing every day that dad had been alive to see me named. Millions of people in thousands of places are like us: baseball lifers. Our family was the Bucs before the Bucs were "We Are Family."
    — *Greg Brown*

To some, a bus means school, senior day trip, or transportation. To me, it's baseball, incongruous how big leaguers line up to get on like kids for class. Sometimes I gape at the financial power trapped in a wheeled tube heading down the highway. In Milwaukee, what would motorists think if they knew All-Stars, Cy Young Award winners, home run champs, Rookies of the Year, MVPs, and a Hall of Fame announcer were seated behind tinted windows? Forget money, fame, and adoration. Players' *real* thread has been the bus since entering baseball: park to park, airport to hotel. Today, it might be Wrigley Field; yesterday Brevard County, Florida, or Round Rock, Texas, or Santiago, Dominican Republic, or Tokyo, Japan, perfecting their God-given talent. Spending my minor-league days hoping to get "off" the bus, I've come to realize that being "on" it means being "in" the game.

— *Brian Anderson*

The morning of 9/11 our seventeen-year-old daughter Stephanie ran into the bedroom to tell us a plane had crashed into one of New York's Twin Towers. Turning the TV on, we saw another plane hit the second tower. A week later we played our first post–9/11 game in Denver. Everyone flew the American flag, not a dry eye in the place. Lee Greenwood stepped to the microphone and sang "God Bless the USA." At its close, I wondered what to say. How could anyone be worthy of the crowd's grief and resolution? I let its noise hold sway, but this was radio: I had to say *something*. Finally, I did, not remembering what. I went quickly to break, really wishing not to talk, unusual for a broadcaster.

— *Greg Schulte*

Without meaning to sound condescending, unless you're from New York or Washington, DC, I don't think you can grasp September 11: one of those six degrees of separation where seemingly everyone has a personal connection, however indirect, with someone who died. If Commissioner Bud Selig had canceled the season, I'd have understood, baseball then irrelevant. Instead, he cited FDR's World War II edict that it continue: in the Mets' case, resuming September 21 at Shea against Atlanta. Both teams shook hands on the field after an extraordinary rendition of the national anthem. By then, our TV network people had talked to my partners and me like kids. Don't emote. Stay even-keeled. Ignore how a live event has an ebb and flow. On one hand, I'd thought it impossible to so soon muster energy and concentration worthy of my audience. On the other, my emotion in the pre-game ceremony took me by surprise. How could you broadcast dispassionately? The night was *about* passion: death and life. In the eighth,

Mike Piazza's home run gave the Mets a one-run lead: my decibel level not high, but now secondary to the screen. Our director found a couple of uniformed firefighters in the stands smiling and high-fiving each other: the most poignant crowd shot I've ever seen. Two men who doubtless had lost friends, perhaps even family, could have a brief respite from tragedy — from hell. The Mets won, and as the crowd left I knew that though September 11 had nothing to do with baseball, recovery did. New York's healing process began September 21, 2001.

— *Howie Rose*

How ironic, if not commensurate: Weeks after America's worst terrorism, baseball staged a great World Series. The D'backs took a 2-0 game lead heading to New York. President Bush threw a perfect strike prior to Game 3 — uncommon for a politician. Games 4 and 5 were even more improbable: Tino Martinez and Scott Brosius homering; Yankee Stadium shaking; a flag flapping in the wind, rescued from the Towers. Security was as heavy as hearts post-9/11. The National Anthem and "God Bless America" never seemed as stirring, nor "America the Beautiful," sung at Bank One Ballpark by legendary Ray Charles. Try topping *that*. Game 7 tried. After Alfonso Soriano's eighth-inning blast gave New York a 2-1 lead, Joe Torre gave the ball to Mariano Rivera, who struck out the side. A day earlier, Randy Johnson threw over 100 pitches to win Game 6. Now, relieving, he got the D'backs last four outs. As Arizona batted in the ninth, the crowd rose, clapped, prayed. Mark Grace singles. Rivera makes a throwing error. Tony Womack's double ties the score. Next, Craig Counsell is hit to load the bases. After fouling a pitch, Luis Gonzalez blooped a hit just over shortstop Derek Jeter. "They're the world champions! Gonzalez did it!" I said. "The Diamondbacks have unseated the New York Yankees as world champions! . . . Honk your horns, stomp your feet, celebrate in Arizona! The Diamondbacks have won the World Series!" Ours was a veteran team, many having never made postseason; some not making it again. What do I remember? In that awful fall, maybe the best Series played.

— *Greg Schulte*

A broadcaster often gets letters from the audience less about your work than, as Jack Buck told me, "As a baseball Voice, connecting with listeners at a personal and emotional level." Anyone familiar with the charitable Make-A-Wish Foundation knows it tries to grant one last wish to a dying child. Three or four times in the last decade Ron Santo and I had an extraordinary request from some unfortunate family, floored and humbled when such a youngster's final wish is to visit us in the booth. The parents are there, suffering terribly, too. Naturally, you try to cheer them up: "You promise to come back and visit us again next year, OK?" Sometimes they do; sadly sometimes not. A few years back Mike Mayers, about fifteen, had leukemia, no hair, not in good shape, nor were his parents. "Mike, come back and see us next year, OK?" we said. To our delight, he did. We said the same thing: "Come back next year, OK?" He did again, and the following year, and year after that. We had absolutely nothing to do with his recovery. That would be preposterous beyond words. But, amazingly, Mike *did* recover. At twenty, a college student, cancer in remission, he visited us: has a nice, pretty girlfriend, is doing great. Baseball can be wonderful escapism, announcers trying daily to give some joy. When Jack said, "You can do good work for a lot of people," he didn't mean balls and strikes.

    — *Pat Hughes*

Asking your greatest memory, people expect a specific game or play. I've done a World Series, ridden in its parade, and visited the White House. None qualify. September 11 altered the 2001 schedule so that instead of ending his career in San Francisco the Padres' Tony Gwynn closed it at home against my Rockies. If fate hadn't intervened, we might have played ball together at San Diego State University. Instead, tearing up my knee, I turned to campus radio, airing Tony's first game and joining the A's in 1981. A year later Tony made the Pads, getting hit 2,000 against Colorado in 1993. Told my partner called it, Gwynn inscribed for me a game-used bat: "Sorry about 2,000." Even this last game couldn't compensate, or could it? I stood at Tony's locker in the clubhouse, wondering about Father Time. We kibitz till he put on a fishing hat to signal his "final walk" on a big-league field. I go to the door, wonder how Tony'll accept the end, take two steps, and hear, "Hey, I said *we* were going on my final walk!" I was stunned. We walked to rightfield, Tony showing where his 1984 LCS hit landed to help the Padres make their first World Series. He talked about his family's opposing retirement, though Tony knew it was the right time to leave. He couldn't wait to start his new job next day as SDSU hitting coach. Emotionally and graciously, he led me around the outfield and eventually to the plate. Everywhere stadium personnel yelled down thanks you's, the "walk" ending in Tony's dugout: two hours of joy for a former collegian who had no right to deserve this privilege. I loved watching Tony hit, yet this day had *nothing* to do with a bat or ball. It had *everything* to do with the heart of a man who shared something special with his friend.

—*Wayne Hagin*

In 2001, Tampa Bay finished 62-100. Next April, after a fine start, the Rays blow a ninth-inning lead to the Twins at home. Losses then began to accumulate: a team-record fifteen in a row, becoming, you might say, a true horror show. The night the streak began, Twins pitcher Matt Kinney, raised in Bangor, Maine, had as a guest his Little League coach, the suspense and science-fiction author Stephen King. As defeat mounted, I had the bright idea to blame the Rays' luck on King: a master of the macabre, jinxing them. "Ya' know, this whole losing streak started when Stephen King was here!" I said. "There must be some connection." Next day I found the King classic *Misery*, telling my audience I'd try to help Rays players and coaches break the "Curse of King" by making the book a catalyst. I had them stick colored pushpins into King's photo on the jacket cover, papers picking the story up. At first King, a self-styled Rays fan, said he shouldn't be blamed, later becoming a good sport, saying I should buy his *real* jinx book: *The Girl Who Loved Tom Gordon*, about the ex–Red Sox reliever who got a sore arm with the Cubs. King himself had an auto accident soon after the book's release: bad karma everywhere. On May 11, Randy Winn's homer beat Baltimore, 6–4, to end the losing streak, the Orioles an expert on losing—twenty-one straight games to start 1988. Misery was over. Sadly, the Rays finished 55-106. As for King, not being much of a book reader, I wonder what became of him?

—*Paul Olden*

Growing up in Needham, outside Boston, I loved the Red Sox: often bad, thus overshadowed by the Celtics. I joined ESPN in 1993. By 1995,

I hosted *Baseball Tonight* five nights a week, in the catbird's seat for every big-league game. Helping raise a generation of baseball fans is not to be taken lightly, and I approach it like a player, with passion, intensity, and detail. In 2004, the team of my childhood, friends, parents, grandparents, and long-sufferers everywhere verged on a World Series title, due to a storybook LCS: the Red Sox as I knew them dead. The Sox had a 3–0 game lead: one out from their first title in eighty-six years. As Keith Foulke fielded Edgar Renteria's comebacker, I stood at the front of a line inside the tunnel at St. Louis. Seconds later, entering the dugout, then field, I saw Terry Francona with tears rolling down his cheeks, players screaming, "I don't believe it!" I didn't, either, unprepared for the emotion. To be from Needham, feel an event so near my heart, and report it for TV's most powerful sports network ever, overwhelmed me. Sometimes I think sports are the greatest link we have.

— *Karl Ravech*

In twelve minor-league years, some events cause a double-, even triple-, take. In 1994, third strike passed balls and wild pitches let Kelly Wunsch become the minors' first starter to fan *five* batters in an inning. We're still waiting for the first big leaguer. I saw a player retire in a game, a manager thrown out before another, even a player pitch against his team. March 2009's World Baseball Classic was held during spring training, many teams playing exhibitions against countries training for the WBC. Houston is the only team in Florida to air even exhibitions that don't count. That year, meeting Panama, we were told the game would go at most nine innings, maybe less, depending on how many pitchers the teams used. Amazingly, some Astros pitchers were used by *Panama* against *Houston*. What's more, three Panamanians had the same number—twenty-one. Try broadcasting a game one step above shirts and skins and call your own fouls. I didn't get a five-strikeout inning, but each game keep hoping.

— *Brett Dolan*

You'd have had to be on Mars in the last two decades to miss players trying to get a legal and illegal edge through steroids, growth hormones, and other performance-enhancing drugs. I don't condone their use, though risking future health is a player's business. Two things do alarm. First, these aids skew records. In 1996, Brady Anderson became the first leadoff batter to hit fifty homers in a year. In no other year did he top twenty-four! The other thing is future salary. Say you and I play the same position, have equal skill, and are trying to make the club. We each have a wife and kids to support. We both want to play in the big leagues. You've been taking steroids for eighteen months and I haven't. You get the job. That's fair? Some players who've been caught say the majors' big money made them do it: think Alex Rodriguez. The discussion inevitably leads to whether these players should make the Hall. To me, that's a matter for voters' conscience. I just know records shouldn't have an asterisk saying they came in the performance-enhancing era.

— *Denny Matthews*

Another strange, but true, story. How often does a visiting team celebrate a *road* walkoff win? In May 2009, the Nationals and visiting Astros traded blown leads, errors, and unearned runs, tied at ten in the eleventh. Rain then began, making the field unplayable. The Astros weren't scheduled to return that year, so the game's completion was moved in July to Houston, where two errors give the Nats an 11–10 win. After waiting sixty-five days for a verdict, the resumption took seven minutes. Nats TV Voice Bob Carpenter called it the best seven minutes of their year. Nyjer Morgan scored the game-winning run, though in May he'd been a Pirate. Even stranger, the Nats' winning pitcher was Joel Hanrahan, traded June 30 to Pittsburgh, taking an off day nap as Morgan crossed the plate.

— *Brett Dolan*

On July 22, 2007, a sweltering night in North Little Rock, Arkansas, I was broadcasting a Double-A Texas League game when Mike Coolbaugh, thirty-five, my friend and Tulsa Drillers' hitting coach, was killed by a foul ball while coaching first base. S. L. Price of *Sports Illustrated* detailed that incident in a fine book on Mike's life, *Heart of the Game: Life, Death, and Mercy in Minor League America*. At such a moment, the personal and professional intersect. I'd gotten to know Mike and his family, including brother Scott. He wound up with 250 professional homers, was a minor-league All-

Star, and even played forty-four games in the bigs. Mike had two kids, a third on the way. The day he died, we had a nice conversation on the bus to the park.

"I haven't had you on the *Dugout Show* yet," I said. "Let me grab my recorder and we'll tape pre-game at the park."

Mike said, "Yeah, great."

The bus arrives. I get the recorder, but arrive after the pre-game Kangaroo Court starts, where players are fined in fun. Entering the Court, *I* get fined. An hour later, it's still going. I tell Mike, "You've got a lot to do. Let's record another day."

Mike is hit in the ninth inning. What irony. His playing career had recently ended, or he wouldn't have been coaching. Orlando Merced had just left as hitting coach, or Mike wouldn't have been in the first-base box. The hitter, Tino Sanchez, nineteen, had lunch with Mike the day before. I still see the drive; Mike hit in the neck, crushing an artery, blocking blood to his brain; falling to the ground, no heartbeat; doctors restarting it as he lay motionless. Mike didn't have a helmet on, now required of baseline coaches.

I had to be sensitive, families listening on the radio and Internet. Needing to avoid panic, I still had to report. An ambulance came on the field, Mike never regaining consciousness. It took about twenty to twenty-five minutes from the moment of impact to leaving the air after the game was canceled. Journalism school doesn't prepare you for someone in uniform dying on the field.

—*Mark Neely*

When you get here, you know that there's really no place like it in the world. It's like Disneyland, except that you don't have to pay for rides. In 2008, I was inducted into Cooperstown, the biggest honor in my life: our Oscar, the Academy Award. You can't go anywhere from here. A couple months earlier I visited for the first time, starting my tour at Doubleday Field, just the name causing goose bumps on your arm. I looked out: church spires, in a distance. Youngsters who play the game they love. An umpire calling balls and strikes the way you're supposed to, for crying out loud, so you don't have to guess. A nice little breeze. To think that they've played there for 150 years is unbelievable. Driving up from New York, about four hours away, as you near the Hall it's like an old *Saturday Evening Post* cover, a Norman Rockwell painting. I was struck by the number of people in the little villages around there who display the American flag: every other house, it seemed, with a flag in the front yard, or sticking out of the house, showing their pride and patriotism. Later, I toured the Hall basement, like going to Fort Knox: temperature controlled, you wear doctor's gloves, hold a bat by my hero, Ted Williams. It's like finding the Holy Grail. Entering the town, you see a sign "Village of Cooperstown." It reminded me of a movie that's become a Christmas favorite, *Polar Express*, where everything is built on belief. The kid goes to the North Pole, and when he gets there Santa gives him a gift. It's this bell. They go back home — Tom Hanks plays every part — and Tom goes to bed, wakes up, and the bell's not there. He thinks it's all been a dream until he goes downstairs and opens the box under the Christmas tree — and there's this bell. It's all if you believe. Seeing that sign, I do.

    — *Dave Niehaus*

I've always thought baseball the most romantic sport, but it took decades to find a woman who felt the same. Even before being romantically involved, I knew Lisa was a baseball person. In 1998, she was at David Wells' perfect game as a spectator. I found out by hearing her report on CBS. Finally dating a decade later, we were meant to be despite liking different New York teams. One Christmas, I gave her the Yankees' broadcast of 1978's Bucky Dent playoff game. Earlier, Lisa had dug up for me her copy of 1969's *Amazin' Mets* album of songs recorded by players presumably hung over from their division-clinching drenching. Our first baseball date was a New Hampshire Fisher Cats Double-A game. I took Lisa for her first visit to the Hall of Fame. We've watched '69 World Series video with Lindsey Nelson in an NBC blazer, unMetsian without a neon jacket. Lisa's the only woman I know who can debate the merits or demerits of Yankee announcers John Sterling and Michael Kay. She loves Ken Singleton, wishes David Cone and Jim Kaat hadn't left, and knows that Bob Gamere and Dom Valentino once had brief and forgettable stints. We laugh with Gary Cohen, Ron Darling and Keith Hernandez, glad that they're well informed, damned funny, and painfully honest when the Mets go bad. We wish Joe

Buck would do every Fox *Game of the Week*, or get out and let someone who really cares take over. We wish Tim McCarver would be more like the '80s McCarver we knew at Shea. We love watching DVDs of Curt, Tony, and Bob on NBC's *Game* and Phil Rizzuto calling the "Pine Tar Game." We wish local Voices still did the Series. We pray that Vin Scully never retires: in fact, when MLB Network debuted New Year's Night 2009, even watched its *countdown* to sign on, the first telecast Vin's and Mel Allen's call of Don Larsen's perfect game. As Scully began his half, Lisa and I remarked how he sounded like he does today. Our *Extra Innings* TV package lets us hear as many Dodger games as we want, Vin lulling us to an East Coast sleep. We love MLB, so addictive we call it "The Crack Channel," and radio baseball in the car, listening no matter the teams involved. We attended the 2010 ALCS in Tampa, then listened to Roy Halladay's no-hitter on the way home. Thank you, XM! Forgive my being personal, but you see, I think we're like you. To us, baseball is less a game than a true love affair—something we now share as newlyweds.

— *Peter King*

Parents tell kids to be careful, knowing how things can change. In 2010, the Marlins' Wes Helms's eleventh-inning single beat Atlanta, 5–4, prompting the usual walkoff celebration. As Helms was being interviewed on live TV, leftfielder Chris Coghlan appointed himself to do the "shaving cream pie-in-the face" routine. Holding a towel piled high, Chris hit Helms square in the face with the white foamy stuff. Sadly, landing at a dangerous angle, he tore the meniscus in his left knee. That week Chris was put on the disabled list, surgery ending his season. What a blow to the 2009 NL Rookie of the Year: a great work ethic, attitude, and cornerstone of the Marlins' future. Even a well-conditioned, well-coordinated athlete can sustain a major injury innocently, instantly. "There's a reason for everything," Chris, a man of faith, told me before surgery. "Maybe in a few months or even a year, I'll figure out the reason for this." One moment in time. No wonder parents worry.

— *Dave Van Horne*

After sixty-five years of baseball, as MLB might say, my "prime nine" top specialists. Leading off, *most spectacular outfielder*: Jimmy Piersall. If he touched a ball, he caught it. *Best-positioned infielder*: Lou Boudreau, almost preternatural in moving to the right position to grab a grounder before the ball was even hit. *Longest batting ritual*: Lou Skizas's wrap bat in the dirt, wipe it between his legs, kiss its end, put right hand in right back pocket, take practice swings with left arm only, and use bat to make a symbol near the box. Lou made Mike Hargrove, the Human Rain Delay, resemble the speed of light. Fourth, *foul ball artist*: If a pitch wasn't hittable, Luke Appling'd chop it foul or take a ball. Dizzy Trout got so upset he threw his glove toward home plate. Since the glove was low and outside, Luke didn't swing. *Greatest windup*: Don Larsen and Bob Turley felt no windup helped control and speed and confused a hitter's timing. By contrast, Satchel Paige'd take one, two, even three windmill windups, a batter unsure when the real pitch would come. Later, he added a "hesitation pitch," making baseball rewrite the rulebook, figuring with Paige's stuff he didn't need another edge. *Best Nail filer*: The knuckleball should properly be called the "fingernail file." Since nails dig into the ball, knuckles resting against it, knucklers fixate on their length. One game was delayed between innings to let 1940s pitcher Roger Wolff get his file in the clubhouse. *Best-balanced tobacco chew*: Few players now chew the stuff. In my day, chewers stuffed their cheeks on just one side. Rocky Bridges put wads in both sides of his mouth, explaining, a) It gave him better balance; and b) if a pitch or bad hop grounder hit his face, he had a cushion on either side. *Poorest rule name*: The "foul pole" should be a "fair pole," since a ball striking it is a homer. Batting ninth, *biggest name player*: Outfielder Carden Edison Gillenwater had twenty-three letters. Where was Ed Ott when I needed him?

— *Bob Wolff*

In this age of being able to tune in and watch any game you want, the local announcer is still special. Maybe it's baseball's nice easy pace: an oasis in today's tumult. Maybe it's the announcer exciting you about a drive toward the bleachers: voice rising, ball soaring. Maybe it's the storytelling. Not a game goes by that I don't reference baseball's past. In 2020, commercial radio will observe its one-hundredth birthday. I'm buying.

— *Greg Schulte*

Chapter Sixteen

Anything You Can Do

In 1943, Bill Stern told his NBC Radio audience how a dying Lincoln begged Gen. Abner Doubleday to "save baseball, please. Protect it for the future." Baseball's task now is to protect the pastime from itself.

On one hand, the 2007 and 2009 bigs sold a record 79 million tickets and made $6.6 billion in revenue, respectively. On the other, the 2010 NFL Pro Bowl and soccer World Cup for the first time out rated the All-Star Game. In a "favorite sport" Gallup survey, football routed baseball, 43–11 percent, leading in each demographic and in video game sales, licensed garb, Fantasy Camp players, and unique Internet users.

"To a baby boomer, baseball was an American child's sun, moon, and stars," said Bob Costas. "It still has a role in our culture, but not nearly what it should." Problem: The game we knew is decreasingly played or televised. Solution: as I wrote in this year's The Cambridge Companion to Baseball, recall past lessons that apply today.

First, announcing matters. "We didn't have models," Ernie Harwell said, prior Voices relying on language to entertain. "Now guys train at radio school and college," sounding robotic and alike. Most "lack background to paint word-pictures," mocking Churchill's "words are bullets to use as ammunition."

Second, TV/radio partnership demands promotion. Quoting Ring Lardner, network carriers frequently deem baseball "a side dish they decline to order." Try respect, like 1950s and '60s CBS and 1980s NBC.

Third, scrap Social Darwinism – survival of the richest. "Football sells itself," said NFL Films' David Plaut, "no matter who's on television." Baseball depends *on a few marquee TV teams: the Red Sox, Yankees, perennial also-ran but beloved Cubs. A sport is no stronger than its weakest franchise.*

Fourth, quicken a pace umpire Joe West famously terms "a disgrace." America took Omaha Beach, split the atom, reached the moon. Baseball can't enforce the strike zone, batter in the box, or bases-empty rule mandating a pitch each twenty seconds. A 1–0 game routinely tops three hours. Game 7 of the 1960 World Series scored nineteen runs in 2:36. As culture turns more impatient, baseball turns more inert.

Fifth, intimacy is indispensable. NBC TV's late director Harry Coyle hailed Fenway Park's "great" coverage, home plate's shot low, yet above an angled backstop. New stadia put the booth above swanky suites, players resembling ants. Worse, vertical guy wire/mesh screens obstruct the camera. Falling ratings are no coincidence: We rarely watch what we cannot see.

At best, radio and TV sing a sonnet upon baseball's heart. So: Hire harmonic Voices. Make baseball less slow motion. Move the weekend World Series to afternoon. Angle the backstop beneath the booth. Make Fenway's coverage standard. For what not to do, see any post–mid-1990s park. For what to do, many announcers have a thought.

If I were Commissioner for a day, I'd move the World Series back to afternoon, so that kids could grow up like we did. Every game you ran home after school to catch the last three innings on radio or TV. In school, teachers put up scores on the blackboard, or kids had a transistor: part of childhood, everywhere. You're trying to sell baseball to kids, for goodness sake! Come on! Let them experience what we did! Games now start at 9:00 o'clock, end at 1:00 in the morning, ridiculous. Kids can't love a game if they can't watch it.
— *Steve Blass*

As Steve says, we raced home to watch postseason, brought a radio to hear at school, and took an extra-long lunch break from work to catch some innings. Loving baseball, we found a way to listen. By contrast, today's sport fears folks at work won't watch, so it cuts daytime postseason, ensuring that kids are asleep during prime-time games. Earth to baseball: Make October count again. Look at the NCAA hoops tournament, Internet

abuzz, people tuning in 1:00 or 8:00 p.m. Let kids catch daytime coverage: memorable, and meaningful. There's a new generation to attract.
—*Denny Matthews*

Growing up, I couldn't wait to watch Saturday's NBC *Game of the Week* and ABC's *Monday Night Baseball*. I pinch myself about doing Fox's *Game*, Fox Sports Net *Thursday Night,* and FX *Saturday Night*: hundreds of events. Also long is my number of partners: nearly fifty alphabetically from Rod Allen and Larry Andersen to Bob Walk and Chris Welsh. They include World Series–winning managers [Joe Girardi and Lou Piniella], MVPs of the Series [Paul Molitor] and each league [Keith Hernandez and Fred Lynn], a sixteen-time Gold Glove award winner [Jim Kaat], perfect game pitcher [David Cone], Cy Young Award winners [Cone and Jim Palmer], and man with the most hits during the 1990s [Mark Grace, 1,754]. What business do I have working with *them*? Each had a different style, but common goal: As Curt Gowdy said, "The game's the thing. Don't get in the way."
—*Kenny Albert*

Baseball's problems include pace, length, and strike zone's height and width. In many new parks, booths are higher and farther from the field, obscuring umpires who don't signal a visible strike. If an ump throws a fist punch in front of him, we can't *see* it. If he doesn't shout loud enough for crowd microphones to catch, we can't *hear* him. Jim Joyce is great, signaling left or right depending on a left- or right-handed batter, then roaring a decision. His call in Washington can be heard in Wilmington. Tim McClelland is different: tall but squatting down, not shouting or signaling till two seconds after standing up. We think it's a ball till Tim calls a strike. The sport is trending toward pitching, defense, and speed. Maybe the next trend—I hope so—will be shorter, better games.
—*Charlie Slowes*

Some people want to speed up baseball. No one wants it to last an eternity. On the other hand, no clock has its charm, as July 28, 2001, our first year at PNC Park, shows. Houston's up, 8–2, with two Bucs out in the ninth. Any other sport, you run out the clock. Here Pat Meares hits a two-run homer, Jack Wilson gets an RBI single, and Brian Giles bombs a game-winning slam. Pirates win, 9–8. I doubt that people there, or following on radio and TV, were clamoring for a clock. Just uphold the rules, and everything will follow.

–Lanny Frattare

In 2009, my high school coach, Ed Kirby, threw out opening day's first ball, celebrating my fifty years with a loyal organization in good times and bad. In 1972, I was 19-8 with eighty-four walks in 249 and 2/3 innings. Next year I was 3-9 and suddenly couldn't throw a strike [eighty-four walks in *88 and 2/3* innings], retiring in 1974. Going good, everyone wants you. Bad, you're on your own. In San Francisco, I called my wife collect. She refused the charges. I get home to find my two sons burning my bubble-gum card. Little indicators. My pitching coach said, "I got a new pitch for you." Me: "What is it?" Him: "A strike." Near the end, Danny Murtaugh, my all-time favorite skipper, says, "We're giving you one more chance tonight." I said, "I want three innings or three hours, whichever comes first." A while back I addressed the Pirates team. Some people say my manager, coach, a close friend motivates. I respect that, but if these people get fired, traded, or leave town, who ya' left with? *You.* The greatest motivational tool can be bought for $39 at Home Depot: a bathroom mirror. That sucker never lies. The other key is pride. "You don't want to be eighty-five years old," I told the Bucs, "saying, 'Boy, I got to the big leagues. Wonder how good I could have been.'" At banquets I say, "You can always tell what kind of a year you've had by the number of invites you receive." In 1968, winning eighteen games, I was invited to speak two or three times a week. In 1971, I could have spoken every night. This year, I tell the dinner, "You're my second invitation." Rim-shot. "The first was from my parents." Fans can't stand guys who don't hustle. Improve baseball by knowing that just getting to the bigs isn't enough.

— Steve Blass

Most PA announcers used to play it straight, voicing and respecting. Today, many sound like a poor disc jockey, cheer the home team, and lower tone for a visitor. Message boards are as immature, telling you to "applaud

. . . clap . . . cheer." We should stop that. Below, Charley Steiner writes of Bob Sheppard, the Yankees' PA Voice and St. John's University public speaking teacher, whom we should emulate. Growing up, I was taught, like Bob, to read, write, and think. Today's priorities may be better, though I'm at a loss to understand how.

— *Bob Wolff*

Sheppard was a native New Yorker who lived in a small suburban town on Long Island, maybe a forty-five-minute drive to Yankee Stadium. He was elegant, graceful, deeply religious, and utterly charming. The "Voice of God" was his: no different in conversation or at the dinner table than he did coming out of a loudspeaker, except there was no echo. But you half heard an echo in his voice even if there wasn't one. I often had my pre-game meal at Bob's circular table, in the corner of the press dining room, at the old Stadium. It sat six, essentially the same crew in the same seats, talking about life and occasionally baseball: Stadium organist Eddie Layton, longtime George Steinbrenner aide Arthur Richman, and writers Frank Dolson and Red Foley, who became a team official and official scorer, respectively. I was the kid at the table. No, I was the kid in the candy store. In the middle of conversation, Bob would ask, "Charles (pause), could you please pass the salt?" The salt was passed. (Another pause) "Thank you." I grew up on Long Island not far from where Bob and his wife Mary lived, and we would occasionally but coincidentally meet at an Italian restaurant during the off season, when I visited my folks. Unfailingly, he'd come to the table and say hello to Mr. and Mrs. Steiner. At first my mom had no idea who this guy, with this voice, was. My mom was never quite sure if they would blow up or sew up a baseball. But that didn't matter. "What a gentleman he is," my mom would inevitably say. As usual, she was right. My mother and father are gone now. So is the Voice of God and as I've noted, The Boss. As Bob would say when completing an announcement or receiving the salt shaker . . . "Thank you." Echo.

— *Charley Steiner*

My recommendation: better radio/TV listening. Many interviewers have a set of questions they want to ask a subject. No matter the answer, each question's asked, announcers talking, not listening. Buddy Blattner told me when we started together he hated if I wasn't listening when he did his innings because he might say something and I'd come on the air and repeat the same thing! Listening is smart. Not listening is also rude, being inattentive to others. God gave us one mouth but two ears. Maybe we're supposed to be listening two-thirds of the time.

— *Denny Matthews*

Improve the broadcast environment. Booth space is paramount to work effectively. Seattle's is wonderful and spacious. In Texas, I was blessed with a cavernous size, the family could come up, hang around. The only drawback was no Logan air conditioning, so we opened windows to circulate air. Bathroom proximity helps, like cuisine. In St. Louis and Yankee Stadium, you're next door to the food and bathroom. Houston has a nice atmosphere and great ice cream. By contrast, in Cleveland you have to dead-on race from the bathroom to make an inning, booth ungainly, no spare space. Boston's near the roof, but you're at Fenway, so no complaints. In Pittsburgh and Washington, you're so high as to be on the moon. Maybe they should put players' numbers on *top* of the hats.

— *Josh Lewin*

Two suggestions to kill two stupid schemes. The AL created the Designated Hitter in 1973 because interest was down, the NL having better players. So, what do we do? Add offense! Sadly, the DH made ours a stand around kind of game. The only hard managerial decision—if you call it that— is whether to pull a pitcher who might be losing stuff. Baseball's not designed to be played with an extra man! So end it—and another gimmick added in 1994–1995, more teams to supposedly fuel regular-season interest. Each league went from two to three divisions, adding a wild card, four taking a World Series, including 2002–2004's Anaheim, Florida, and Boston. I'm sorry, but that defeats the Series' purpose: crowning the best team. A team with the league's best record feels October pressure. Feeling none, the wild card, not supposed to win, often does. Want three divisions? Fine. Eliminate the wild card and give the best record a first-round bye, letting the other two teams collide. As the cliché says, the regular season *is* a marathon. Don't treat it like a sprint.

— *Denny Matthews*

More than any game, baseball radio/TV flows from personality. Someone timed a three-hour game, finding eight minutes of action. As I tell kids,
this gives you two hours and fifty-two minutes to make a complete fool of
yourself. [The 2010 postseason gave even more. Twenty-three of thirty-two
games topped three hours, including 3:36, 3:38, 3:39, 3:40, 3:41, 3:47 (twice),
3:48, 3:50, 3:52, and 4:05. Only five took less than 2:56.] You can't decide
when you're eighteen or twenty that you want to do this for your life. It has
to be a life-long pursuit, growing up on baseball's language and history,
watching it on TV, and learning its pace and rhythms. It also means being
literate: reading everything you can about everything, not just baseball.
Without reading you can't write, let alone learn to speak.
— *Gary Cohen*

Growing up, I'd get to Busch Stadium early for batting practice. Radio
had made me feel I knew the players. Now to view them in person was a
dream come true. This is one area baseball could improve upon. The home
team hits first, followed by the visitors. By the time fans are let inside the
park, the home team has wrapped up BP and visitors are hitting. Why not
switch it, have visitors hit first, and let fans watch *their* team go deep?
— *Greg Schulte*

Al Michaels once talked about having a satellite dish at his home and
watching eight or nine games a night. He said most were "absolutely boring. In every game, the local announcer always has the same conversation — should they send the man over to second? It's a baseball seminar —
it's starting to bug me." Al's right. At fifteen I became Voice of Hayward
High School near San Francisco, which is, you must admit, an honor. Next
morning I'd hear myself on the school intercom. My sophomore year in
college I broadcast at a new TV station in Santa Rosa. The pay was awful, hours worse, and experience spectacular. Remember Harry Caray. He
didn't say, "You can't beat a seminar or statistics at the old ballpark." He
said, "You can't beat *fun*."
— *Jon Miller*

Baseball should remember it's fighting for attention. In Texas, the joke
is that the two sports are football and spring football: an exaggeration, but

not by much. Come August the landscape shifts, especially Friday night, when high school football starts. [A 2010 NFL *regular*-season Cowboys game routed the Rangers' same-day *Division* Series, 34.1 to 9.7 percent of Dallas-area TV homes.] I know people who just want balls and strikes, and to them I apologize for trying to balance informing and entertaining. I don't mean emulating a Danny Gans, God bless him, but knowing that if people feel a game's dragging, there's *American Idol*, a new episode of *The Office*, forty different movies, Facebooking, Tweeting. A guy works all day, nine-to-five becomes eight-to-eight, looks forward to coming home, and putting the feet up. I owe him a great time. God knows, I've learned I'm not everyone's cup of tea [leaving the Rangers after the 2010 season]. I just try to follow guys I admire: Please the greatest amount of people, cheese off the fewest, don't lose sight of yourself, and show that you love the game.
    — *Josh Lewin*

Stress storytelling. In the 1950s and '60s I did more than a hundred TV player interviews, a mike in one hand, stopwatch in the other, done on film in one take, since players didn't have time for their mistakes, or mine. Ultimately a DVD was released called *Legend to Legend*. Curiosity is key. Every person has a spot in the heart—cars, golf, singing—where you and he can bond. I met manager Joe McCarthy late in his career, having found he loved vaudeville. I boned up, and we hit it off. Roger Maris topped Babe Ruth's record, but hated the spotlight: a family man, liked to hunt and fish. Respecting this, I chitchat as if he weren't a player. Later Roger chose me to interview him for a *Look* magazine national TV show because I *didn't* treat him as a star. Bonding means respecting your subject. I asked Ty Cobb about his reputation for cursing and spiking people. "They personified me as slashing left and right," he said. "No one's asked about the cuts on *my* legs! Look at old movies. You see fielders coming down, with their spikes, to injure *me*. I had to defend myself." I didn't interrupt. Everyone deserves to tell their story, even if you don't agree.
    — *Bob Wolff*

In many ways, baseball is extremely healthy. More people go to games, are exposed to the sport, follow its controversy: There's more of that, too. Our biggest challenge isn't *on* the field, but getting kids *to* the field. A lot

play video games or another sport. Baseball needs to spend some money, like its RBI program [Reviving Baseball in Inner Cities]. Be more proactive getting the players out of, and kids into, the park. Broadcasters need to help. The worst thing I hear in the booth or press box is, "I hope they get this game over with fast." What? This is in your way? You need to be somewhere else? What exactly *would* you rather do? Baseball announcers are the most fortunate people in the world. [In 2010, Jon Miller felt fortune's whim. The Giants won his thirteenth ESPN Radio World Series. Jon then rode in San Francisco's victory parade, "hundreds of thousands of people . . . all joined in joyful celebration." At City Hall, Miller emceed a salute to "the whole panorama" of the post–1957 Jints: Willie Mays and Willie Mc-Covey hailing Buster Posey and Tim Lincecum. That week ESPN ended his twenty-one-year *Sunday Night Baseball* TV reign, moving Jon to radio.]
— *Jon Miller*

As a kid growing up in the late '50s and early '60s, baseball had no serious competition. The other sports were filler until next spring, when *our* sport reappeared. At least twenty of us would go to elementary and junior high school with our arms holding gloves, not just books. Class ended with the Pavlovian ring of the bell at precisely 3:17. By 3:25, we'd be out in the schoolyard choosing up sides and playing until dark, or till someone's mom said it's time for dinner, whichever came first. Game over. Years passed. Society changed. Kids don't bring gloves to school anymore. They don't need twenty others to play basketball. They just need a ball and hoop. The NFL? A perfect TV sport on a winter's Sunday afternoon. Point spreads and office pools don't hurt it any. Baseball, competition-free forty or more years ago, now fights other sports for fan interest (and the entertainment dollar). Little League and high school fields, which used to be packed, simply aren't anymore. Baseball must re-seed its fan base, or watch it slowly wither on the vine.
— *Charley Steiner*

Somewhere in a small town in the country, when you talked about the team, the broadcaster pictured the game for them night after night. There's not much of that left anymore, and baseball has to decide, given changes inside and beyond the sport, how to replace what's gone.
— *Gary Thorne*

Sources

Brief portions of this book have appeared in slightly different form in *Pull Up a Chair* and *What Baseball Means to Me*. Grateful acknowledgment is made for permission to excerpt from the 2005–2009 XM Satellite Radio *Voices of The Game* series at the National Baseball Hall of Fame and Museum and 1993 *Voices of The Game* series at the Smithsonian Institution.

Stories from Milo Hamilton's and Dan Schlossberg's *Making Airwaves: 60+ Years at Milo's Microphone*, with Bob Ibach (Sports Publishing, 2007), Denny Matthews' *Hi, Anybody! Why I Love Baseball and What I'd Do to Fix It*, with Matt Fulks (Ascend Books, 2009), and Chris Wheeler's *View from the Booth: Four Decades with the Phillies*, as told to Hal Gullan (Camino Books, 2009), are reprinted with each Voice's permission.

Special appreciation is due Chicago Cubs announcer Pat Hughes, the producer, writer, and narrator of the CD programming *Baseball Voices: Hall of Fame Series*, whose audio tributes include Red Barber, Marty Brennaman, Jack Buck, Harry Caray, Milo Hamilton, Dave Niehaus, Bob Prince, and Bob Uecker. Information is available at www.baseballvoices.com.

Index

About the Author

Curt Smith, writes *USA Today*, "is the voice of authority on baseball broadcasting." The columnist, radio host, and Senior Lecturer in English at the University of Rochester wrote more speeches than anyone for former President George H. W. Bush. Bob Costas says, "Curt Smith stands up for the beauty of words."

Smith is a columnist for GateHouse Media, Major League Baseball's official website MLBlog.com, and *Jewish World Review*'s PoliticalMavens .com. He hosts the National Public Radio affiliate series *Perspectives,* and is a frequent guest on network and cable radio/TV programming. Associated Press has voted his radio commentary "Best in New York State."

Smith's fourteen books include *Voices of The Game, The Voice, What Baseball Means to Me, The Storytellers, Long Time Gone,* and most recently *Pull Up a Chair* (Potomac Books, 2009). Other recent book essays include the presidential memoir as art, thirty-two greatest presidential speeches, thirty-two greatest TV/film presidential portrayals, and Cambridge University's 2011 *The Cambridge Companion to Baseball.*

Raised in New York, Smith was a Gannett reporter, speechwriter for presidential candidate John B. Connally, and the *Saturday Evening Post* senior editor. In 1989, he joined the Bush White House. Among speeches for the forty-first President were the "Just War" Persian Gulf address, Margaret Thatcher's Medal of Freedom, and speech aboard the USS *Missouri* on Pearl Harbor's fiftieth anniversary. The *New York Times* terms his work "the high point of Bush familial eloquence."

Leaving the White House in 1993, Smith headed the ex-president's speech staff, writing Bush's moving 2004 eulogy to President Reagan. He has keynoted events like the Cooperstown Symposium on Baseball and American Culture, hosted Smithsonian Institution and XM Satellite Radio series, and helped write ABC/ESPN's *SportsCentury* and ESPN's *Voices of The Game*. The latter title has become shorthand for baseball radio/TV.

Smith has written for, among others, the *Boston Globe*, *Newsweek*, *New York Times*, *Reader's Digest*, *Sports Illustrated*, and the *Washington Post*. He has appeared on such network programs as ABC's *Nightline,* Armed Forces Radio, BBC, *CBS This Morning*, CNBC, CNN, ESPN, Fox News Channel, History Channel, MSNBC, Mutual Radio's Larry King and Jim Bohannon, and Radio America.

The State University of New York at Geneseo alumnus has been named among the SUNY system's "100 Outstanding Alumni." He is a member of the Judson Welliver Society of former White House speechwriters; Baseball Hall of Fame Ford C. Frick Award committee; and National Radio Hall of Fame committee, helping create its Franklin D. Roosevelt Award in Political Communication. In 1999, Smith joined the University of Rochester faculty, teaching Presidential Rhetoric and Public Speaking. He lives with his wife, Sarah, and their two children in Rochester, New York.